Teaching
Ethically

Teaching
Ethically

Challenges and
Opportunities

EDITED BY

R. Eric Landrum and
Maureen A. McCarthy

American Psychological Association • Washington, DC

Published by
American Psychological Association
750 First Street, NE
Washington, DC 20002
www.apa.org

To order
APA Order Department
P.O. Box 92984
Washington, DC 20090-2984
Tel: (800) 374-2721; Direct: (202) 336-5510
Fax: (202) 336-5502; TDD/TTY: (202) 336-6123
Online: www.apa.org/pubs/books
E-mail: order@apa.org

In the U.K., Europe, Africa, and the Middle East, copies may be ordered from
American Psychological Association
3 Henrietta Street
Covent Garden, London
WC2E 8LU England

Typeset in Goudy by Circle Graphics, Inc., Columbia, MD

Printer: Maple-Vail Books, York, PA
Cover Designer: Mercury Publishing Services, Rockville, MD

The opinions and statements published are the responsibility of the authors, and such opinions and statements do not necessarily represent the policies of the American Psychological Association.

Library of Congress Cataloging-in-Publication Data

Teaching ethically : challenges and opportunities / edited by R. Eric Landrum and Maureen A. McCarthy. — 1st ed.
    p. cm.
  Includes bibliographical references and index.
  ISBN-13: 978-1-4338-1086-2
  ISBN-10: 1-4338-1086-7
  1. Psychology—Study and teaching (Higher) 2. Teacher-student relationships.
3. Teaching—Moral and ethical aspects. 4. Teachers—Professional ethics. 5. Cultural awareness. I. Landrum, R. Eric. II. McCarthy, Maureen A.

  BF77.T415 2012
  174'.937—dc23
                                    2011026965

British Library Cataloguing-in-Publication Data

A CIP record is available from the British Library.

Printed in the United States of America
First Edition

DOI: 10.1037/13496-000

CONTENTS

CONTRIBUTORS

Scott C. Bates, PhD, Utah State University, Logan
Douglas A. Bernstein, PhD, University of South Florida, Tampa
Karen Brakke, PhD, Spelman College, Atlanta, GA
David W. Carroll, PhD, University of Wisconsin–Superior
Stephen L. Chew, PhD, Samford University, Birmingham, AL
Melanie M. Domenech Rodríguez, PhD, Utah State University, Logan
Patt Elison-Bowers, PhD, Boise State University, Boise, ID
Regan A. R. Gurung, PhD, University of Wisconsin–Green Bay
Diane F. Halpern, PhD, Claremont McKenna College, Claremont, CA
Mitchell M. Handelsman, PhD, University of Colorado, Denver
Allen H. Keniston, PhD, University of Wisconsin–Eau Claire
Meera Komarraju, PhD, Southern Illinois University at Carbondale
R. Eric Landrum, PhD, Boise State University, Boise, ID
Maureen A. McCarthy, PhD, Kennesaw State University, Georgia
Blaine F. Peden, PhD, University of Wisconsin–Eau Claire
Vincent Prohaska, PhD, Lehman College, City University of New York, Bronx
Thomas P. Pusateri, PhD, Kennesaw State University, Kennesaw, GA

Bryan K. Saville, PhD, James Madison University, Harrisonburg, VA

Beth M. Schwartz, PhD, Randolph College, Lynchburg, VA

K. Bryant Smalley, PhD, PsyD, Georgia Southern University, Statesboro

Chareen Snelson, EdD, Boise State University, Boise, ID

Elizabeth V. Swenson, PhD, JD, John Carroll University, University Heights, OH

Holly E. Tatum, PhD, Randolph College, Lynchburg, VA

Phylicia Thompson, BA, Spelman College, Atlanta, GA

Sonja Trent-Brown, PhD, Hope College, Holland, MI

Scott VanderStoep, PhD, Hope College, Holland, MI

Wayne Weiten, PhD, University of Nevada, Las Vegas

Jerry W. Wells, BA, Randolph College, Lynchburg, VA

Janie H. Wilson, PhD, Georgia Southern University, Statesboro

C. Thresa Yancey, PhD, Georgia Southern University, Statesboro

ACKNOWLEDGMENTS

This book is the culmination of the efforts of authors who are devoted to teaching with integrity. These scholars worked diligently to provide evidence-based guidelines where available. In a number of instances, these authors wrote about topics on which (a) there is not much existing literature or (b) they added a new perspective or twist to the story. We are thankful for their efforts to summarize the existing literature and provide so many practical applications of ethical principles.

Of course, we would never have hit an orbit like this without Linda McCarter as our support system. Her enthusiasm for psychology education is impressive, her patience is legendary, and her encouragement is refreshing and motivating. We are appreciative of all the key players at the American Psychological Association's Books Department. Jessica Kamish's attention to detail made this a better book, and she helped to keep us on track and on time. Susan Herman, our development editor, did her typical outstanding work to help us focus on delivering the clearest messages possible. We appreciate the expertise and generous contributions of both Debbie Felder (our copyeditor) and Dan Brachtesende (our production editor) and all of those individuals who helped to bring these ideas to fruition. Thank you so much.

We admit that it has been great fun to work together, but the greater reward is working with our colleagues and recognizing the impact their words and ideas can have to improve psychology education. All students deserve teachers who teach ethically, and we hope this volume furthers that goal for faculty and students alike.

Teaching
Ethically

INTRODUCTION

R. ERIC LANDRUM AND MAUREEN A. McCARTHY

Psychologists, as a community of scholars, strive to meet the highest standards of their profession. Amid these efforts they are faced with complicated challenges requiring careful analysis. Psychologists' actions are shaped by a rapidly changing academic and social landscape that forces them to interpret and reinterpret what constitutes ethical practice. As teachers, psychologists must work to ensure that their teaching is effective and that students are treated with integrity. To that end, this book has been crafted to identify some of the ethical challenges facing the professoriate. Invited authors examined the literature in search of solutions that allow teachers to act ethically. Case studies are included throughout the book so that readers can see a direct application from the conceptual issues into the classroom.

The book is divided into four parts. Part I addresses ethical issues associated with pedagogical concerns. Thomas P. Pusateri provides an overview of issues related to academic freedom and provides guidance for balancing academic freedom with the responsibility of faculty to deliver a curriculum that is pedagogically sound (Chapter 1). Elizabeth V. Swensen and Maureen A. McCarthy tackle the difficult topic of how to conduct research on the scholarship of teaching and learning. They distinguish among legal mandates, ethical codes, and ethical practices (Chapter 2). Bryan K. Saville asks readers to consider the importance of carefully constructing grading criteria in an objective and equitable manner. He also offers suggestions for attending to the increasing incidence of plagiarism (Chapter 3). Wayne Weiten, Diane F. Halpern, and Doug A. Bernstein build on the literature from the medical community to offer guidance for ethically selecting textbooks (Chapter 4). Patt Ellison-Bowers and Chareen Snelson address ethical challenges of online teaching. They identify digital privacy, intellectual property, and professional practice as critical issues that must be addressed as psychologists move forward into an increasingly technological forum (Chapter 5). In the final chapter of this section, Regan A. R. Gurung suggests that ethical faculty use evidence-based pedagogies to improve their classroom practice (Chapter 6).

In Part II of this book, authors consider the challenges of how to encourage ethical student behaviors. Vincent Prohaska offers practical advice for attending to student cheating and plagiarism (Chapter 7). Beth M. Schwartz, Holly E. Tatum, and Jerry W. Wells provide a comprehensive model for systemically addressing student infractions through the use of a campuswide honor system (Chapter 8).

The special focus of Part III is diversity. Melanie M. Domenech Rodríguez and Scott C. Bates build on personal experiences and provide vivid examples that introduce challenges of attending to diversity in the context of teaching. They consider the intersection of ethics and multicultural guidelines in meeting the challenges of ethically providing sensitive solutions (Chapter 9). Stephen Chew offers specific suggests for challenging student belief systems as one mechanism for increasing cultural sensitivity (Chapter 10). David W. Carroll completes this section by offering specific suggestions for addressing the needs of students with disabilities in an ethically and practically sensitive manner (Chapter 11).

The final section of this volume addresses faculty behavior. Janie H. Wilson, Bryant Smalley, and C. Thresa Yancey identify ethical issues confronting undergraduate faculty in particular. They offer practical suggestions for maintaining professional boundaries both inside and outside the classroom (Chapter 12). Blaine F. Peden and Allen H. Keniston provide readers specific guidance for infusing research ethics into the curriculum across the undergraduate experience (Chapter 13). Karen Brakke and Phylicia Thompson address the complex issues associated with supervision of undergraduate students in community-based settings. They place these experiences in the context of the broader undergraduate experience, identify common issues that are often present in these experiences, and offer clear recommendations for addressing the unique challenges of providing service learning experiences (Chapter 14). Scott VanderStoep and Sonja Trent-Brown address the benefits and the potential pitfalls of faculty collaboration with undergraduate research assistants, offering a number of different models for successful collaboration of this type (Chapter 15). Maureen A. McCarthy provides suggestions for addressing the complicated set of issues associated with determining the role of undergraduate students in establishing authorship (Chapter 16). Meera Komarraju and Mitch M. Handelsman bring the book full circle by discussing psychologists' responsibilities to train the next generations of faculty with an emphasis on current graduate student teachers of psychology (Chapter 17).

It is our hope that this book provides valuable guidance for navigating the many ethical challenges facing faculty in a rapidly changing society and assists faculty in evaluating challenges and using solutions in a local context. This book may also be a useful vehicle for promoting discussion around issues of ethical practice in centers for excellence in teaching and learning. Ultimately, we hope that faculty will use this text as a way to promote open discussion leading to a more ethical culture of teaching.

I

PEDAGOGICAL CONCERNS

1

TEACHING ETHICALLY: ONGOING IMPROVEMENT, COLLABORATION, AND ACADEMIC FREEDOM

THOMAS P. PUSATERI

Ethical teachers habitually reflect on their teaching effectiveness and actively seek professional development opportunities that increase their mastery and repertoire of teaching pedagogies and methods of assessing student learning. Ethical teachers also view their teaching in the context of a broader program of study and collaborate with colleagues in ways that promote individual and institutional academic freedom. In this chapter, I identify resources for faculty interested in enhancing their teaching effectiveness and for documenting their professional development in applications for promotion and tenure. I argue that the ethics of effective teaching involves two potentially conflicting perspectives related to academic freedom. Teachers exercise individual academic freedom and responsibility to develop and deliver courses on the basis of their professional expertise, but they also teach courses in the context of a curriculum offered by an academic department (e.g., a baccalaureate degree in psychology) or institution (e.g., a general education program) that has the

I thank Bill Hill for suggestions on the contents of this chapter.

9

responsibility to identify program requirements.[1] Effective teachers find ethical ways of collaborating with colleagues to support both individual and institutional academic freedom.

I begin by describing the elements of the American Psychological Association's (APA's) *Ethical Principles of Psychologists and Code of Conduct* (hereinafter referred to as the Ethics Code; APA, 2010) that refer directly to teaching, students, and education. Although the Ethics Code specifically pertains to those who have a doctorate in psychology, it also applies to graduate students, secondary school teachers, and others who teach psychology but do not have a doctoral degree as affiliate members of APA. I discuss how the concepts of individual and institutional academic freedom provide opportunities and potential ethical dilemmas for evaluating effective teaching. I identify criteria for effective teaching that emerged from science experts, discuss how these criteria are consistent with sections of the APA Ethics Code, and suggest a strategy for collaboration in departments and institutions to design and improve their courses and curricula. I conclude by recommending discipline-specific resources that teachers of psychology may consult to improve their teaching, to develop a statement of teaching philosophy, and to document effective teaching in applications for promotion and tenure.

SECTIONS OF THE APA ETHICS CODE RELATED TO TEACHING, STUDENTS, AND EDUCATION

Several sections of the APA Ethics Code make direct reference to teachers, students, and education. The Introduction and Applicability section indicates that the Ethics Code applies to "psychologists' activities that are part of their scientific, *educational* [emphasis added], or professional roles as psychologists" including "teaching and supervision of trainees" (APA, 2010). General Principle C (Integrity) specifically stipulates, "Psychologists seek to promote accuracy, honesty, and truthfulness in the science, *teaching* [emphasis added], and practice of psychology," and several ethical standards make direct reference to teaching, students, or education. I focus here on standards that address the ethical obligations of psychology teachers to develop and teach courses and to contribute to the design and delivery of educational programs.

Standards 2.01, Boundaries of Competence; 7.03, Accuracy in Teaching; and 7.06, Assessing Student and Supervisee Performance, focus, respectively,

---

[1]There are similar ethical and legal issues concerning conflicts between the academic freedom of faculty members and students that are beyond the scope of this chapter. Interested readers may consult statements by the American Association of University Professors (http://www.aaup.org/AAUP/issues/AF/).

on teachers' ethical obligations to teach courses within their boundaries of competence, to provide students accurate information in their teaching and course descriptions, and to establish timely and specific processes for assessing student performance. Two additional standards place teachers' courses within the broader context of an educational program such as a baccalaureate degree in psychology or a general education requirement. Standards 7.01, Design of Education and Training Programs, and 7.02, Descriptions of Education and Training Programs, address the responsibility of teachers to contribute to the design of educational programs and to provide students accurate information about program requirements. These standards imply that teachers of psychology are ethically obligated not only to teach their courses well but also to consider how their courses contribute to the objectives of the larger program of study such as student attainment of content knowledge, written and oral communication skills, research skills, collaborative skills, and career and personal development. A faculty member who focuses only on content knowledge may not be contributing sufficiently to the larger program's objectives if the teacher does not address other skills that may be relevant to the course.

INDIVIDUAL ACADEMIC FREEDOM AND INSTITUTIONAL ACADEMIC FREEDOM

The requirements for an institution's general education program or a department's degree program may entail widespread adoption of pedagogies and methods for assessing student learning outcomes that require faculty members to modify the way they teach courses that contribute to the program. Faculty members may perceive these requirements as a violation of their academic freedom to rely on their professional expertise when choosing pedagogies and assessment methods when teaching courses. However, this perception may be inaccurate in that it fails to consider that academic freedom applies not only to individual faculty members but also to institutional governance structures. Academic administrators and those who serve on academic committees are collectively responsible for setting the curriculum, approving and reviewing courses, and determining faculty qualifications to teach courses; their decisions place constraints on a faculty member's full expression of academic freedom (Gerber, 2010). Nelson (2009)—past president of the American Association of University Professors—identified occasions when faculty members may have legitimate reasons for challenging these constraints (e.g., when administrative decisions affecting courses and curricula are made for arbitrary or political reasons) but indicated that there are currently few guidelines for resolving conflicts between individual and institutional academic freedom. For resources and additional discussion of academic freedom, visit http://www.aaup.org/AAUP/issues/AF/.

To increase the likelihood that conflicts are resolved on sound academic principles and not for arbitrary or political purposes, Gerber (2010) recommended that faculty members with teaching assignments constitute the membership of governance structures responsible for academic policies and decision making. In their statement, *Academic Freedom and Educational Responsibility*, the Board of Directors of the Association of American Colleges and Universities (2006) made a similar argument concerning the obligations of faculty to collaborate in designing educational programs (to read the full statement, visit http://www.aacu.org/about/statements/academic_freedom.cfm).

RECOMMENDED CRITERIA FOR EVALUATING EFFECTIVE TEACHING IN SCIENCE, TECHNOLOGY, ENGINEERING, AND MATHEMATICS DISCIPLINES

I raise the conflict between individual and institutional academic freedom because I believe it is relevant to discussing the ethics of effective teaching. This opinion is supported by a report from a committee of 15 educators representing disciplines in science, technology, engineering, and mathematics that included two psychologists (National Research Council, 2003). The committee recommended that academic institutions and departments in science, technology, engineering, and mathematics disciplines consider adopting five criteria for evaluating teaching effectiveness:

- knowledge of and enthusiasm for the subject matter;
- skill, experience, and creativity with a range of appropriate pedagogies and technologies;
- understanding of and skill in using appropriate testing practices;
- professional interactions with students within and beyond the classroom; and
- involvement with and contributions to one's profession in enhancing teaching and learning.[2]

Readers may refer to the report (National Research Council, 2003) for detailed descriptions and examples of the types of knowledge, skills, and attitudes that illustrate each criterion.

The first four criteria pertain to a faculty member's individual academic freedom and responsibility to develop and deliver courses and to interact

---

[2]From *Evaluating and Improving Undergraduate Teaching in Science, Technology, Engineering, and Mathematics* (pp. 101–106), by the National Research Council, 2003, Washington, DC: The National Academies. Copyright 2003 by the National Academy of Sciences. Reprinted with permission.

professionally with students in ways that are consistent with the APA Ethics Code. Teachers demonstrate integrity (General Principle C) and mitigate potential harm to students (Standard 3.04, Avoiding Harm) when they know their subject matter; use appropriate pedagogies, technologies, and assessment strategies; and maintain professional interactions with their students. Teachers who reflect on their current knowledge of their subject matter can assess when they are teaching within their boundaries of competence (Standard 2.01, Boundaries of Competence) and when they are presenting information accurately to their students (Standard 7.03, Accuracy in Teaching). Teachers who develop skills with a range of appropriate pedagogies, technologies, and assessment strategies are likely to design course activities consistent with the goals of the course and curriculum (Standard 7.01, Design of Education and Training Programs) and provide timely and specific feedback to students concerning their attainment of those goals (Standard 7.06, Assessing Student and Supervisee Performance). Teachers maintain professional interactions with students when they provide accurate descriptions of the content and requirements of their courses and programs (Standards 7.02, Descriptions of Education and Training Programs, and 8.04, Client/Patient, Student, and Subordinate Research Participants), avoid exploitative and multiple relationships (Standards 2.05, Delegation of Work to Others; 3.02, Sexual Harassment; 3.08, Exploitative Relationships; 7.05, Mandatory Individual or Group Therapy; 7.07, Sexual Relationships With Students and Supervisees; and 8.12, Publication Credit), and maintain confidentiality of student information (Standards 4.07, Use of Confidential Information for Didactic or Other Purposes, and 7.04, Student Disclosure of Personal Information).

The fifth criterion pertains to institutional academic freedom and a faculty member's responsibility to collaborate with departmental and institutional colleagues to improve courses and curricula (Standards 7.01, Design of Education and Training Programs, and 7.02, Descriptions of Education and Training Programs). In addition, teachers who are involved with and contribute to their profession are likely to seek professional development opportunities (e.g., attending or presenting at teaching workshops, reading or authoring articles or other resources on the teaching of psychology) that help them increase their levels of competency (Standard 2.01, Boundaries of Competence).

BALANCING INDIVIDUAL AND INSTITUTIONAL ACADEMIC FREEDOM

The statements by the American Association of University Professors and Association of American Colleges and Universities on academic freedom and responsibility; the criteria for evaluating effective teaching in science, technology, engineering, and mathematics disciplines; and Standards 7.01, Design of Education and Training Programs, and 7.02, Descriptions of Education and Training Programs, of the APA Ethics Code suggest an ideal academic climate that would address both individual and institutional academic freedom. In this context, faculty members would work collaboratively, perhaps as members of a general education committee or departmental curriculum committee, to develop, articulate, and implement a shared set of desired learning outcomes for students who complete the program and a curricular structure designed to help students attain the outcomes.

Such committees would create task forces that consist of faculty members who teach required courses in the curriculum. If the curriculum allows students to select one or more options from a set of equivalent courses (e.g., a social sciences requirement in a general education curriculum), task forces would include faculty members who teach courses in each respective option. Task force members would consult the research literature on general and discipline-specific issues of student learning and good teaching relevant to the courses they teach. They would also consider institutional documents that address policies and procedures relevant to curricular issues such as the institution's mission statement, strategic plan, and requirements for assessment reports. Task force members would refer to these resources in their deliberations and in their recommendations to the larger committee concerning a set of learning outcomes, pedagogies, and assessments for all sections of the courses under their purview.

The task forces and committee would favor consensus building that allows faculty members who follow the recommendations sufficient latitude to incorporate their unique expertise and creativity into their courses. The relative importance that task force and committee members assign to consensus building versus individual faculty autonomy might vary on the basis the nature of the course. Consensus building may receive more weight when decisions involve courses that are core requirements or prerequisites, and individual faculty autonomy may receive more weight for electives and special topics courses.

Periodically, the committee or task force would meet to share and review evidence from their courses (e.g., syllabi, course materials, student performance on tests and assignments) to assess whether the implementation was having desirable or adverse effects on student learning outcomes with the goal of improving the course and curriculum. Successful implementation of these changes may provide opportunities for faculty members to present or publish their work in the scholarship of teaching and learning. For an extensive list of journals that publish scholarship of teaching and learning research, visit http://www.kennesaw.edu/cetl/resources/journals.html.

This ideal climate extends the concept of peer review of teaching outside of classroom observations to include other types of formal and informal faculty interactions. Hoyt and Pallett (1999) suggested that peers can evaluate a colleague's contributions to the general learning climate of the department or institution, to the development of courses and curricula, and to the teaching effectiveness of other peers (e.g., through consultations and sharing of teaching strategies). Berk (2006) and Bernstein (2008) provided additional recommendations and resources for peer review of teaching that include, but are not restricted to, classroom observations.

RESOURCES FOR EFFECTIVE TEACHING OF PSYCHOLOGY

With this ideal climate in mind, I suggest several resources that teachers of psychology may find useful for assessing and improving their teaching effectiveness in ways that address both individual and institutional academic freedom.

Discipline-Specific Standards, Guidelines, and Principles

Table 1.1 lists discipline-based resources that articulate disciplinary standards, guidelines, and principles for psychology courses and curricula. Individually, teachers of psychology could use these resources to reflect on how well their courses align with expert recommendations and how they should adjust their courses accordingly. Collectively, faculty members in psychology departments could consult these resources to examine and consider changes to curricula and courses. For example, Levy, Burton, Mickler, and Vigorito (1999) suggested that department members collaborate to construct a "curriculum matrix" that displays how each course in the curriculum contributes to desired student learning outcomes and use this matrix for discussing potential curricular changes.

Empirically Supported Statements of Teaching Philosophy

Many advertisements for teaching positions in APA's *Monitor on Psychology*, the Association for Psychological Science's *Observer*, and *The Chronicle of Higher Education* include requests for applicants to submit a statement of teaching philosophy, and institutions often request that faculty members include such statements with supporting evidence in their applications for promotion and tenure. Haggerty (2010) expressed the concern that statements of teaching philosophy can easily degenerate to a literary exercise in which faculty members endorse a list of institutionally approved buzzwords like critical thinking and collaborative learning rather than reflect on how and why they teach. To avoid this pitfall, ethical teachers of psychology

TABLE 1.1
Discipline-Based Resources for Effective Teaching in Psychology

Resource[a]	Relevance to effective teaching
National Standards for High School Psychology Curricula (APA, 2005)	Includes a set of learning objectives initially developed for psychology courses in secondary schools that are equally appropriate for introductory courses at the college level. Visit http://www.apa.org/ed/precollege/topss/national-standards.pdf
APA Guidelines for the Undergraduate Psychology Major (APA, 2007)	Describes 10 goals and learning outcomes for baccalaureate psychology degrees. Five goals are specific to psychological science. Five goals indicate how psychology contributes to the liberal arts (e.g., for general education and institutionwide outcomes assessment). Visit http://www.apa.org/ed/precollege/about/psymajor-guidelines.pdf
The Assessment Cyberguide for Learning Goals and Outcomes (APA, Education Directorate, 2009)	Discusses how to conduct outcomes assessment for goals in the *APA Guidelines for the Undergraduate Psychology Major* and provides abstracts of articles illustrating how to assess each goal. Visit http://www.apa.org/ed/governance/bea/assessment-cyberguide-v2.pdf
Teaching, Learning, and Assessing in a Developmentally Coherent Curriculum (APA, 2008)	Argues that students acquire the goals in the *APA Guidelines for the Undergraduate Psychology Major* at basic, intermediate, and advanced levels of competency as they progress from introductory to advanced courses and provides rubrics for assessing students on the first five goals. Visit http://www.apa.org/ed/governance/bea/curriculum.pdf
"Quality Benchmarks in Undergraduate Education" (Dunn, McCarthy, Baker, Halonen, & Hill, 2007)	Proposes benchmarks to assess the quality of undergraduate psychology programs in eight domains including curriculum, assessment, and student learning outcomes.
Undergraduate Education in Psychology: A Blueprint for the Future of the Discipline (Halpern, 2010)	Argues that psychology teachers should prepare students to be psychologically literate citizens, presents a scientist-educator model for psychology teachers, proposes a model curriculum, and offers quality principles for undergraduate education in psychology.
Office of Teaching Resources in Psychology	Provides a collection of peer–reviewed syllabi and other pedagogical resources for teaching psychology. Visit http://teachpsych.org/otrp/
Teaching Tips	A regular column in the Association for Psychological Science's monthly *Observer* magazine. Visit http://www.psychologicalscience.org/teaching/tips/
Course-specific websites	http://www.intropsychresources.com/ http://www.socialpsychology.org/ http://personalitypedagogy.arcadia.edu/

Note. APA = American Psychological Association. [a]For additional resources, visit http://www.apa.org/ed/precollege/

should consider how APA policy on evidence-based practice in psychology (APA, Presidential Task Force on Evidence-Based Practice, 2006) might apply to their teaching ("Educators Advised to Use Evidence-Based Assessment," 2006). Meyers (2008) suggested a further analogy between clinical practice and teaching by applying the psychotherapeutic concept of the working alliance to student–teacher interactions.

Bernstein et al. (2010) proposed a scientist–educator model for the professional development of teachers of psychology in which teachers should increase their skills in articulating course goals, selecting and adapting pedagogies, assessing student learning, adjusting their teaching, and communicating with their peers about their teaching. This model assumes that teachers are most likely to develop these skills when they consult the literature in content and pedagogies and adopt a conceptual framework for their teaching. Bransford, Brown, and Cocking (1999) provided a conceptual framework based on human learning research from cognitive psychology, developmental studies, social psychology, and neuroscience, and they make recommendations for effective teaching practices based on this research. It is possible for faculty members to individualize their statements of teaching philosophy while still grounding their teaching in empirically supported theory. Mayo (2010) advocated using constructivist theory to design a coherent curriculum in psychology and provided examples of assignments and assessments appropriate for students at various stages of cognitive development.

Guidelines for Promotion and Tenure

There are some discipline-specific guidelines and principles to assist faculty members in psychology departments when drafting promotion and tenure policies. The *Guidelines for Conditions of Employment of Psychologists* (APA, Committee on Academic Freedom and Conditions of Employment, 1987) addressed the rights and responsibilities of employees and employers in recruitment, selection, and evaluation of psychologists and made several direct references to teaching and academic freedom. In 1994, APA adopted its *Principles for Quality Undergraduate Psychology Programs*,[3] which identified best practices for psychology students, faculty, and curricula, and an updated and expanded set of these principles is undergoing public review (at the time of this writing) for possible adoption by APA (Halpern, 2010). The authors of the new set of principles call on teachers of psychology to strive to become scientist–educators who adopt evidence-based teaching practices and who collaborate to design and deliver a coherent curriculum.

---

[3] http://www.apa.org/ed/precollege/about/principles.aspx

SUMMARY

Ethical teachers of psychology consider how the pedagogies and assessments they use in their courses contribute to a student's development within the context of a program of study (e.g., a general education program or a degree program) designed to facilitate student attainment of an articulated set of knowledge and skills. Within this context, they collaborate with their colleagues to honor both the individual academic freedom of faculty to use their expertise in designing their courses and the institutional academic freedom of departments and institutions to design programs of study that set expectations for the objectives, pedagogies, and assessments for required courses in the curriculum. Ethical teachers seek professional development opportunities and consult discipline-specific resources and literature in the scholarship of teaching and learning to improve their use of evidence-based teaching pedagogies and assessments, and they collaborate with colleagues to design courses and curricula based on disciplinary standards and guidelines. These collaborations provide formal and information opportunities, in addition to classroom observations, for peers to review their contributions to teaching and student learning.

REFERENCES

American Psychological Association. (2005). *National standards for high school psychology curricula*. Retrieved from http://www.apa.org/ed/precollege/topss/national standards.pdf

American Psychological Association. (2007). *APA guidelines for the undergraduate psychology major*. Retrieved from http://www.apa.org/ed/precollege/about/psymajor-guidelines.pdf

American Psychological Association. (2008). *Teaching, learning, and assessing in a developmentally coherent curriculum*. Retrieved from http://www.apa.org/ed/governance/bea/curriculum.pdf

American Psychological Association. (2010). *Ethical principles of psychologists and code of conduct (2002, Amended June 1, 2010)*. Retrieved from http://www.apa.org/ethics/code/index.aspx

American Psychological Association, Committee on Academic Freedom and Conditions of Employment. (1987). Guidelines for conditions of employment of psychologists. *American Psychologist, 42,* 724–729. doi:10.1037/0003-066X.42.7.724

American Psychological Association, Education Directorate. (2009). *The assessment cyberguide for learning goals and outcomes*. Retrieved from http://www.apa.org/ed/governance/bea/assessment-cyberguide-v2.pdf

American Psychological Association, Presidential Task Force on Evidence-Based Practice. (2006). Evidence-based practice in psychology. *American Psychologist, 61,* 271–285. doi:10.1037/0003-066X.61.4.271

Association of American Colleges and Universities. (2006). *Academic freedom and educational responsibility.* Washington, DC: Author.

Berk, R. A. (2006). *Thirteen strategies to measure college teaching.* Sterling, VA: Stylus.

Bernstein, D. J. (2008). Peer review and evaluation of the intellectual work of teaching. *Change, 40*(2), 48–51. doi:10.3200/CHNG.40.2.48-51

Bernstein, D. J., Addison, W., Altman, C., Hollister, D., Kmoarraju, M., Prieto, L., . . . Shore, C. (2010). Toward a scientist-educator model of teaching psychology. In D. F. Halpern (Ed.), *Undergraduate education in psychology: A blueprint for the future of the discipline* (pp. 29–45). Washington, DC: American Psychological Association. doi:10.1037/12063-002

Bransford, J. D., Brown, A. L., & Cocking, R. R. (Eds.). (1999). *How people learn: Brain, mind, experience, and school.* Retrieved from http://www.nap.edu/catalog.php?record_id=9853

Dunn, D. S., McCarthy, M. A., Baker, S., Halonen, J. S., & Hill, G. W., IV. (2007). Quality benchmarks in undergraduate psychology programs. *American Psychologist, 62,* 650–670. doi:10.1037/0003-066X.62.7.650

Educators advised to use evidence-based assessment. (2006, November). *Monitor on Psychology, 37*(10), 36. Retrieved from http://www.apa.org/monitor/nov06/evidence-based.aspx

Gerber, L. G. (2010). Professionalization as the basis for academic freedom and faculty governance. *AAUP Journal of Academic Freedom, 1,* 1–26. Retrieved from http://www.academicfreedomjournal.org/VolumeOne/Gerber.pdf

Haggerty, K. D. (2010, February 9). Teaching statements are bunk. *The Chronicle of Higher Education, 56*(23). Retrieved from http://chronicle.com/article/Teaching-Statements-Are-Bunk/64152/

Halpern, D. F. (Ed.). (2010). *Undergraduate education in psychology: A blueprint for the future of the discipline.* Washington, DC: American Psychological Association. doi:10.1037/12063-000

Hoyt, D. P., & Pallett, W. H. (1999, November). *Appraising teaching effectiveness: Beyond student ratings* (IDEA Paper # 36). Retrieved from The IDEA Center website: http://www.theideacenter.org/sites/default/files/Idea_Paper_36.pdf

Levy, J., Burton, G., Mickler, S., & Vigorito, M. (1999). A curriculum matrix for psychology program review. *Teaching of Psychology, 26,* 291–294.

Mayo, J. A. (2010). *Constructing undergraduate psychology curricula: Promoting authentic learning and assessment in the teaching of psychology.* Washington, DC: American Psychological Association. doi:10.1037/12081-000

Meyers, S. A. (2008). Working alliances in college classrooms. *Teaching of Psychology, 35,* 29–32. doi:10.1080/00986280701818490

National Research Council. (2003). *Evaluating and improving undergraduate teaching in science, technology, engineering, and mathematics.* Retrieved from http://www.nap.edu/catalog.php?record_id=10024

Nelson, C. (2009, July-August). Whose academic freedom? *Academe, 95*(4), 54–55.

2

ETHICALLY CONDUCTING THE SCHOLARSHIP OF TEACHING AND LEARNING RESEARCH

ELIZABETH V. SWENSON AND MAUREEN A. McCARTHY

Boyer (1990) first articulated that a scholarship of teaching would be one way to "define the work of faculty in ways that reflect more realistically the full range of academic and civic mandates" (p. 16). Bowden (2007) noted that the "inability to refine the scholarship of teaching across disciplines and institutions suggests the waters have become more turbulent" (p. 2). In response to external pressures, both Boyer and Bowden suggested that conducting scholarship of teaching and learning (SoTL) research has become (a) increasingly important for assessing effectiveness of teaching and learning and (b) potentially difficult to measure. What do psychology educators want their students to learn? How do they know students in their classes have learned anything? How can this information be used to improve teaching? These are sample questions that often guide SoTL (Hutchings, 2002). Answers to these questions, if they are documented, generalizable, and public, constitute the research outcomes of SoTL. Halpern et al. (1998) suggested that SoTL research is a new paradigm of scholarship that should include the creation, synthesis, and application of knowledge. Ultimately SoTL research should contribute to excellence in teaching and learning.

Conducting ethical pedagogical research is possible with guidance from federal regulations that address research with all human participants (U.S.

Department of Health and Humans Services [DHHS], Protection of Human Subjects, 2009). For teachers of psychology, additional guidance is also provided by the American Psychological Association's (APA's; 2010) *Ethical Principles of Psychologists and Code of Conduct* (hereinafter referred to as the Ethics Code). We begin this chapter with a broad view of research ethics, the protective nature of the institutional review board (IRB), and avoiding coercion and dual relationships and end with practical advice about using student work when experimenting in the classroom.

ETHICS OF RESEARCH WITH HUMAN PARTICIPANTS

Historically, egregious violations of basic human rights were evident in the research conducted on concentration camp prisoners during World War II and in the Tuskegee Syphilis Study conducted by U.S. Public Health Service from the 1930s to the 1970s. These flagrant violations led to the creation of many regulations, national and international, designed to protect the welfare of humans participating in research. Federal guidelines were established in 1974 when the U.S. Congress passed the National Research Act creating the National Commission for the Protection of Human Subjects of Biomedical and Behavioral Research. The commission was charged with developing ethical principles and guidelines for research involving human participants and in 1979 produced the Belmont Report (U.S. Department of Health, Education, and Welfare, National Commission for the Protection of Human Subjects of Biomedical and Behavioral Research, 1979), which set forth the principles of justice, beneficence, and respect for persons (autonomy). Although the Belmont Report established these principles for conducting research, additional regulations (U.S. DHHS, Protection of Human Subjects, 1991) were developed, and revisions of these guidelines have continued, with the most recent revisions occurring in 2009 (U.S. DHHS, Protection of Human Subjects, 2009).

APA, in the first codified version of the APA Ethics Code (APA, 1953), addressed human subjects research as a separate category (Section 4). This earliest version also included an extensive discussion of teaching ethics, including whether students should be required to participate in research (APA, 1953; Nagy, 2011). Throughout each of the 10 revisions of the Ethics Code, the goal has been to define the standards and values that unite psychologists as a profession and as a discipline that treats and studies behavior. In the case of pedagogical research, faculty must attend to competence in teaching by using scientifically sound practice and safeguarding the very students who are participants in the pedagogical research.

INVOLVEMENT OF THE INSTITUTIONAL REVIEW BOARD

Although the Nuremberg Code established important tenets for basic human rights and the Belmont Report addressed the importance of human protections, the U.S. DHHS enacted the legal requirement for reviewing federally funded research for the express purpose of protecting human subjects. Under this legislation, an institution that applies for federal research funds is required to establish an IRB (U.S. DHHS, Protection of Human Subjects, 2009). Institutions are required to provide evidence of an approved assurance certification with all applications for federal funding (§ 46.103(f)), which ensures that an institutional review board (IRB) is appropriately configured and regularly reviews all research involving human subjects. Adherence to federal regulations is required for most colleges and universities because they accept federal funds (e.g., student financial aid). Additionally, consistent with the guidelines from the Belmont Report, many federal agencies (e.g., the National Science Foundation) require compliance with the "Common Rule" or protections for human subjects. Thus, most institutions register IRBs consistent with the federal guidelines to ensure that they will be eligible for a wide range of federal grants. For nonfederally funded research, it is advisable to review the treatment of human participants because many publication and presentation venues, as well as university policies, require review by the IRB. An IRB's mission is to ensure the safety and ethical treatment of human subjects, and the APA Ethics Code, in Standard 8.01, Institutional Approval, reinforces the importance of obtaining IRB approval for all research with human participants (APA, 2010).

Some SoTL research, because of its educational nature, qualifies as exempt from regulations set forth by the U.S. DHHS on the protection of human subjects (2009). Still, it is in the best interest of the researcher to seek IRB approval (E. E. Bartlett, Office for Human Research Protections, personal communication, October 5, 2010). The first step in drafting the application for review of the research by an IRB is to consider whether the investigation is "research" (U.S. DHHS, Office for Human Research Protections [OHRP], 2004). As specified in the regulations that follow, if research is conducted only in established or commonly accepted educational practices (e.g., colleges and universities), then it is exempt from all requirements:

> Research conducted in established or commonly accepted educational settings, involving normal educational practices, such as (i) research on regular and special education instructional strategies, or (ii) research on the effectiveness of or the comparison among instructional techniques, curricula, or classroom management methods. (U.S. DHHS, Protection of Human Subjects, 2009, 45 C.F.R. 46.101(b)(1)).

Wilson (2008) argued that trying new techniques in class and then evaluating and discussing the outcomes with colleagues is ordinary classroom practice. At what point does educational practice become SoTL? (See also http://www.hhs.gov/ohrp/policy/checklists/decisioncharts.html.) Burman and Kleinsasser (2004) suggested that SoTL is important for improving educational practices. In this context, they emphasized using appropriate ethical practice and invoking the necessary procedures for exempting educational research from a full IRB review. Who decides when SoTL research is exempt from IRB review? The IRB, the IRB chair, or an IRB administrator makes this decision. If the institution requires all research to undergo review, then regardless of whether the research qualifies as exempt from all regulations, SoTL research must be reviewed by at least one person associated with the IRB.

It is important to attend to each of the criteria set forth by the local IRB. Institutions determine whether research must be reviewed by the IRB, and they determine the level of review required (i.e., exempt, expedited, or full). Not all research must be reviewed by the IRB. However, the local IRB determines whether they will allow research to proceed without review, so a local IRB may require all research to be reviewed. The IRB reviews research protocols to ensure that, during research, humans do not experience any more than minimal risk, or no more than the risk typically incurred during daily living. The IRB reviews the experimental procedure, the informed consent process, the description and recruitment of the participants to be used, the debriefing, the anonymity of the individuals, and the rationale for the research.

If an IRB requires review of all research, approval must be obtained even if the SoTL research qualifies for exemption from all regulations. Proceeding with an IRB review is especially important to protect the safety and rights of human participants in research, particularly when conducting research with one's own students. Because of the evaluative authority teachers have over their own students, proper care must be taken to be sure students are not exploited. The APA Ethics Code (APA, 2010) is particularly useful for guiding research when potential conflicts of interest may arise. It is essential to ensure that students as research participants are protected.

INDUCEMENTS TO PARTICIPATE IN RESEARCH

The 2010 APA Ethics Code addresses the use of students as research participants in two standards: 8.04 (Client/Patient, Student, and Subordinate Research Participants) and 8.06 (Offering Inducements for Research Participation). These two standards illustrate the need to be cautious and offer students the opportunity to withdraw from some types of SoTL research because students could be exploited. Consider the following example:

> Professor Michaelson wanted to understand how students might react to his use of an actual televised trial in his forensic psychology class. This trial would take up 3 weeks of class time, but Professor Michaelson had a hunch that students would not only have a deeper understanding of trial and jury dynamics but also have more fun in class. He explained that he would be giving the students a questionnaire covering both their reactions to the trial and some questions covering the trial facts and procedures. He asked them to be completely honest in their assessment of the educational usefulness of the trial and advised them that their answers to the factual questions would not affect their grade in the course. He then asked students to sign an informed consent to be a participant in this research, saying he planned to write a manuscript detailing the procedure and he planned to use verbatim student comments. A graduate student collected the consent forms to minimize coercion. However, Dr. Michaelson did not leave the room while the students were completing the informed consent form. Reluctant students felt as though it was in their best interest to agree to participate.

Faculty regularly implement new teaching techniques that may improve learning. Implementing a new technique does not require IRB approval. However, if Dr. Michaelson wants to evaluate the effectiveness of the new technique, and the local IRB requires review of all research, it is incumbent on Dr. Michaelson to submit the protocol for review. Additionally, if a researcher wishes to use verbatim responses, it is wise to submit the research protocol to the IRB for review regardless of the local requirements.

Dr. Michaelson attempted to obtain informed consent; however, he did not ensure that participants would not be coerced. In this scenario, it is possible that the students did not feel protected from any adverse consequences of declining to participate. Informed consent can only be obtained when participants do not feel coercion. One might argue that Professor Michaelson's errors in coercing students to be participants in his research would surely violate Ethics Code Standard 8.06, Offering Inducements for Research Participants; a more appropriate solution would have been to simply ask students to complete an online questionnaire related to the change in course format.

A second solution is also possible within the guidelines provided by the U.S. DHHS, Protection of Human Subjects (2009). If the research did not meet the standard as nonexempt as required by the local IRB, then Dr. Michaelson should have considered whether informed consent was necessary. An IRB may approve a study that does not include or alters the informed consent process. The questions used to make this determination are contained in the regulations as follows:

> (d) An IRB may approve a consent procedure which does not include, or which alters, some or all of the elements of informed consent set forth in this section, or waive the requirements to obtain informed consent provided the IRB finds and documents that:
>   (1) The research involves no more than minimal risk to the subjects;
>   (2) The waiver or alteration will not adversely affect the rights and welfare of the subjects;
>   (3) The research could not practicably be carried out without the waiver or alteration; and
>   (4) Whenever appropriate, the subjects will be provided with additional pertinent information after participation. (U.S. DHHS, Protection of Human Subjects, 2009)

In other words, simply asking for feedback about the videos can be done without informed consent if the four criteria are met and the institution has a provision for waiving informed consent. Nevertheless, it is imperative that students be provided with the option not to participate in the evaluation of pedagogical change.

MULTIPLE RELATIONSHIPS

Multiple relationships are not uncommon in higher education. A student in a professor's class may also be an advisee, a research or teaching assistant, or a work-study student. When a person is both a research participant and a student in a class, a multiple relationship exists. Ethics Code Standard 3.05, Multiple Relationships, provides guidance for multiple relationships, and Standard 3.05(a) posits that all multiple relationships are not unethical, and this ambiguity makes interpretation of the Code at times difficult. Fortunately, Standard 3.05(a) provides guidance that allows teaching faculty to determine if a particular relationship is ethical.

> A psychologist refrains from entering into a multiple relationship if the psychologist's objectivity, competence, or effectiveness in performing his or her functions as a psychologist, or otherwise risks exploitation or harm to the person with whom the professional relationship exists.

In Professor Michaelson's study, some of the students felt that the videos lasted too long. Although the students felt their time may have been wasted, they were reluctant to express their concerns. If students were asked to share their perceptions anonymously, it is unlikely that the multiple relationship (i.e., teacher and researcher) would result in harm to the student.

INFORMED CONSENT TO USE STUDENT WORK

Ensuring informed consent when needed is critical; however, with SoTL research informed consent is not always required (OHRP, personal communication, October 5, 2010). If students are asked by the instructor of record to participate in SoTL research, is it possible to obtain informed consent, given the power differential in the classroom? Students might believe that the failure to give informed consent could affect their grade or a future request for a letter of recommendation. To alleviate student concerns about declining or withdrawing from research, it is critical to ensure anonymity. Burgoyne (2002), in an analysis of power relationships between students and faculty, suggested that professors should never be privy to knowing who consented. The Ethics Code defines the requirements for informed consent in Standard 8.02, Informed Consent to Research:

> (a) When obtaining informed consent as required in Standard 3.10, Informed Consent, psychologists inform participants about (1) the purpose of the research, expected duration, and procedures; (2) their right to decline to participate and to withdraw from the research once participation has begun; (3) the foreseeable consequences of declining or withdrawing; (4) reasonably foreseeable factors that may be expected to influence their willingness to participate such as potential risks, discomfort, or adverse effects; (5) any prospective research benefits; (6) limits of confidentiality; (7) incentives for participation; and (8) whom to contact for questions about the research and research participants' rights. They provide opportunity for the prospective participants to ask questions and receive answers.

Informed consent refers to the basic moral principle of autonomy. If faculty are conducting a study that requires informed consent, then students need to be able to think through the consequences of making decisions and make a decision freely.

EXPERIMENTING WITH METHODOLOGY: GROUPS OF STUDENTS TAUGHT DIFFERENTLY

SoTL research often involves evaluating the efficacy of a particular teaching technique or activity. Consider the following scenario:

> Professor Bingham wondered if student learning might differ on the basis of whether she assigned the e-book version or the traditional print version of her favorite introductory psychology textbook. So Professor Bingham decided that she would assign the e-book to one section and the print copy of the text to a second section of the course. Both were midmorning classes with a cap of 30 students. She flipped a coin and assigned the

e-book to the 10:00 a.m. section and the print copy to the 11:00 a.m. section. Professor Bingham used well-defined learning objectives as the basis for comparing the two classes.

In this scenario, the class using the print version of the text served as the control group and the class using the e-book constituted the experimental group. Similarly, in an interesting variation on group division, Franz and Spitzer (2006) presented a case study in teaching two groups of students APA Style. If the experimental group outperforms the control group, then protections must be in place to protect the control group, similar to control group protections in therapeutic intervention research. It is not unusual for faculty to use a new technique in comparable course sections to evaluate the effectiveness of pedagogy. Faculty often explore new procedures or techniques for the purpose of improving their teaching; updating a course is part of being a good teacher. Conducting SoTL research is advantageous for faculty and students. SoTL research is essential if faculty are to remain compliant with the APA Ethics Code's stipulation that teachers are to be effective and current in their teaching.

CONCLUDING REMARKS

Faculty regularly strive to improve teaching techniques. In this chapter, we discussed some of the ethical responsibilities that should be considered when conducting SoTL research. Some might argue that it is important for faculty to evaluate the efficacy of their teaching practices. So, in one sense, it is important to act ethically by evaluating educational practice.

Concomitantly, research involving human subjects should be carefully evaluated, both in terms of legal requirements and ethical guidelines, to ensure that people are protected when they participate in research. Because educational research (SoTL) is conducted on standard educational practice, it is research that is potentially exempt from IRB review. Nevertheless, it is within the purview of an IRB to review all research and to impose more rigorous review. It also is important to ensure that all research is undertaken ethically. Psychologists must ensure that all students are treated with respect, that teachers are using sound teaching practice, and that teachers are obtaining empirical evidence for their teaching.

REFERENCES

American Psychological Association. (1953). *Ethical standards of psychologists*. Washington, DC: Author.
American Psychological Association. (2010). *Ethical principles of psychologists and code of conduct (2002, Amended June 1, 2010)*. Retrieved from http://www.apa.org/ethics/code/index,aspx

Bowden, R. G. (2007). Scholarship reconsidered: Reconsidered. *Journal of the Scholarship of Teaching and Learning, 7*, 1–21.

Boyer, E. L. (1990). *Scholarship reconsidered: Priorities of the professoriate*. Princeton, NJ: Carnegie Foundation for the Advancement of Teaching.

Burgoyne, S. (2002). Case 3: Refining questions and renegotiating consent. [Peer commentary on "Suzanne Burgoyne's case" by P. J. Markie]. In P. Hutchings (Ed.), *Ethics of inquiry: Issues in the scholarship of teaching and learning* (pp. 40–43). Menlo Park, CA: Carnegie Foundation for the Advancement of Teaching.

Burman, M. E., & Kleinsasser, A. (2004). Ethical guidelines for use of student work: Moving from teaching's invisibility to inquiry's visibility in the scholarship of teaching and learning. *The Journal of General Education, 53*, 59–79. doi:10.1353/jge.2004.0018

Franz, T. M., & Spitzer, T. M. (2006). Different approaches to teaching the mechanics of American Psychological Association style. *Journal of Scholarship of Teaching and Learning, 6*, 13–20.

Halpern, D. F., Smothergill, D. W., Allen, M., Baker, S., Baum, C., Best, D., & Weaver, K. A. (1998). Scholarship in psychology: A paradigm for the twenty-first century. *American Psychologist, 53*, 1292–1297. doi:10.1037/0003-066X.53.12.1292

Hutchings, P. (2002). Introduction. In P. Hutchings (Ed.), *Ethics of inquiry: Issues in the scholarship of teaching and learning* (pp. 1–17). Menlo Park, CA: Carnegie Foundation for the Advancement of Teaching.

Nagy, T. F. (2011). *Essential ethics for psychologists: A primer for understanding and mastering core issues*. Washington, DC: American Psychological Association. doi:10.1037/12345-000

U.S. Department of Health and Human Services (1991). *Federal policy for the protection of human subjects: Notices and rules*. Fed. Reg. 46, No. 117 (June 18): 28001-32.

U.S. Department of Health and Human Services, Protection of Human Subjects, 45 C.F.R. pt. 46. (2009). Retrieved from http://www.hhs.gov/ohrp/policy/ohrp regulations.pdf

U.S. Department of Health and Human Services, Office for Human Research Protections. (2004). *Is an activity research involving human subjects covered by 45 CFR part 46?* Retrieved from http://public.health.oregon.gov/ProviderPartnerResources/EvaluationResearch/InstitutionalReviewBoard/Documents/isresearch.pdf

U.S. Department of Health, Education, and Welfare, National Commission for the Protection of Human Subjects of Biomedical and Behavioral Research. (1979). *The Belmont report: Ethical principles and guidelines for the protection of human subjects of research*. Retrieved from http://ohsr.od.nih.gov/guidelines/belmont.html

Wilson, J. H. (2008). The value and ethics of the scholarship of teaching and learning. In S. A. Meyers & J. R. Stowell (Eds.), *Essays from e-xcellence in teaching* (Vol. 8, pp. 13–15). Retrieved from http://teachpsych.org/resources/e-books/eit2008/eit08-04.pdf

3

THE ETHICS OF GRADING

BRYAN K. SAVILLE

Grading—the very word can create anxiety for some psychology teachers. Along with the frustration that comes with students underperforming on assignments, grading often means taking time away from other activities such as class preparation and research. Nevertheless, many teachers view grading as an innocuous activity, one that may be time- consuming but is, for the most part, fairly uncomplicated. Have no doubt, though—grading can be tricky business.

Consider, for instance, a teacher who has to decide whether to allow a student to make up a missed exam. The student—who also happens to be the teacher's research assistant—insists that his roommate accidentally unplugged the alarm clock but has no proof to support his claim. Although the teacher is fairly certain that the student is telling the truth, students with similar excuses were not allowed to make up a missed exam. Should the teacher allow this student to make up the exam? Consider, now, another situation in which two thirds of a teacher's students failed miserably on an exam. Although the teacher wonders whether the students prepared adequately, the exam may

I would like to thank Tracy Zinn for her helpful comments on an earlier draft of this chapter.

have been exceedingly difficult and may not have accurately measured student knowledge. Should the teacher adjust students' grades or offer them an opportunity to earn extra credit? In short, the preceding examples exemplify the ethics of grading. Although many readers might assume that the ethicality surrounding grading-related issues is relatively unambiguous, in fact, ethical dilemmas involving grading are, somewhat paradoxically, among the most perplexing dilemmas that many psychology teachers face. In the paragraphs that follow, I hope to convince psychology teachers that they would do well to consider the ethical issues that surround grading practices as well as how these practices potentially affect students' lives. First, I briefly describe some general principles that psychology teachers can use to guide their decisions when confronting a grading-related ethical dilemma; I also review the extant literature on the ethics of grading and explain why I believe the ethics of grading is an important issue.

ETHICAL PRINCIPLES RELATED TO GRADING

For over half a century, the American Psychological Association's (APA's) *Ethical Principles of Psychologists and Code of Conduct* (hereinafter referred to the Ethics Code; APA, 2010) has provided guidance to psychologists in determining the best course of action to take when confronted with ethical dilemmas (Keith-Spiegel, Tabachnick, & Allen, 1993; Tabachnick, Keith-Spiegel, & Pope, 1991); however, the Ethics Code devotes relatively little space to the practice of teaching (Keith-Spiegel et al., 1993). In fact, the latest version of the Ethics Code (APA, 2010) contains only seven standards under the heading "Education and Training," the section devoted specifically to teaching. Even then, many of those standards do not address ethical issues that are likely to affect the daily activities of many teachers, especially those whose primary teaching responsibilities fall at the undergraduate level (Keith-Spiegel, 1994). Furthermore, the Ethics Code has even less to say about grading, an activity that affects most, if not all, teachers (Kienzler, 2004). Specifically, the only standard that addresses grading is Standard 7.06, Assessing Student and Supervisee Performance, which contains two specific guidelines:

(a) In academic and supervisory relationships, psychologists establish a timely and specific process for providing feedback to students and supervisees. Information regarding the process is provided to the student at the beginning of supervision.

(b) Psychologists evaluate students and supervisees on the basis of their actual performance on relevant and established program requirements. (APA, 2010)

Other than these two statements, the Ethics Code is lacking information that might provide guidance to teachers of psychology who are confronted with grading-related ethical dilemmas—dilemmas that arise more frequently and have the potential to be more serious in nature than some educators might believe or wish to admit.

WHY EDUCATORS SHOULD DISCUSS THE ETHICS OF GRADING

Given the relatively small amount of space in the Ethics Code devoted to grading-related teaching issues, one might wonder whether the ethics of grading is that important. Maybe the Ethics Code contains little discussion of grading because, in the grand scheme of teaching-related ethical issues, grading is of little consequence to most teachers. Perhaps, as Keith-Spiegel et al. (1993) noted, because teaching occurs in settings where institutional policies already provide guidelines for what faculty can and cannot do, teachers are unlikely to engage in unethical grading practices. Maybe, in short, the ethics of grading is not that big of a deal.

When taken at face value, this assumption may seem valid—grading seems to be relatively innocuous and probably does not pose a major ethical threat to either teachers or students. In reality, though, the extant research on the ethics of grading, although small in size, seems to suggest otherwise. In a series of studies, Keith-Spiegel and her colleagues asked faculty (Tabachnick et al., 1991) and students (Keith-Spiegel et al., 1993) to rate the ethicality of various teaching-related behaviors. The researchers found that a large majority of faculty and students (at least 80%) rated the following grading-related behaviors as unethical under most circumstances: ignoring evidence of cheating, using invalid grading procedures, and allowing students' likeability to influence grading. (To provide a comparison, only a slightly higher percentage [90%] of the faculty in the Tabachnick et al., 1991, study reported that getting sexually involved with a student was unethical under most circumstances.) Students in Keith-Spiegel et al.'s (1993) study also reported that giving good grades regardless of the quality of students' work, giving too few good grades, not returning exam grades within a reasonable time period, changing the grading criteria midsemester, and including material on exams that was not covered in the lectures or assigned readings were also unethical practices (see also Kuther, 2003).

So, if both faculty and students view grading as an important ethical issue, why are there so few empirical studies on the topic? Although there are likely several reasons for the paucity of articles (see, e.g., Goodstein, 1981; Keith-Spiegel, Tabachnick, Whitley, & Washburn, 1998; Matthews, 1991; Wittig, Perkins, Balogh, Whitley, & Keith-Spiegel, 1999), one primary reason seems to stand out: Although educators do view grading as an important ethical issue, they do not view it to be as important as other ethical issues (Barrett, Headley, Stovall, & Witte, 2006; Quatrella & Wentworth, 1995; Rodabaugh, 1996). Again, at first glance, this assumption may seem warranted: Certainly the ethics involved in giving a few particularly hardworking students a couple of extra points so they can get a higher grade pales in comparison to the ethical issues that surround a teacher engaging in a romantic relationship with a student.

In reality, though, it is important to consider the ethics of grading because the *opportunity* for grading-related violations arises so frequently. Teachers, for instance, probably have relatively few opportunities to participate in romantic relationships with their students. In contrast, the opportunity for grading-related ethical violations arises much more frequently (see Koocher & Keith-Spiegel, 1998). Take, for instance, the act of grading essay exams. Because teachers have many obligations, they may be tempted to read the essays less carefully than they should, assuming that a missed point here or there is not a big deal. But multiply a point or two across several exams (and maybe even several classes) and the result may be the difference between gaining admission to graduate school and receiving one of those depressing "We're-sorry-to-inform-you" letters in the mail. Thus, when one considers the frequency with which teachers make grading-related decisions, the act of grading becomes a more serious ethical issue—one that educators would do well to spend some time considering.

TWO EXAMPLES AND SOME ISSUES AND PRACTICES TO CONSIDER

Most likely, teachers who spend their days grading student assignments will encounter a dilemma that may have ethical implications. Consider, for instance, the case of Sally and Juanita:

> Sally and Juanita took your introductory psychology course last semester and are just about to finish your statistics course this semester. Sally—an outgoing freshman who earned a C in introductory psychology and who frequently commented on how she just did not "get it"—performed, surprisingly, really well this semester, earning As or Bs on most of the course assignments. In contrast, Juanita—a somewhat reserved but intelligent sophomore who came to class every day last semester and earned one of the highest grades in your introductory course—missed quite a few classes this semester, put in minimal effort on assignments that were only worth a few points, and showed little overall interest in learning about statistics. Nevertheless, she still earned decent grades on most of the bigger assignments.

After grading the final exams, you find that Sally and Juanita are each two points away from an A in the course. Because you believe that Sally worked very hard during the semester, you really want to give her a few extra points as a reward for her effort and to let her know you think she has a promising future if she continues to work hard. You are less certain, however, that Juanita deserves the higher grade given her seeming lack of effort and interest all semester. The question arises: Is it ethical to give Sally a few extra points on the basis of effort, or is this somehow unfair to Juanita (and your other students), who, although she did not show a lot of effort, still ended up with the same number of points as Sally? Although some teachers might argue that you should reward Sally for her hard work and that a higher grade might boost her confidence and provide benefits in the long run (Principle A, Beneficence and Nonmaleficence), others could argue that "playing favorite" with Sally violates Principle D, Justice, which states that teachers need to treat students equally. One might also argue, however, that, according to Principle E, Respect for People's Rights and Dignity, which includes the right to self-determination, it was Juanita's choice to work as much (or as little) as she did and that you should not punish her for making that decision.

Now consider the case of William, a bright and motivated student who just finished your research methods course.

> William did very well on the exams, participated during class discussions, showed a real penchant for research methods, and unfortunately, plagiarized a small portion of his final paper. The policy outlined on your syllabus states that any form of plagiarism will result in a failing grade in the course. Although you initially considered "looking the other way" because the amount of plagiarism was minimal, you realized that you needed to address the issue. After meeting with William, you are fairly certain (although you cannot be 100% sure) that the plagiarism was accidental and that he— along with many other undergraduate students (see Roig, 1997)—was unaware of some of the more subtle forms of plagiarism.

Do you follow Principle A (Beneficence and Nonmaleficence) and give William the benefit of the doubt, knowing that the plagiarism was probably unintentional and that a failing grade in the course could have negative, potentially long-lasting effects on this promising researcher-to-be? Or do you follow through with your policy, knowing that you need to treat all students equally (Principle D, Justice) and that you have given other students failing grades when they have plagiarized on their writing assignments? What if the plagiarism was intentional, though? (And how would you know?) If you downplay the incident and only give William a little "talking to," will it give him the impression that minor cases of plagiarism are harmless? What if he plagiarizes again in the future but does not have a teacher who is as "understanding" as you are? Could your decision not to enforce your syllabus policy this time around actually harm William in the long run?

Although APA's principles will likely provide you with some guidance as you contemplate a decision, finding the best solution is not always so straightforward. In fact, as Strike (1988) noted, ethical dilemmas often have more than one acceptable solution. Moreover, teachers need to consider the policies of their own institutions when making such decisions. At my institution (James Madison University), we have both formal and informal procedures in place for matters of academic dishonesty. In the case of first-time offenders, teachers may submit an informal complaint that goes into a student's file but has no long-term consequences as long as the student does not commit another violation. If, however, the student commits a second violation, the informal complaint becomes official, and the student is listed as a repeat offender, the outcome of which is a failing grade in the course and a one-semester suspension. (This is also a good reason to keep track of as much information as possible when confronted with ethical dilemmas; the information might be helpful to you and your institution when deciding what to do.) Thus, being aware of institutional policies might clarify which course of action to take when confronted with grading-related ethical dilemmas. For instance, what if you found out that William had plagiarized in another course, that his teacher had submitted an informal complaint to the university, and that your university has a zero-tolerance policy for repeat offenders? Presumably, giving William the benefit of the doubt in this case would not be the most ethical decision.

In sum, deciding the ideal course of action when confronted by grading-related ethical dilemmas can be difficult and complicated. In fact, the complexity of ethical dilemmas may be one additional reason why educators have spent so little time discussing the ethics of teaching (e.g., Keith-Spiegel et al., 1998). Nevertheless, because most teachers will likely confront a grading-related ethical dilemma at one time or another, it is important to consider some ways that teachers can put themselves in a position to avoid as many ethical dilemmas as possible. Next I describe just a few grading-related suggestions and issues that teachers might wish to consider as they ponder the ethics of grading.

Syllabi and Grading Policies

Ethical Standard 7.03, Accuracy in Teaching, states that teachers should provide their students with an accurate course description, usually in the form of a syllabus, that highlights how the teacher will measure student progress. One way for teachers to avoid many grading-related ethical dilemmas, then, is to clearly outline exactly how they will assess student assignments (Baiocco & DeWaters, 1998; Zlokovich, 2004). For instance, teachers might state that there will be no "rounding up" at the end of the semester; that they will add a certain number of points to a student's grade if other criteria (e.g., perfect attendance) have been met during the semester; that assignments will lose 10% for each day they are late; and that they will deal with instances of plagiarism on a case-by-case basis, using the institution's stated policy on academic dishonesty as a guide. In addition, teachers should give their students a realistic course preview and explain clearly why these policies are in place (Brinthaupt, 2004; see also Morse & Popovich, 2009). Teachers might also consider including a grading rubric in their syllabi that students can follow when preparing to complete assignments (Andrade, 2005). Regardless of what information teachers choose to include, a detailed syllabus seems to give students the impression that their teachers are fair and caring (Saville, Zinn, Brown, & Marchuk, 2010). Moreover, when students have a good idea of how teachers will assess their performance, they are less likely to be confused about the grades they receive (Matthews, 1991).

Number and Types of Assessments

In general, most educators believe that it is better to have more, rather than fewer, assessments (Halpern et al., 1993). Rather than having only a midterm exam and a cumulative final exam, for instance, teachers might instead give five or six smaller exams, daily or weekly reading quizzes, and several personal application papers. Using such low-stakes assessment, with each assignment worth a relatively small percentage of a student's grade, teachers obtain a larger sample of behavior to consider, which may capture and provide a more valid measure of student learning. As Halpern et al. (1993) noted, "[Because] measurement is imperfect . . . assessment will be most useful when multiple methods are used to examine clearly specified objectives" (p. 37).

Teachers should also spend some time thinking about the types of assessments they include in their courses and how they might affect grading (e.g., Davis, 2009; Halpern et al., 1993; McKeachie, & Svinicki, 2006). For instance, multiple-choice exams are relatively easy to grade and thus may help teachers preclude certain grading-related ethical dilemmas. On the other hand, although well-written multiple-choice questions can be designed to measure complex learning (Appleby, 1990; Cantor, 1987), when used to measure basic knowledge, a common practice among teachers (see Frederiksen, 1984), they may not do a good job of assessing student learning, which raises further ethical questions. Likewise, although essay exams and papers may be superior for assessing certain aspects of students' knowledge, grading is arguably more difficult and may be more prone to subjective bias. And what about grading based on even more subjective criteria, such as perceived student effort? Whereas some teachers might like to reward students who show good effort, especially in cases in which there is a borderline grade involved (see Burke, 2008), grading based on such subjective criteria is arguably even more difficult than grading essay exams and, as in the case of Sally and Juanita presented earlier, likely to compound the problem.

Grading Assignments

Providing students with detailed grading criteria can go a long way toward helping to preclude many of the ethical dilemmas that teachers are likely to encounter when engaging in grading-related activities. Next I discuss a few additional issues that teachers should consider when examining their grading practices. Again, this list is by no means exhaustive, but rather it touches on a few issues that are likely to arise for most teachers.

Provide Prompt Feedback

Ethical Standard 7.06, Assessing Student and Supervisee Performance, states that teachers need to provide their students with timely feedback. This edict coincides nicely with a growing body of research showing that immediate rewards tend to have a more powerful effect on learning than delayed rewards (for reviews, see Green & Myerson, 2004; Jaehnig & Miller, 2007; Renner, 1964; Tarpy & Sawabini, 1974). Once again, though, when considering the ethics of grading, the issue may not be so cut-and-dried. Whereas one teacher could argue that prompt feedback will ultimately benefit students (Principle A, Beneficence and Nonmaleficence), another teacher might counter that rapid grading might produce more mistakes and that students may come to distrust the teacher (see Principle C, Integrity) if such grading errors continue. Of course, there are ways to provide prompt feedback and grade assessments accurately. For instance, on the day after an exam, teachers could spend a few minutes going over the correct answers with students. Although the teacher may not be finished with grading at that point, students will nonetheless receive some feedback on how they performed, which may ultimately benefit their learning.

Grading and Teaching Assistants

Another way that some teachers expedite the grading process is by using teaching assistants (TAs). Although grading can be educational for TAs (e.g., Keith-Spiegel, 1994), it can also be a source of ethical concern, as expressed in Standard 2.05, Delegation of Work to Others. One major ethical concern of using TAs to help grade constructed response or essay assignments is that they may not be as knowledgeable when it comes to identifying correct answers, the differences between which are sometimes subtle and hard to detect for the untrained eye. As Standard 2.05 states, though, teachers may be able to avoid this ethical issue simply by taking the time to train their TAs how to grade effectively. For instance, providing TAs with well-constructed grading rubrics and taking the time to discuss the types of answers they might encounter while grading will go a long way in avoiding various grading-related dilemmas. In addition, one relatively simple way to ensure that TAs are grading effectively is to establish interrater reliability; this can be accomplished by having the teacher independently grade a subset of the assignments and comparing his or her grading with the TA's grading. Teachers might also give students the opportunity to appeal their grades if they feel that the TA has made a mistake (see Goss Lucas, 2004). Finally, because confidentiality is an important ethical issue (see Section 4, Privacy and Confidentiality), teachers need to ensure that their TAs take steps to keep students' grades confidential.

CONCLUSION

At its most basic level, the primary function of grading should be to provide students with feedback regarding their learning. Unfortunately, grading may no longer serve this function. Rather, grades continue to be one of the primary ways that people—educators, employers, society at large—differentiate which students have the ability, intelligence, and motivation to succeed in an increasingly complex world, a practice that, as Bain (2004) noted, is relatively new to education. At the very least, then, teachers need to be aware that the outcomes of their grading practices can influence how others view their students and thus can have far-reaching consequences—consequences that may extend well beyond the walls of their classrooms.

At first glance, grading seems relatively harmless and certainly not on the same ethical plane as other issues that have received the majority of educators' attention. But when examined more closely, it becomes clear that grading-related activities have important ethical implications. In this chapter, I have attempted to highlight a few of the issues that teachers would do well to consider when thinking about the ethics of grading. Certainly, there are other important issues to ponder, not the least of which is an analysis of the situational variables that might lead some teachers to commit grading-related violations. For instance, it would be interesting to know whether a heavy reliance on student evaluations during tenure reviews might lead to an increase in grading-related ethical violations.

In sum, as with many ethical dilemmas, determining the course of action to take when confronted with a grading-related dilemma can be difficult, even emotionally and mentally taxing. Nevertheless, teachers need to consider the ethical issues that surround their grading practices, how these practices might affect their students, and how existing principles can guide them in their quest to be ethical teachers.

REFERENCES

American Psychological Association. (2010). *Ethical principles of psychologists and code of conduct (Amended June 1, 2010)*. Retrieved from http://www.apa.org/ethics/code/index.aspx

Andrade, H. G. (2005). Teaching with rubrics: The good, the bad, and the ugly. *College Teaching, 53*, 27–31. doi:10.3200/CTCH.53.1.27-31

Appleby, D. C. (1990). A cognitive taxonomy of multiple-choice questions. In V. P. Makosky, C. C. Sileo, L. G. Whittemore, C. P. Landry, & M. L. Skutley (Eds.), *Activities handbook for teaching of psychology* (Vol. 3, pp. 79–82). Washington, DC: American Psychological Association.

Bain, K. (2004). *What the best college teachers do*. Cambridge, MA: Harvard University Press.

Baiocco, S. A., & DeWaters, J. N. (1998). *Successful college teaching: Problem-solving strategies of distinguished professors*. Boston, MA: Allyn & Bacon.

Barrett, D. E., Headley, K. N., Stovall, B., & Witte, J. C. (2006). Teachers' perceptions of the frequency and seriousness of violations of ethical standards. *The Journal of Psychology: Interdisciplinary and Applied, 140*, 421–433. doi:10.3200/JRLP.140.5.421-433

Brinthaupt, T. M. (2004). Providing a realistic course preview to students. *Teaching of Psychology, 31*, 104–140. doi:10.1207/s15328023top3102_6

Burke, B. L. (2008). For the "grader" good: Considering what you grade and why. In B. Perlman, L. I. McCann, & S. H. McFadden (Eds.), *Lessons learned: Vol. 3. Practical advice for the teaching of psychology* (pp. 121–130). Washington, DC: Association for Psychological Science.

Cantor, J. (1987). Developing multiple-choice tests items. *Training & Development Journal, 41*, 85–88.

Davis, B. G. (2009). *Tools for teaching* (2nd ed.). San Francisco, CA: Jossey Bass.

Frederiksen, N. (1984). The real test bias: Influences of testing on teaching and learning. *American Psychologist, 39*, 193–202. doi:10.1037/0003-066X.39.3.193

Goodstein, L. D. (1981). Ethics are for academics too! *Professional Psychology, 12*, 191–193. doi:10.1037/h0078093

Goss Lucas, S. (2004). Returning graded assignments is part of the learning experience. In B. Perlman, L. I. McCann, & S. H. McFadden (Eds.), *Lessons learned: Vol. 2. Practical advice for the teaching of psychology* (pp. 265–273). Washington, DC: American Psychological Society.

Green, L., & Myerson, J. (2004). A discounting framework for choice with delayed and probabilistic rewards. *Psychological Bulletin, 130,* 769–792. doi:10.1037/0033-2909.130.5.769

Halpern, D. F., Appleby, D. C., Beers, S. E., Cowan, C. L., Furedy, J. J., Halonen, J. S., & Pittenger, D. J. (1993). Targeting outcomes: Covering your assessment concerns and needs. In T. V. McGovern (Ed.), *Handbook for enhancing undergraduate education in psychology* (pp. 23–46). Washington, DC: American Psychological Association. doi:10.1037/10126-001

Jaehnig, W., & Miller, M. L. (2007). Feedback types in programmed instruction: A systematic review. *The Psychological Record, 57,* 219–232.

Keith-Spiegel, P. (1994). Teaching psychologists and the new APA ethics code: Do we fit in? *Professional Psychology: Research and Practice, 25,* 362–368. doi:10.1037/0735-7028.25.4.362

Keith-Spiegel, P. C., Tabachnick, B. G., & Allen, M. (1993). Ethics in academia: Students' views of professors' actions. *Ethics & Behavior, 3,* 149–162. doi:10.1207/s15327019eb0302_1

Keith-Spiegel, P., Tabachnick, B. G., Whitley, B. E., & Washburn, J. (1998). Why professors ignore cheating: Opinions of a national sample of psychology instructors. *Ethics & Behavior, 8,* 215–227. doi:10.1207/s15327019eb0803_3

Kienzler, D. S. (2004). Teaching ethics isn't enough: The challenge of being ethical teachers. *Journal of Business Communication, 41,* 292–301. doi:10.1177/0021943604265974

Koocher, G. P., & Keith-Spiegel, P. (1998). *Ethics in psychology: Professional standards and cases* (2nd ed.). New York, NY: Oxford University Press.

Kuther, T. L. (2003). A profile of the ethical professor. *College Teaching, 51,* 153–160. doi:10.1080/87567550309596431

Matthews, J. R. (1991). The teaching of ethics and the ethics of teaching. *Teaching of Psychology, 18,* 80–85. doi:10.1207/s15328023top1802_3

McKeachie, W. J., & Svinicki, M. (2006). *McKeachie's teaching tips: Strategies, research, and theory for college and university teachers* (12th ed.). Boston, MA: Houghton Mifflin.

Morse, B. J., & Popovich, P. M. (2009). Realistic recruitment practices in organizations: The potential benefits of generalized expectancy calibration. *Human Resource Management Review, 19,* 1–8. doi:10.1016/j.hrmr.2008.09.002

Quatrella, L. A., & Wentworth, D. K. (1995). Students' perceptions of unequal status dating relationships in academia. *Ethics & Behavior, 5,* 249–259. doi:10.1207/s15327019eb0503_4

Renner, K. E. (1964). Delay of reinforcement: A historical review. *Psychological Bulletin, 61,* 341–361. doi:10.1037/h0048335

Rodabaugh, R. C. (1996). Institutional commitment to fairness in college teaching. *New Directions for Teaching and Learning, 1996*, 37–45. doi:10.1002/tl.372199 66608

Roig, M. (1997). Can undergraduate students determine whether text has been plagiarized? *The Psychological Record, 47*, 113–122.

Saville, B. K., Zinn, T. E., Brown, A. R., & Marchuk, K. A. (2010). Syllabus detail and students' perceptions of teacher effectiveness. *Teaching of Psychology, 37*, 186–189. doi:10.1080/00986283.2010.488523

Strike, K. A. (1988, October). The ethics of teaching. *Phi Delta Kappan, 70*, 156–158.

Tabachnick, B. G., Keith-Spiegel, P., & Pope, K. S. (1991). Ethics of teaching: Beliefs and behaviors of psychologists as educators. *American Psychologist, 46*, 506–515. doi:10.1037/0003-066X.46.5.506

Tarpy, R. M., & Sawabini, F. L. (1974). Reinforcement delay: A selective review of the last decade. *Psychological Bulletin, 81*, 984–997. doi:10.1037/h0037428

Wittig, A. F., Perkins, D. V., Balogh, D. W., Whitley, B. E., Jr., & Keith-Spiegel, P. (1999). Treating students differentially: Ethics in shades of gray. In B. Perlman, L. I. McCann, & S. H. McFadden (Eds.), *Lessons learned: Practical advice for the teaching of psychology* (pp. 219–224). Washington, DC: American Psychological Society.

Zlokovich, M. S. (2004). Grading for optimal student learning. In B. Perlman, L. I. McCann, & S. H. McFadden (Eds.), *Lessons learned: Vol. 2. Practical advice for the teaching of psychology* (pp. 255–264). Washington, DC: American Psychological Society.

4

A TEXTBOOK CASE
OF TEXTBOOK ETHICS

WAYNE WEITEN, DIANE F. HALPERN, AND DOUGLAS A. BERNSTEIN

Traditional paper textbooks continue to play a central role in most psychology courses despite the premature obituaries written by education pundits enthusiastic about content-delivery innovations such as video, computer-assisted instruction, and the Internet. Indeed, textbook prices have recently become a hot issue, generating legislative hearings, new laws, and extensive hand-wringing in the press (Ayres, 2005; Bartlett, 2004; Chaker, 2006; Granof, 2007; Helderman, 2006; Silverstein, 2006). College textbook publishing is a $4 billion-a-year industry, and though students are the publishers' customers, teachers decide which books these customers buy. Ideally, decisions about textbook adoptions are based solely on judgments about which of the available books best serve the educational needs of teachers and students. But a teacher's choice of one book over another can have significant economic repercussions for students, authors, publishers, and bookstores. As a result, financial considerations may come to influence adoption decisions, and when money enters the picture, ethical issues are sure to follow.

We outline here the nature of these issues and offer some guidance about whether various practices are ethical or unethical. As veteran textbook authors, we have probably thought more than most of our colleagues about the ethics of the adoption process, but readers, please take note: The knowledge and experience that have enhanced our sophistication about the intricacies of adoption considerations, the publishing business, and the economics of both have undoubtedly exerted some influence on our views about what is ethical and what is not ethical. We are all also experienced teachers, though, so we hope our experience as authors has not left us overly biased or out of touch with the real world of textbook adoptions.

We organized this chapter around a series of issues about textbook adoption; we conferred about our responses; and we reached consensus on each with little guidance from previously published material. Our strategy was based partly on the fact that there is not much literature in this area. The American Psychological Association's *Ethical Principles of Psychologists and Code of Conduct* (APA, 2010) does not address textbook adoptions even tangentially. An excellent book titled *The Ethics of Teaching: A Casebook* (Keith-Spiegel, Whitley, Balogh, Perkins, & Wittig, 2002) touches briefly on several textbook issues, but its coverage of these matters amounts to only a few paragraphs. So, to be candid, we had to wing it. We hope our analyses will foster discussion and raise awareness of the ethical issues and dilemmas surrounding textbook adoptions.

CONTAINING THE COST OF TEXTBOOKS

The primary obligation that instructors have on behalf of their students is to provide a sound educational experience. Cost must be part of any professor's decision when selecting learning materials, but cost must be considered in a broader context. The College Board (2009) estimated the annual cost of books and supplies at between $1,098 and $1,116 a year. If we assume that 15% of these costs relate to supplies, then the average textbook costs per semester are between $933 and $948. So although textbook costs can strain any budget, they are a relatively small proportion of the total cost of a college education. Yet we believe that instructors need to consider costs when selecting course materials, but the focus should be on value: Do the materials warrant their cost? A quality textbook will advance students' understanding of complex topics and help students remember what they learned when the course is completed. Cost is one factor in deciding if a textbook is a good value, but it is not the only factor in selecting books or other materials. In addition to being sensitive to price when selecting textbooks, instructors can help to contain students' costs by submitting their textbook orders early and posting online information about the book well before the course begins. Doing so allows students to explore alternatives to buying the book at the campus bookstore (Advisory Committee on Student Financial Assistance, 2007).

Fair Use and Duplication of Materials

Is it ethical for instructors to post text materials online for duplication by students? The contents of textbooks are protected by copyright law. Distributing these materials without permission violates publishers' copyrights. The *fair use* doctrine does allow for very limited distribution (to students enrolled in a class) of very small portions of books, such as a table or a couple of diagrams, but wholesale duplication of textbook material would be a clear violation of copyright law. A key factor weighed in legal assessments of fair use is whether the use would harm the copyright owner's ability to exploit (i.e., sell) the work. Obviously, duplicating large portions of a textbook would harm a publisher's ability to market the book. Even the TEACH Act, a federal law passed in 2002 that liberalized the use of digital works in distance education, explicitly excludes textbooks from its coverage (TEACH Act, 2002). So, not only is unauthorized online distribution of textbook material unethical, it is also illegal.

Deciding Not to Use the Adopted Text

Is it ethical to require a textbook and then not use it? For example, suppose a teacher did not examine a book carefully prior to its adoption, but as the course progressed realized the mismatch between the textbook and student learning. Or perhaps on return from a teaching conference, a teacher makes the last-minute change to teach from a set of readings rather than the ordered textbook. A quality textbook is like a second teaching "voice" that provides background and reinforces concepts presented in class, extends student knowledge and understanding, and help students become independent learners. We cannot think of any justification for requiring a textbook and then not using it. If circumstances change at the last minute, arrange for the bookstore to buy back the book at full cost so as not to financially harm students.

Reselling Examination Copies

Is it ethical for instructors to sell examination copies of textbooks? To us, the only justifiable rationale for selling exam copies is that it puts more used books in the marketplace, thereby providing students with more opportunities to purchase less expensive texts. However, it seems likely that most faculty who sell exam copies do so because of the cash they will receive. Some faculty argue that selling exam copies is a convenient way to prune their book collections, but they could accomplish the same goal just as easily by giving the books to students or putting them in a departmental library.

Publishers point out that when faculty sell exam copies they deprive authors of the entitled royalties as partial compensation for the countless hours dedicated to planning, researching, writing, revising, and proofreading their books. When this argument is made in the case of authors of successful large-market books, it is not likely to generate much sympathy, but faculty need to realize that 90% to 95% of textbook authors earn very modest remuneration for their work. Publishers also note that each complimentary copy sold to a book buyer displaces the sale of a new book. Publishers factor these revenue losses into their book budgets, which forces them to increase text prices, so selling exam copies fuels inflationary pressures on textbook prices. Selling exam copies can also be viewed as a betrayal of publishers' trust in instructors' professionalism. An exam copy is a valuable commodity that publishers provide gratis to instructors, mainly in the hope that the latter will seriously consider adopting the book. When this hope goes unfulfilled because professors really only wanted to add the book to their personal library, publishers can live with that. They ask only that the text not be placed into the used book market instead. True, the exam copy becomes the instructor's property, but it strikes us as ethically questionable to accept something of value for free from publishers and then turn around and sell the text.

ACCEPTING GIFTS AND INCENTIVES FROM PUBLISHERS

We believe that, other than exam copies, instructors should not accept anything of value from a publisher, period. Although small items such as a coffee mug or a pen embossed with the company name are unlikely to sway a textbook decision, it is possible that they may influence the outcome, and even these small items can create the appearance of bribery.

Many professions are taking stronger positions against the acceptance of any gift that could possibly create a conflict of interest. For example, the National Academies, which includes the U.S. National Academy of Sciences, National Academy of Engineering, Institute of Medicine, and National Research Council, released new voluntary and regulatory measures with the goal of ending "long-accepted practices that create unacceptable conflicts of interest" (National Academies, 2009, para. 2). The new guidelines call on researchers and private practice physicians to "forgo gifts of any amounts from medical companies" (para. 3). We believe that college faculty should adhere to similar guidelines. There is no "bright line" indicator between the cost of gifts that are small and insignificant and those that might influence an instructor when selecting a textbook. Research in psychology has shown that people are often unaware of the influences on how they think and make decisions. In a series of experiments, Williams and Bargh (2008) demonstrated that just holding a hot cup of coffee for a few seconds can cause people to judge a person they are interacting with as warmer than when they hold a cup of iced coffee. Another example of unconscious influences on behavior is the finding that college students walk slower when they finished learning a list of words related to being old than when they learned a different list of words (Bargh, Chen, & Burrows, 1996). These and other studies make it likely that even if people do not believe that receiving a small gift affects their decision making, in fact, it is possible, and maybe even probable, that it does. Research on the impact of the gifts physicians receive from pharmaceutical and medical devices companies has suggested that even trivial gifts can influence physicians' treatment practices (Dana & Loewenstein, 2003; Rothman & Chimonas, 2008). In short, when in doubt about the ethics of receiving any gift (including an expensive meal), we believe that the ethical option is to politely decline any gift that might appear to compromise one's decision about which textbook to use.

Dinners and Junkets

Is it ethical for instructors to let publishers' sales representatives take them out to expensive dinners before making their adoption decisions? In thinking about this question, the fundamental issue is whether an expensive dinner is a bribe. Bribery to secure a contract is illegal, and it is often considered more egregious when the contract is with a public institution, which would include state-supported universities. We think that when selecting class-related materials—and in all of their decisions regarding their courses—instructors should adopt standards that put the education of their students first. It is clearly unethical if instructors allow themselves to be "bought" by the highest bidder. One can imagine a scenario in which competing book sales people offer ever more extravagant dinners to the decision makers in large-scale adoptions in an attempt to persuade these professors that their book is the best choice for that large enrollment class. When a meal exceeds the cost of a dinner at a typical family restaurant, the entire situation becomes suspect.

Is it ethical for instructors to attend publisher-sponsored trips during which they may provide publishers with updates on course trends and marketing feedback? There are times when instructors may travel to a distant location to participate in a focus group relating to a textbook or to learn about materials that are under development. However, if it is not clear that the purpose of the trip is to accomplish the work that has been planned, it may actually be a junket. A *junket* is a trip that is ostensibly taken for business purposes but really is more like a vacation. For example, to us, a 3-day trip to a sandy beach resort where an instructor is expected to work 1 hour a day seems more like a bribe than a legitimate business trip. If the trip can best be described as a junket, we recommend that the instructor ask to join the working group through a conference call from his or her home campus. If an expensive dinner can compromise an instructor's ability to dispassionately select a textbook on the basis of its educational merits alone, then a junket is even more suspect. We recommend against participating in publisher-paid junkets.

Incentives and Extravagant Honoraria

Is it ethical for instructors or departments to accept incentives for making adoptions? If an incentive is offered to an instructor, the answer is simple: No, it is not ethical. It is a kickback and similar to a public official accepting a bribe to give a company its government business. Some small, new publishing houses have tried to disguise the bribe by paying professors extravagant honoraria (up to $4,000) for reviewing texts, but the professors only receive the honorarium if they adopt the book in question (Bartlett, 2003). Given that these honoraria are 10 to 20 times higher than normal and are tied to an adoption, they clearly represent bribery in our opinion. Although not illegal in most states, Arkansas passed a law in 2007 that prohibits professors from accepting incentives from publishers in return for adoptions (Vu, 2007). However, just because a practice may be legal does not mean that the practice is ethical.

If the incentive is provided to the department to enhance instructional efforts, the situation is much more complicated and ambiguous. For example, if a department obtained a free computer for student use in a lab, one could argue that the department took advantage of an adoption situation for a worthwhile purpose. But there is no free lunch. The computer truly is not free—somebody paid for it. The publishers have one primary source of revenue—income from students who purchase texts and other learning materials. So some students, somewhere, paid for that "free" computer. It may be the department's own students, in that the publisher may have factored the computer's cost into the bookstore price negotiated for the adoption. In such cases, the department is really passing on a hidden student fee. It may not be unethical, but it is messy.

The heart of the problem that arises when departments seek incentives in return for adoptions is that the process can lead to an unseemly bidding war. In essence, the department is auctioning off its adoption. Furthermore, it is perhaps even more important in this situation that the adoption decision hinges not on which book the department believes would be the best fit for its students but on which publisher is most willing to provide attractive incentives. Unless the various adoption alternatives offer demonstrably equal value for students, it seems unlikely that students are well served by such a bidding process.

This practice also sends the wrong message to publishers and their representatives. The implicit message is that faculty and departmental administrators care less about book quality or how a text fits with departmental goals than about getting a piece of the publisher's financial action. We think that when departments have an opportunity to play publishers off against each other in return for a big adoption of texts of virtually equal value, it would be better to short-circuit the bidding war by negotiating a direct benefit for the students, such as a substantial discounting of the book's retail price at the bookstore.

FINDING THE BEST FIT FOR STUDENTS

Departments and faculty should consider how best to serve students and intended learning outcomes. This might entail the packaging of multiple works together (bundling) or tailoring an existing work specific to one institution's needs (customization). We address both of these approaches here.

Bundling Text-Related Ancillaries

Is it ethical for instructors to adopt shrink-wrapped bundles of text-related materials that preclude students' purchase of used books? Bundling of texts with supplementary materials is controversial for several reasons. First, it impairs or prevents students' efforts to purchase less expensive used books because bundles are available only at a student's local bookstores. Second, once students break into a bundle it typically cannot be resold, even locally, thus depriving the students of the opportunity to recoup some of their textbook costs later. Third, students complain because bundles sometimes include relatively insignificant ancillaries that are not fully integrated into the course. Concern about bundling has spiked dramatically in recent years, leading to the introduction of federal and state laws that regulate the practice. Most of these laws require that bundled materials also be made available by publishers and bookstores as individual elements (Reed, 2008).

Although bundling can add to students' educational expenses, we think it would be imprudent to characterize all bundling as unethical. In some cases, text ancillaries play a crucial role in an instructor's educational plan. Some instructors carefully assemble multifaceted learning packages designed to facilitate their educational efforts. Bundling can ensure that all students receive the instructional materials that they need in a course, and by arranging for bundling, professors can sometimes negotiate meaningful price discounts for their students because publishers are reassured that they will actually be able to sell new textbooks.

So to us, the ethical status of bundling depends on the motivation underlying it. If a bundle is assembled to maximize teaching efficacy and all of the elements in the bundle play a genuine role in instruction, there would seem to be no ethical dilemma. However, when a bundle includes trivial elements that are not clearly related to instructional goals or is primarily intended to promote the sale of new books, bundling appears ethically questionable.

Adding complexity to this issue is the fact that faculty members' good intentions can go awry. Publishers' sales representatives can be very convincing in touting the educational benefits of bundles that are created for the purpose of selling more new books. Surely, many instructors with pure intentions have been coaxed and cajoled by persuasive salespeople into ordering bundles that they genuinely hoped would improve learning outcomes but that they probably never would have assembled themselves. It is hard to criticize these optimistic and sometimes gullible instructors, and one cannot really condemn the sales representatives for being persuasive because that is their job. But instructors should be aware that the creation of bundles is more likely to be justified if the idea grows naturally out of their teaching goals and strategies rather than out of the salesmanship of publishers' representatives.

Customized Textbooks

When instructors or departments customize textbooks, is it ethical for them to receive royalties on these materials? It is hard to say how frequent this practice is, but according to an article in *The Wall Street Journal* (Hechinger, 2008), various academic departments are collecting tens of thousands of dollars in royalties from department-sponsored custom texts. True, many departments are strapped for funds, and these royalties can be used for worthwhile purposes, but we think the practice is regrettable if not unethical. First, when departments ask for royalties on customized adoption sales, those royalties are factored into the retail price of the book and thus become a hidden fee to be paid by students. We think that student fees should be explicit, not disguised. Second, like incentives for adoptions, these royalty arrangements send the message that departments want to muscle in on publishers' income, and they appear likely to foster unseemly negotiations (read collusion) between publishers and departments. The economics of textbooks are already severely strained. Publishers complain about inadequate profit margins; most authors earn relatively little for their work; college bookstores must compete with online distributors; and students feel as though they are paying too much for their texts. If academic departments were to become yet another financial stakeholder in this distressed economic system, the system seems likely to reach the breaking point. Finally, departmental royalty arrangements raise concerns about conflict of interest because the forces behind them may lead to decisions that benefit departments more than their students.

Instructor–Authors Adopting Their Own Book for Their Course

Is it ethical for instructors who are text authors to adopt their own book? We begin by considering what might be wrong about instructor–authors adopting their own books. Some argue that it is unseemly for instructors to make money from their own students. For example, in a speech to college students in Texas, President Obama said, "I taught law at the University of Chicago for 10 years, and one of the biggest scams is law professors write their own textbooks and then assign it to their students. They make a mint. It's a huge racket" (Dorning, 2008). Other critics assert that authors have a conflict of interest and obviously cannot make an unbiased assessment regarding which book is the best book for their students.

The first argument seems curious to us in that no one seems to mind when authors earn profits from other instructors' students. As long as the book is a legitimate text published by a reputable company that has been vetted through peer review, there is no obvious reason why one's own students should be exempted from paying the royalties that other students must pay. On the other hand, if the author's required text is a locally produced "vanity" text that has not been subjected to peer review, there is some reason for concern. A locally produced text could be excellent, but given the absence of any objective quality control, it does seem ethically questionable for instructors to profit from their own students. If faculty are convinced that their locally produced book represents the optimal text for their course, fine, but we think that they should decline royalties for the work or donate those royalties to their department.

The assertion that instructor–authors are unable to make an objective evaluation about which book is best for their students is undeniably true. But this may not be the problem that it appears to be at first glance. Textbooks certainly vary in quality, but assessments of textbook quality are multidimensional (involving evaluations of accuracy, currency, readability, pedagogy, etc.) inherently subjective, and eminently debatable. The notion that professors who are not authors can evaluate text options without bias and wisely select the best textbook is oversimplistic and naive. It is more realistic to hope that instructors can make informed judgments about which texts are likely to be the best fit for their course goals, teaching strategies, content emphases, and student clientele. When one thinks about textbook selection in terms of seeking the *best fit*, as opposed to the *best book*, the issue of author bias seems less problematic. Obviously, a textbook written by the instructor of a course is likely to be an excellent fit for the course. Moreover, authors' intimate familiarity with their own texts should facilitate well-thought-out linkages between text content, lectures, and other classroom activities.

Another consideration, and one that would only occur to authors, is that adopting a competitor's book rather than one's own can be viewed as a repudiation of one's own text. This perception may be inaccurate, but in the cutthroat world of textbook adoptions, sales representatives would quickly spread the word that because an author was not using her or his own text, there must be something wrong with it. (It is a little like what happens to a company's share price when Securities and Exchange Commission's filings show that top executives are dumping all their stock and options.) Thus, an open-minded decision to use a competitor's text could backfire on an author and result in economic harm for him or her and for the book's publisher. Given these realities, we venture to say that instructor-authors are virtually compelled to use their own texts.

In sum, it strikes us that few if any ethical problems arise when instructor–authors adopt their own texts. Still, many authors, accustomed as they are to the noncommercial milieu of academia, feel awkward or sheepish about making profits from their own students, so they voluntarily donate their locally generated royalties to their college, department, or student organizations. Although we do not think this admirable option should be mandated, we think it should be encouraged. Authors who choose to donate their local royalties probably should make note of this fact in their syllabi.

CONCLUSION

Are there general guidelines for thinking about the many ethical issues surrounding textbook adoptions? As we admitted in our opening paragraphs, there is very little published that provides guidelines for thinking about the many issues related to textbook adoptions. A good strategy for anyone who makes decisions about the use of textbooks is to consider how the consequences will support student learning, long-term retention, and the ability to apply what has been learned in appropriate out-of-class contexts. Of course, instructors may have other learning goals for students that should also be considered when making decisions about textbooks, such as developing critical thinking or ethical reasoning. The main idea is to consider how a decision about a textbook supports the instructor's goals for the class.

Given that textbooks involve costs to students, royalties for authors, and profits (or losses) for publishers, other ethical considerations concern the value of the textbook for students and the avoidance of even the appearance that an instructor or department has been bribed to make a particular decision about a textbook. Faculty members are role models for undergraduate and graduate students as these students develop their own ethical standards. There are also possible legal ramifications to accepting what might appear to be a bribe, so as noted previously, faculty should think carefully about accepting any gifts from publishers.

In addition to these very broad ideas, we think it would be prudent for instructors to keep several principles in mind. First, faculty should be mindful of the costs of textbooks and other learning materials and strive to contain these costs as long as they can do so without compromising the quality of students' educational experiences. Second, faculty should avoid accepting incentives of any kind from publishers because these incentives can undermine their objectivity in assessing learning materials and create conflicts of interest. Third, when it comes to bundling and customizing, intentions matter; if the primary goal of these practices is to constrain the availability of used books, then the practices appear ethically questionable. We hope that this chapter will spur deliberation and debate about the many ethical issues related to textbooks and, by extension, to other types of learning materials. We look forward to discussing our views on the ethics of textbooks with interested readers.[1]

REFERENCES

Advisory Committee on Student Financial Assistance. (2007). *Turn the page: Making college textbooks more affordable*. Retrieved from http://www2.ed.gov/about/bds comm/list/acsfa/turnthepage.pdf

American Psychological Association. (2010). *Ethical principles of psychologists and code of conduct (Amended June 1, 2010)*. Retrieved from http://www.apa.org/ethics/code/index.aspx

Ayres, I. (2005, September 16). Just what the professor ordered. *The New York Times*. Retrieved from http://www.nytimes.com

Bargh, J. A., Chen, M., & Burrows, L. (1996). The automaticity of social behavior: Direct effects of trait concept and stereotype activation on action. *Journal of Personality and Social Psychology, 71*, 230–244. doi:10.1037/0022-3514.71.2.230

Bartlett, T. (2003, June 27). Selling out: a textbook example. *The Chronicle of Higher Education*. Retrieved from http://chronicle.com

Bartlett, T. (2004, July 21). Witnesses at congressional hearing accuse textbook publishers of price gouging. *The Chronicle of Higher Education*. Retrieved from http://chronicle.com

Chaker, A. M. (2006, September 28). Efforts mount to cut costs of college textbooks. *The Wall Street Journal*. Retrieved from http://online.wsj.com

---

[1]We welcome readers' thoughts and comments on ethical issues related to textbook adoptions. Our email addresses are as follows: weitenw@unlv.nevada.edu, diane.halpern@cmc.edu, and douglas.bernstein@att.net.

College Board. (2009). *Trends in college pricing*. Retrieved from http://www.trends collegeboard.com/college_pricing/pdf/2009_Trends_College_Pricing.pdf

Dana, J., & Loewenstein, G. (2003). A social science perspective on gifts to physicians from industry. *JAMA, 290,* 252–255. doi:10.1001/jama.290.2.252

Dorning, M. (2008, February 22). Obama on a college textbook "racket." *The Swamp.* Retrieved from http://www.swamppolitics.com

Granof, M. (2007, August 12). Course requirement: Extortion. *The New York Times.* Retrieved from http://www.nytimes.com

Hechinger, J. (2008, July 10). As textbooks go "custom," students pay. *The Wall Street Journal.* Retrieved from http://online.wsj.com

Helderman, R. S. (2006, March 9). Virginia assembly passes bill to cut college textbook costs. *The Washington Post.* Retrieved from http://www.washingtonpost.com

Keith-Spiegel, P., Whitley, B. E., Jr., Balogh, D. W., Perkins, D. V., & Wittig, A. F. (2002). *The ethics of teaching: A casebook.* Mahwah, NJ: Erlbaum.

National Academies. (2009, April 28). *NEWS Voluntary and regulatory measures needed to reduce conflicts of interest in medical research, education, and practice.* Retrieved from http://www8.nationalacademies.org/onpinews/newsitem.aspx?RecordID= 1259

Reed, J. (2008, January 9). New state law to break book bundles. *Oregon Daily Emerald.* Retrieved from http://www.dailyemerald.com

Rothman, D. J., & Chimonas, S. (2008). New developments in managing physician–industry relationships. *JAMA, 300,* 1067–1069. doi:10.1001/jama.300.9.1067

Silverstein, S. (2006, November 7). When you can't afford to go buy the book. *Los Angeles Times.* Retrieved from http://www.latimes.com

TEACH Act, Pub. L. No. 107-273, 116 Stat. 1758, Title III, Subtitle C § 13301. §§ 110 and 112 of the Copyright Act, as amended by the TEACH Act. (2002).

Vu, P. (2007, August 28). States, colleges work to cut textbook costs. *Stateline.* Retrieved from http://www.stateline.org

Williams, L. E., & Bargh, J. A. (2008, October 24). Experiencing physical warmth promotes interpersonal warmth. *Science, 322,* 606–607. doi:10.1126/science.1162548

5

ETHICAL CHALLENGES OF ONLINE TEACHING

PATT ELISON-BOWERS AND CHAREEN SNELSON

Online technologies (e.g., e-mail, websites, course management systems) provide alternatives to traditional face-to-face instruction that have made it possible to offer courses either partially or completely online. Allen and Seaman (2010) identified four categories of course delivery that are based on the proportion of content delivered online: (a) traditional (0% online delivery), (b) web facilitated (1%–29% online delivery), (c) hybrid (30%–79% online delivery), and (d) online (80%–100% online delivery). In this chapter, we focus primarily on the fourth category, in which most or all of the course content is delivered virtually with the aid of online technologies.

The growth of online education has been phenomenal. The seventh annual Sloane Survey of Online Learning (Sloan-C, 2009) revealed that approximately 4.6 million students were enrolled in at least one online course in fall 2008, an increase of nearly 17% from the previous year (Allen & Seaman, 2010). As more students enroll in virtual courses, questions and concerns about ethical teaching practice in digital classrooms will continue to emerge.

Strike and Soltis (2004) described several types of ethical challenges within the educational context (e.g., punishment and due process, intellectual freedom, equal treatment of students, diversity, professionalism). These types of ethical issues are also present in virtual (online) classrooms, albeit with the added complexities of online course delivery. The online educator shoulders the solemn responsibility of handling student records, instructional materials, and private communications, which are stored and distributed in digital form. Additionally, the educator assumes the added responsibility of maintaining sufficient technical knowledge to avoid unfortunate breaches of confidential information. Although many additional ethical challenges emerge in an online format, we limit our discussion to the specific issues of digital privacy, intellectual property, and professional practice in the online classroom.

ETHICAL CHALLENGES OF DIGITAL PRIVACY IN ONLINE TEACHING

According to Burbules (2000), information and communication technologies have contributed to "a transformative moment in education" (p. 38). The information technology of today, although creating enormous opportunity for students, will simultaneously introduce instructors to a new set of ethical challenges inherent to virtual learning environments (Burbules, 2000; Kellner, 2000). As educators make the transition from traditional to virtual classrooms, they may be unprepared to face these new challenges. This is particularly true if their knowledge of best practice is grounded in what works within the face-to-face environment (Haughton & Romero, 2009) rather than the very different world of online teaching (Yoshimura, 2008). Nevertheless, educators have an obligation to provide students the highest quality education possible by the most effective means available (Dibiase, 2000).

Online education provides the flexibility of convenient access; however, a potential threat to privacy is present because of the necessity of digital file transmission and storage within an online course in which communications, assignments, and grades are transmitted electronically. This problem is further compounded by the fact that sensitive information may be stored on any combination of computers, including student and instructor machines as well as web servers where course sites are hosted for online access. Even student usage of the course website can be digitally tracked and recorded from the moment they login. There are significant digital data in an online course, and the potential for either abuse or unintentional disclosure of sensitive information is a grave concern (Ackay, 2008).

One ethical issue that may arise with assigned roles in the learning management system (LMS) is with respect to teaching assistants who may have access to student attendance records, assignments, and grades. Without proper supervision and training, the teaching assistant for the online course may have complete access to all student records, which would not typically be the case if assisting a course taught in a brick-and-mortar classroom. The opportunity is available for online teaching assistants to disclose private student information or to help a friend get a good grade. Consequently, it is imperative to ask teaching assistants to sign a confidentiality agreement and specify clear standards of ethical practice with respect to grading procedures. Furthermore, training in ethical teaching is suggested as an important strategy for the preparation of teaching assistants (Branstetter & Handelsman, 2000).

Guest access to online courses is another source of concern related to student privacy. Varvel (2009) argued that student identities must be protected from those who are outside of the course as per legal requirements under the Family Educational Rights and Privacy Act of 1974 (for an overview of this act, see http://www2.ed.gov/policy/gen/guid/fpco/ferpa/index.html). Guest access poses an ethical dilemma for online instructors who would like to bring in an expert guest lecturer yet hesitate because of privacy concerns. A similar issue occurs when another instructor requests guest access to review the course when preparing to teach online. In all situations related to guest access, caution is warranted to protect student privacy.

Information contained within an LMS is protected from unauthorized viewing when it remains within the course website. Privacy can be violated when information leaves the system. For example, a discussion forum is often composed of text entries. In some LMSs, registered users can subscribe to discussion posts so that they arrive via e-mail without the need to first log in to the system. The instructor may be able to turn off subscriptions so that this cannot occur. However, text can be copied and pasted for external storage very easily, thus removing the privacy afforded by the LMS. Anderson and Simpson (2007) referred to this as *textual permanence*. In other words, when text is submitted to a discussion forum or sent in an e-mail message, it can be copied and pasted to other locations or forwarded to any number of people. Once submitted, text messages can be redistributed forever. The ethical dilemma here is whether to allow anonymous posting and protect privacy or to keep names attached to posts for grading purposes. The decision may depend on the nature of the discussion and intended learning outcomes.

Another ethical issue closely related to privacy is that of surveillance of online students. Instructors, in their desire to promote the development of online learning communities and reduce isolation of individual students, might go online and pose as students. Actions of this nature have the potential to jeopardize the overall student–teacher relationship and evoke questions about trust, confidentiality, and informed consent (Parry, 2009). It is sometimes difficult to assess the kind of scrutiny that occurs in online courses and make ethical judgments about the use of such data (Anderson & Simpson, 2007; Parry, 2009). However Nagel, Blignaut, and Cronje (2007) made specific surveillance recommendations from their study of an undisclosed virtual student: obtain permission and ethical clearance, allow external supervision and monitoring, do not use a virtual student to spy on students or violate their trust or privacy, and do not manipulate students deliberately. The reactions of students when discovering one of their classmates was a virtual student controlled by the instructor ranged from benign to a sense of shock and betrayal (Nagel et al., 2007; Parry, 2009). Online teaching requires changes in the classroom, which takes a virtual form in online education, in areas such as engagement and trust and particularly how that trust is gained by the instructor in the online classroom (Haughton & Romero, 2009; Moore & Kearsley, 2005). We present here a digital privacy example:

> Dr. Smith teaches at a small midwestern university and has received a grant to assist him in developing his first online course. After taking several workshops on the subject of online teaching, Dr. Smith decided an important goal for his class should be to promote the development of online communities and reduce isolation of individual students in the online environment. After much study, Dr. Smith decided to approach this goal by assigning a teaching assistant for his course the role of virtual student. He believed there was enough evidence to support his assumption that a "phantom student" could stimulate participation in his course by embedding discussion questions and reduce isolation of students in the online learning environment by asking direct questions soliciting student opinion. However, at the conclusion of the course, when Dr. Smith shared this teaching method with his online class, he was surprised by some student reactions. Whereas many students reported no issues with the use of a virtual student in the course, some students reported strong feelings of shock and betrayal. In addition, two students sent Dr. Smith e-mails attacking his effectiveness and ethics as an instructor.

This example illustrates the practical problems associated with embedding a student in the virtual classroom. Following the recommendation of Nagel et al. (2007), Dr. Smith could have informed the class at the start of the semester that online interactions would be monitored. Perhaps more important than the legal issues are the difficulties introduced by compromising the trust of the students.

ETHICAL CHALLENGES OF INTELLECTUAL PROPERTY IN ONLINE TEACHING

When teaching an online course, it is important to use media appropriately. It is particularly important to follow the legal guidelines governing the use of the media. Two comprehensive resources that provide information about copyright and fair use of media are the U.S. Copyright Office (http://www.copyright.gov) and the Center for Social Media (http://www.centerforsocial

media.org). Individual instructors are responsible for current knowledge in areas such as changes in technology, policies, and guidelines as well as regulations in how material may be used in the online classroom. Often electronic material cannot be used in the same way materials are used in the traditional classroom, and differences in regulations can become confusing (Mitchell, 2009; Sweeney, 2006).

Copyright and fair use practices related to online video streaming serve to illustrate the confusion that can arise when using media in an online course as opposed to a live classroom. An instructor may lawfully play a DVD movie for students in a face-to-face classroom. However, if the same DVD is streamed online to students who view the movie remotely, then fair use provisions may fail to protect against charges of copyright infringement. This is exactly what happened at the University of California, Los Angeles, when the Association for Information Media and Equipment (http://www.aime.org) charged the university with copyright violation as a result of online video streaming of DVDs that had been purchased by the university (Hampton, 2010; Lutzker, 2010). The ensuing debate raises difficult questions about fair use exemptions in online education. One of these questions is whether a password-protected online course may be defined as a classroom. Another question is whether the exemption that allows live viewing in a face-to-face classroom may be extended to the virtual learning space? The complicated debate continues (Kolowich, 2010).

Managing intellectual property is a grave concern for the online educator. Unless the instructor creates original materials for the entire course, he or she will face the problem of how to distribute works created by others in an online classroom, if this practice is permissible at all. The central issue is how ownership is governed by copyright, which is "a form of protection grounded in the U.S. Constitution and granted by law for original works of authorship fixed in a tangible medium of expression" (U.S. Copyright Office, 2006, para. 1). In traditional classroom settings, educators have used the provisions of fair use to reproduce copyrighted materials for their classrooms ("Educational Uses of Non-coursepack Materials," 2007). However, the rules of fair use for distance programs "become much more rigorous when the materials are uploaded to websites, transmitted anywhere in the world and easily downloaded, altered, or further transmitted by students and other users, posing possible threats to the interests of copyright owners" (American Library Association, 2010, Background of Copyright Law section, para. 2). The TEACH Act, signed into law in 2002, was designed to help clarify how copyrighted materials could be used fairly in distance education. It is in every online educator's best interest to become familiar with the rules governing how copyrighted materials must be used.

With respect to intellectual property, there are several pragmatic strategies that an online educator could use when preparing materials for a course.

These include creating original content, linking to materials rather than making copies, teaching students how to obtain their own copies of materials such as articles, obtaining permission from the copyright owner, and using public domain materials or using materials released under a Creative Commons license. There are six main licenses available to authors who choose to publish their work under a Creative Commons license. Each license specifies the conditions under which the materials may be used (for an overview, see http://creativecommons.org/about/licenses/).

Online instructors should seek out information and strive to comply with individual policies governing online classrooms (Gearhart, 2001; Hallam, 1998; Mitchell, 2009). More specifically, it is prudent to be proactive about the latest rules governing intellectual property because local institutional policy may be found inadequate. In fact, institutional support in the form of policies on intellectual property has been rated as below average in a survey of colleges and universities across the United States (Seaman, 2009). We present here a scenario illustrating the complicated issues associated with online use of digital media.

> Dr. Jones teaches a course that includes a unit on psychological disorders. In the past, she purchased DVDs of video case studies showing people with various types of disorders. Dr. Jones would play these videos for her students to watch and discuss in class. Then, she was asked to design an online version of the course. The DVDs Dr. Jones used previously are expensive, and posting them online introduces some tricky legal and technical challenges. Instead, Dr. Jones turns to YouTube, where she has found numerous video clips of people who either discuss or display symptoms of psychological illnesses. These videos are public, and all Dr. Jones needs to do is add a link to each video in her online course materials. The YouTube videos make wonderful case studies because they are public, already online, and easy to link into the course materials. However, although it is true that the videos are publically available, is it ethical to use them as case studies in class?

Using online video may be simple and efficient, but it raises additional ethical concerns. Just because a YouTube video is publicly available does not imply that the creative work is in the public domain (from a legal perspective). Thus, faculty should ensure that online media are legally obtained and posted in accordance with existing regulations.

ETHICAL CHALLENGES OF PROFESSIONAL PRACTICE IN THE ONLINE CLASSROOM

Professional educators play a role as the guardians of academic integrity in the online classroom. Instructors who are aware of ethical responsibilities should be good role models for students as they teach or participate in the online environment. Unfortunately, this has not always been the case. Recently, a professor's acerbic and expletive-ridden e-mail reply to a student went viral after being forwarded to many people and resulted in an embarrassing situation about student course performance (Carter, 2010). Instructors have even lost their positions after posting information on social networking sites (Carter, Foulger, & Ewbank, 2008). Rules of netiquette (online etiquette) should be applied to every online correspondence with students (Shea, 2004). Anything that leaves the computer in an e-mail or online posting has been released into cyberspace, where it can be redistributed with ease.

Information about academic integrity should be shared with students early in the online experience. It is important to create learning opportunities for students that allow them to evaluate personal online activity by questioning the legality, violation of ethical codes, or the likelihood of harm of online activity (Ackay, 2008; Bodi, 1998; Lanier, 2006; Russell, 2006). Although professional educators should be working toward promoting academic integrity in an online environment, Mize, Rogers, and Gibbons (2002) maintained there are specific design features that, when used, promote academic integrity in online classes. The first feature is to clearly state that academic dishonesty is not acceptable and to provide specific examples. The second feature provides online course materials with a high degree of interaction. Finally, they recommend that an online course include a variety of evaluation materials. Using a plan for an online class that specifically factors in these design elements will encourage academic integrity at the onset of the course and assist the instructor in discouraging a climate of academic dishonesty.

Online instructors need to make themselves aware of institutional policies developed by their college or university as well as those developed by accreditation bodies regarding ethics and e-learning whenever such policies are available. Currently, most of these policies provide a set of standards in areas such as academic values, academic freedom, equality and diversity, and ethical student and staff behavior (Brey, 2006; International Society for Technology in Education, 2008; Woody, 2008). The Accreditation Board of Engineering and Technology (2004) requires schools to demonstrate an understanding of professional ethical responsibility (Chachra, 2005). It is equally important that colleges and universities have widely published use policies covering ethics in online learning environments in areas such as privacy, sanctions, and resources (Brey, 2006). Institutional support for students and instructors struggling with ethical issues is critical (Haughey, 2007).

The ethics codes of academic disciplines should address how ethical questions are solved in the online learning environment. Ethical instructors model appropriate behavior to students and have an impact far beyond the online classroom (Fulton & Kellinger, 2004; Woody, 2008). At this time it is possible for new faculty members and graduate students to teach without having taken a single class in ethics. In fact, only 6% of new psychology faculty or graduate students have taken an ethics course (Branstetter & Handelsman, 2000; Woody, 2008).

CONCLUSION

The ethical challenges of online teaching discussed in this chapter were in three broad areas: (a) digital privacy, (b) intellectual property, and (c) professional practice in the online classroom. Teaching in cyberspace requires working with digital communications and content that is distributed easily on the Internet. As a result, there are two primary responsibilities that online educators face beyond that of those in traditional classrooms. First, it is imperative that online educators are knowledgeable about policies governing privacy as well as how information and intellectual property should be managed in an online environment. It is also critical to maintain up-to-date technical skills, to be aware of how LMSs handle sensitive information, and to avoid unfortunate breaches of privacy. Both policy and technology have a tendency to be complicated and fraught with change. Yet, the rewards of maintaining knowledge in these areas are protection of both student records and professional reputation. As online education grows, educators need to be prepared for the challenges they may face before encountering avoidable problems.

REFERENCES

Accreditation Board of Engineering and Technology. (2004). *Criteria for accrediting engineering program*. Retrieved from http://www.abet.org/forms.shtml

Ackay, B. (2008). The relationship between technology and ethics: From society to schools. *Turkish Online Journal of Distance Education, 9*, 120–127.

Allen, I. E., & Seaman, J. (2010). *Learning on demand: Online education in the United States, 2009*. Retrieved from http://sloanconsortium.org/publications/survey/pdf/learningondemand.pdf

American Library Association. (2010). *Distance education and the TEACH Act*. Retrieved from http://www.ala.org/Template.cfm?Section=Distance_Education_and_the_TEACH_Act&Template=/ContentManagement/ContentDisplay.cfm&ContentID=25939

Anderson, B., & Simpson, M. (2007). Ethical issues in online education. *Open Learning: The Journal of Open and Distance Learning, 22*, 129–138. doi:10.1080/02680510701306673

Bodi, S. (1998). Ethics and information technology: Some principles to guide students. *Journal of Academic Librarianship, 24,* 459–463. doi:10.1016/S0099-1333(98) 90007-6

Branstetter, S., & Handelsman, M. (2000). Graduate teaching assistants: Ethical training, beliefs and practices. *Ethics & Behavior, 10,* 27–50. doi:10.1207/S15327019 EB1001_3

Brey, P. (2006). Social and ethical dimensions of computer-mediated education. *Journal of Information, Communication and Ethics in Society, 4,* 91–101. doi:10.1108/ 14779960680000284

Burbules, N. C. (2000). Response: Why philosophers of education should care about technology issues. In L. Stone (Ed.), *Philosophy of education yearbook* (pp. 37–41). Carbondale, IL: Philosophy of Education Society.

Carter, D. (2010, March 9). Professors, beware: Your nasty eMail could go viral. *eCampus News: Technology for Today's Higher-Ed Leader.* Retrieved from http:// www.ecampusnews.com/2010/03/09/professors-beware-your-nasty-email-could-go-viral/

Carter, H. L., Foulger, T. S., & Ewbank, A. D. (2008). Have you Googled your teacher lately? *Phi Delta Kappan, 89,* 681–685.

Chachra, D. (2005). Beyond course-based engineering ethics instruction: Commentary on 'Topics and cases for online education in engineering.' *Science and Engineering Ethics, 11,* 459–461. doi:10.1007/s11948-005-0015-2

Dibiase, D. (2000). Is distance education a Faustian bargain? *Journal of Geography in Higher Education, 24,* 130–135. doi:10.1080/03098260085216

Educational uses of non-coursepack materials. (2007). Retrieved from Stanford University Libraries and Academic Information Resources website: http://fairuse. stanford.edu/Copyright_and_Fair_Use_Overview/chapter7/7-b.html

Family Educational Rights and Privacy Act, 20 U.S.C. § 1232 (1974).

Fulton, J., & Kellinger, K. (2004). An ethics framework for nursing educators on the Internet. *Nursing Education Perspectives, 25,* 62–66.

Gearhart, D. (2001). Ethics in distance education: Developing ethical policies. *Online Journal of Distance Learning Administration, 4*(1). Retrieved from http://www.west ga.edu/~distance/ojdla/spring41/gearhart41.html

Hallam, S. (1998). Misconduct on the information highway: Abuse and misuse of the Internet. In R. N. Stichler & R. Hauptman (Eds.), *Ethics, information and technology readings* (pp. 241–254). Jefferson, NC: McFarland.

Hampton, P. (2010, March). Campus to restart streaming of instructional video content. *UCLA Newsroom.* Retrieved from http://newsroom.ucla.edu/portal/ucla/ campus-to-re-start-streaming-of-154601.aspx

Haughey, D. (2007). Ethical relationship between instructor, learner and institution. *Open Learning: The Journal of Open and Distance Learning, 22,* 139–147. doi:10. 1080/02680510701306681

Haughton, N., & Romero, L. (2009). The online educator: Instructional strategies for effective practice. *MERLOT Journal of Online Learning and Teaching, 5*, 570–576. Retrieved from http://jolt.merlot.org/vol5no3/haughton_0909.pdf

International Society for Technology in Education. (2008). *National educational technology standards for teachers*. Retrieved from http://www.iste.org/Content/NavigationMenu/NETS/ForTeachers/2008Standards/NETS_T_Standards_Final.pdf

Kellner, D. (2000). New technologies/new literacies: Reconstructing education for the new millennium, *Philosophy of Education 2000*, 21–36. Retrieved from http://www.ed.uiuc.edu/EPS/PES-yearbook/2000/kellner%2000.pdf

Kolowich, S. (2010, February). Who's right on video copyright? *Inside Higher Ed*. Retrieved from http://www.insidehighered.com/news/2010/02/04/copyrightredux

Lanier, M. (2006). Academic integrity and distance learning. *Journal of Criminal Justice Education, 17*, 244–261. doi:10.1080/10511250600866166

Lutzker, A. (2010). Educational video streaming: A short primer. *Association for Media and Equipment News, 24*. Retrieved from http://www.aime.org/news.php?download=nG0kWaN9ozI3plMlCGZ%3D&u=100614120000

Mitchell, R. L. G. (2009). Ethics in an online environment. *New Directions for Community Colleges, 2009*(148), 63–70. doi:10.1002/cc.387

Mize, C., Rogers, K., & Gibbons, A. (2002). That's my story and I'm sticking to it: Promoting academic integrity in the online environment. In P. Barker & S. Rebelsky (Eds.), *Proceedings of World Conference on Educational Multimedia, Hypermedia and Telecommunications 2002* (pp. 604–609). Chesapeake, VA: Association for the Advancement of Computing in Education. Retrieved from http://www.editlib.org/p/10116

Moore, M., & Kearsley, G. (2005). *Distance education: A systems view* (2nd ed.). Belmont, CA: Thomson Wadsworth.

Nagel, L., Blignaut, S., & Cronje, J. (2007). Methical Jane: Perspectives on an undisclosed virtual student. *Journal of Computer-Mediated Communication, 12*(4), Art. 10. Retrieved from http://jcmc.indiana.edu/vol12/issue4/nagel.html doi:10.1111/j.1083-6101.2007.00376.x

Parry, M. (2009, May 20). Online professors pose as students to encourage real learning. *The Chronicle of Higher Education, 55*(38), A10.

Russell, G. (2006). Globalisation, responsibility and virtual schools. *Australian Journal of Education, 50*, 140–154.

Seaman, J. (2009). *Online learning as a strategic asset: Vol. II. The paradox of faculty voices: Views and experiences with online learning*. Retrieved from http://www.sloan-c.org/publications/survey/APLU_Reports

Shea, V. (2004). *Netiquette*. Retrieved from http://www.albion.com/netiquette/book/index.html

Sloan-C. (2009). *Learning on demand: Online education in the United States, 2009*. Retrieved from http://sloanconsortium.org/publications/survey/learning_on_demand_sr2010

Strike, K., & Soltis, J. F. (2004). *The ethics of teaching*. New York, NY: Teachers College Press.

Sweeney, P. C. (2006). Faculty, copyright law and online course materials. *Online Journal of Distance Learning Administration*, 9(1). Retrieved from http://www.westga.edu/~distance/ojdla/spring91/sweeney91.htm

TEACH Act, Pub. L. No. 107-273, 116 Stat. 1758, Title III, Subtitle C § 13301. §§ 110 and 112 of the Copyright Act, as amended by the TEACH Act. (2002).

U.S. Copyright Office. (2006). *Copyright in general*. Retrieved from http://www.copyright.gov/help/faq/faq-general.html

Varvel, V. E. (2009). Student privacy issues, ethics, and solving the guest lecturer dilemma in online courses. *eLearn Magazine*. Retrieved from http://www.elearnmag.org/subpage.cfm?section=articles&article=28-1

Woody, W. D. (2008). Learning from the codes of the academic disciplines. *New Directions for Higher Education, 2008(142)*, 39–54. doi:10.1002/he.302

Yoshimura, M. (2008). Educators in American online universities: Understanding the corporate influence on higher education. *Journal of Education for Teaching, 34*, 295–305. doi:10.1080/02607470802401412

6

CONSUMING SCHOLARSHIP OF TEACHING AND LEARNING: USING EVIDENCE-BASED PEDAGOGY ETHICALLY

REGAN A. R. GURUNG

Picture this. You just read a research article in your disciplinary area that inspires you to significantly change what you do in the classroom. You think it will help your students perform better. You implement the new technique in one section of your course (and not the other). At the end of the semester, you scan student evaluations to see if students liked the new approach, and you examine the grade distribution for changes in student performance from previous semesters. Is there anything wrong with this picture? It all depends on what safeguards you put in place, how much attention you paid to the modification of your class, and whether there were significant differences in performance. What if one class did worse than the other (either the class in which you implemented your new technique or the one in which you did not)? How will you know if your intervention helped?

There are at least four major areas in which ethics plays a role in teaching: (a) ethical considerations for classroom pedagogy or course design, (b) faculty–student interactions, (c) the use of pedagogical research, and (d) conducting pedagogical research or the Scholarship of Teaching and Learning (SoTL; covered in depth in Chapter 2, this volume). Many faculty conduct SoTL research, and still more faculty strive to use SoTL to change how they teach and how their students learn (Gurung, Kerns, Ansburg, Alexander,

& Johnson, 2008; Weimer, 2006). Unfortunately, directly implementing the results of SoTL research without considering the implications of doing so and without adequate modifications of the methodology for one's class can result in negative outcomes for students. In this chapter, I consider the issues involved in using SoTL or what I believe is best described as ethical scholarly teaching. I begin by clarifying some key definitions (e.g., SoTL, scholarly teaching), describing ethical pedagogy and, consequently, the ethical use of evidence-based pedagogy.

CRITICAL DEFINITIONS

Empirical research on pedagogy, teaching, and learning is referred to as *Scholarship of Teaching and Learning* (SoTL; see Irons & Buskist, 2008; Pan, 2009; Smith, 2008). SoTL is best described as intentional, systematic reflection on teaching and learning that results in peer-reviewed products made public (Gurung & Burns, 2011). Scholarly teaching occurs when a teacher intentionally and systematically reflects on and modifies his or her teaching (Richlin, 2001). A scholarly teacher who shares the empirically based evidence collected in a peer-reviewed public format, presentation, or publication is doing what is traditionally referred to as SoTL. Although the term *SoTL* is relatively new, teachers have been striving to improve teaching and learning for centuries (see Gurung & Schwartz, 2009, for a review). *Pedagogical research* (Gurung & Schwartz, 2009) is a more general term that captures the essence of scholarly work conducted to enhance teaching and advance learning. Pedagogical research encompasses SoTL and scholarly teaching, but it does not imply that the results are published or presented (a key part of being labeled *SoTL*). However, pedagogical research implies a rigorous methodological investigation that goes beyond mere scholarly teaching.

Of direct relevance to this chapter is the concept of scholarly teaching. Some instructors use evaluative techniques that go beyond student evaluations as a means for evaluating their teaching. They may engage in self-reflection and consult with colleagues on course design, syllabi, lectures, and methods of effectiveness. These instructors explore the published literature on teaching and learning for the purpose of modifying their own teaching. They also use the scientific method to ensure that the modifications are effective. Essentially, scholarly teachers begin by identifying a problem; they then review the literature, modify their techniques, and measure student outcomes to determine if the pedagogical modifications resulted in changes in student learning. A systematic approach not only informs SoTL but also improves subsequent courses. The results of these instructors' reflections and course modifications may be summarized in a teaching portfolio and may be used to review the instructor for merit or promotion, but the results are not submitted for publication. The classroom essentially becomes the teacher's laboratory (Smith, 2005).

Using SoTL to modify and evaluate teaching effectiveness (i.e., scholarly teaching) is the hallmark of a skillful teacher (Brookfield, 2009). As Shulman (2002) stated, "an educator can teach with integrity only if an effort is made to examine the impact of his or her work on the students" (p. vii), an obligation that Shulman referred to as the *pedagogical imperative*. Similarly, others (Bernstein & Bass, 2005) have argued that pedagogical research of this sort should be seen as part as one's professional responsibility as a teacher. However, to teach effectively through the practice of SoTL may result in overlooking the ethical obligations. Is it ethical to give one group of students material (e.g., a study guide) while withholding the material from another group of students to test the efficacy of that material? To help answer this question and set the stage for a full discussion of ethical obligations, I first describe ethical scholarly teaching.

ETHICAL SCHOLARLY TEACHING: USING PEDAGOGICAL RESEARCH

Not everyone has the time or inclination to conduct his or her own pedagogical research. Those who do conduct SoTL follow the ethical guidelines in their respective disciplines or rely on the ethical guidelines generated by organizations focused on SoTL, such as the International Society for the Scholarship of Teaching and Learning or the Carnegie Foundation (Gurung & Martin, 2007; Hutchins, 2002). However, an element of practicing ethical pedagogy is the conscientious monitoring of whether one's teaching innovations are making a difference. Teaching innovations are often based on personal reflections and conversations with peers, but innovations can and should also be fueled by reviewing the empirically based literature. Scholarly teachers rely on the published literature to modify their own teaching and almost always apply basic rudiments of the scientific method to measure effectiveness. Essentially, they begin by identifying a problem, reviewing the literature, modifying what they do, and measuring student outcomes to determine if the pedagogical changes resulted in changes in student learning (Richlin, 2001). For example, a scholarly teacher may create a course portfolio to document systematic observations and course modifications. This approach allows teachers to identify problem areas and search the literature for solutions. Putting in the time and effort to be an ethical scholarly teacher is commendable, but one should not implement new techniques without considering implications of new pedagogies. It is critical to keep in mind that one teacher's students may be very different from students in other settings. Ethical scholarly teaching requires careful evaluation of the implications of the innovations teachers want to incorporate into their class. Teachers also have to be cognizant that other factors may change (e.g., student motivation), implicitly or explicitly, when they try to incorporate a pedagogical innovation. Key questions to ask are, Will these findings work for my students? What will changing this assignment or using this new technique do to my other assignments and to the other pedagogical strategies I use? Consider the following scenario:

> Dr. Marteen read a journal article discussing how role play seems to get students engaged. He wonders if using role play in his abnormal psychology class will work better than using scenarios. He decides to use the role-play technique in one section of his class and scenarios in the other section. Students in one section of the course engage in role playing (i.e., clients or therapists), and a second section reads scenarios that include similar content. Students in the role-playing class appear to enjoy the experience and seem to be more excited about coming to class. Dr. Marteen also feels more enthusiastic about the role-playing section of his course.

Did Dr. Marteen use SoTL ethically? To answer this question, it is important to know whether he considered the research in light of his local context; for example, did he ascertain whether students would be comfortable participating in a role play? Also, did he have a plan for collecting data that would help him to see whether the new technique improved learning outcomes? Did he consider how role playing might change the nature of the faculty–student interaction? If the answer to each of these questions is yes, then it is likely that Dr. Marteen was using SoTL ethically.

ETHICAL PEDAGOGY

There are explicit guidelines for how clinical psychologists should interact with their clients. What about guidelines for interacting with students? Clinical licensing guidelines can be translated to teaching (Hatcher, 2009). A second source of guidance is available from guidelines for institutional review boards (IRBs).

Many countries have some form of human subject protection programs and guidelines (Gurung & Martin, 2007). For example, in the United States, most universities have statements for their researchers mandating adherence to the requirements set forth in Title 45, Part 46 of the *Code of Federal Regulations* (U.S. Department of Health and Human Services, Protection of Human Subjects, 2009). The Belmont Report (U.S. Department of Health, Education, and Welfare, National Commission for the Protection of Human Subjects of Biomedical and Behavioral Research, 1979) also provides a general framework for what constitutes ethical research. Three general ethical principles (i.e., respect for persons, beneficence, and justice) from the Belmont Report directly apply to the use of pedagogical research in class. For example, teaching methods, classroom design, assignments, and assessments should be designed solely to enhance the well-being of an individual student, and there should be a reasonable expectation that the pedagogy will work. Those teaching practices that may not have a reasonable expectation of success (i.e., novel untested approaches that deviate substantially from standard approaches that could potentially be too challenging or inappropriate) should become the subject of scientific scrutiny. For example, an instructor of a counseling psychology class may want students to get a hands-on look at counseling. To achieve this goal, the instructor may require students to work in a mental health clinic. Allowing undergraduate students to deliver psychological services is both unethical and potentially dangerous. Furthermore, even if the students did have an ethical and legally acceptable role in the clinic, would that close contact with patients be pedagogically appropriate? When applying the reasonable expectation standard for successful innovation, the teacher should conduct a robust assessment of the pedagogical modification. In other words, the teacher should design and carry out a research study to determine the effectiveness of the new technique. Thus, teachers carry the ethical obligation of exploring new or different teaching strategies and techniques and evaluating the efficacy of those techniques. Teachers must also consider the rights of the participants, or students, when testing pedagogical innovations.

Respect for Students

Respect for persons (U.S. Department of Health, Education, and Welfare, National Commission for the Protection of Human Subjects of Biomedical and Behavioral Research, 1979) requires researchers to treat participants with autonomy, and participants must be free to withdraw from a research study. This basic principle becomes particularly relevant when a teacher is conducting an assessment of a pedagogical innovation. Students, or more explicitly, participants, are at risk for coercion in SoTL-based research. There are at least two ways coercion can occur within this context. First, a student who is asked to complete an evaluation or participate in a study of a new technique may feel coerced because of the difference in power between the instructor (researcher) and student (participant). The student may elect to participate because he or she fears a negative outcome as a result of not participating. Second, a student may feel coerced to participate because he or she appreciates or likes the professor. In this case, a student may feel uncomfortable with a particular innovation but participate because he or she wants to do the teacher a favor. Although this second type of coercion may appear to be less negative, it still infringes on the student's right to make an autonomous decision about whether to participate and is, therefore, potentially unethical.

To address this potential for coercion, it is imperative that researchers take steps to minimize the degree to which students feel pressured to participate in SoTL. For example, strategies like ensuring that the person responsible for collecting evaluation data is unknown to the students can decrease the potential for coercion. Unlike research studies, in which a participant has the right to withdraw, a student cannot be expected to drop a class because he or she does not want to experience a new technique. However, if a student decides not to complete the evaluation, the student retains the ability to withhold his or her data from the study. Students should be provided with the opportunity to refuse to complete the evaluation. In other words, in the earlier scenario, it would be ethical for Dr. Marteen to require all students to take an exam or write an essay based on the material presented in the role play or scenarios, but it may not be ethical for him to force all students to evaluate how they felt about the role playing—that a student could withhold his or her data is a desirable option. Faculty can request that students evaluate the pedagogy, but steps should be taken to ensure that the assessments are optional and anonymous.

Beneficence

Beneficence, or the need to maximize possible benefits and minimize possible harm, is a second critical ethical assurance that should be provided to research participants. The need to minimize possible harm should also be obvious within the context of teaching and SoTL. Implementing a new technique without a thorough understanding of the potential for harm may result in poor teaching or harmful circumstances. Sometimes teachers may hear about a pedagogical innovation (e.g., using online exams or weekly quizzes) and implement change without consulting the literature. Every effort should be made to ensure that innovations are not harmful, and regulations (U.S. Department of Health and Human Services, Protection of Subjects, 2009) provide specific guidance for conducting educational research that is consistent with standard educational practice. For example, most classroom changes in pedagogy constitute no more than minimal risk of harm to a subject, and such research does not require the investigator to obtain written informed consent from the student (U.S. Department of Health and Human Services, Protection of Subjects, 2009; see § 46.117, para. (c)). Of course, even if implementing something that a teacher has just heard about presents no more than minimal risk (and does not require written informed consent), due diligence requires considerable thought. Before implementing a new technique, it is still important to thoroughly and critically evaluate the merits of the pedagogy. If a faculty member knows ahead of time that he or she is going to implement a new teaching approach and he or she plans to make the outcomes part of the SoTL literature, it is best to seek IRB approval before making and assessing the change.

One could argue that the risk of a new intervention is that it may result in less student learning or lower grades. Regardless of interpretations of federal regulations, the IRB has the power to set more stringent standards for pedagogical research. For example, Section 46.405 of the U.S. Department of Health and Humans Services, Protections of Human Subjects (2009) concerns research "involving more than minimal risk but presenting the prospect of direct benefit to the individual subjects." Paragraph (a) cautions that the IRB must find the risks are justified by the anticipated benefit to the students. Similarly, Paragraph (b) suggests that "the relation of the anticipated benefit to the risk is at least as favorable to the subjects as that presented by available alternative approaches."

Teachers also have a great opportunity to maximize possible benefits as they implement SoTL research. Students learn more effectively because of new pedagogies. Consider a second example:

> Dr. Luddite notices that more students are bringing laptop computers to class. The students say they use their laptops to type their notes, but often they can be found surfing the Internet, updating their profiles on social networking sites, and playing computer games. Dr. Luddite becomes frustrated, and he decides to ban laptops and other wifi-enabled devices during class. Dr. Luddite finds two studies indicating that students who use laptops in class learn less, and he uses SoTL research to justify his decision.

Dr. Luddite's decision to ban wifi-enabled devices may indeed allow students to be more engaged and learn more effectively. If students are distracted during class, it seems intuitive that they will not learn well. Research also indicates that using a computer is detrimental to learning (Fried, 2008). However, if Dr. Luddite did not consider valid uses of the laptop as a means for justifying his personal philosophy against technology, he may have inadvertently restricted students from viable learning resources. Using SoTL to justify a teaching philosophy may not seem unethical, but using SoTL to build a philosophy that then drives a pedagogical choice is a sound practice.

Justice

Research participants should benefit from the pedagogical research. There are many instances when research conducted with undergraduate students does not directly benefit the student. Improved pedagogies benefit all students. If an instructor is using the literature ethically and implementing new pedagogies based on empirical evidence, students benefit from improved learning. Both case examples illustrate that using SoTL can benefit students.

Here I offer a more vivid and explicit example. After reading articles showing that online exams reduce student stress and save class time (Landrum, 2007; Stowell & Bennett, 2010), I moved all my exams for my introductory psychology class online. This gave me more class time to go into great depth, saved resources (e.g., printing, answer sheets), and most important, gave my students the opportunity to take the exam at a convenient time. I minimized the likelihood of academic dishonesty by using an honor code and applying recommendations from the pedagogical literature (Gurung & Daniel, 2005). My students reported being significantly less stressed while taking the exams, and preliminary analyses suggest learning was positively influenced. In this instance, students directly benefited from the use of SoTL.

CONCLUSION

Teachers should not be dissuaded from trying new SoTL-based techniques. In fact, teaching innovations are a sign of outstanding teaching. By the same token, teachers need not attempt to make changes in response to every published SoTL recommendation. If a technique does not fit a teacher's style, or if it is not developmentally appropriate for his or her student population, it may not be useful. The biggest challenge for faculty is to conduct sound research in which the instructor is keeping all other elements beyond what is manipulated or changed as equal as possible.

It is a teacher's responsibility to assess pedagogy using sound methodology. It is not enough to replicate a validated method without evaluating effectiveness in multiple settings. One way to be an ethical teacher and to use evidence-based pedagogy ethically is to be an active pedagogical researcher. As SoTL becomes more accessible, teachers must attend to conducting ethical research. They should use pedagogical research to change their pedagogy in the same way that research guides the larger psychological practice.

REFERENCES

Bernstein, D., & Bass, R. (2005, July–August). The scholarship of teaching and learning. *Academe*, 91(4), 37–43. doi:10.2307/40253429

Brookfield, S. D. (2009). *The skillful teacher: On technique, trust, and responsiveness in the classroom.* San Francisco, CA: Jossey-Bass.

Fried, C. B. (2008). In-class laptop use and its effects on student learning. *Computers & Education, 50*, 906–914.

Gurung, R. A. R., & Burns, K. (2011). The social psychology of teaching and learning. In E. Y. Hammer & D. Mashek (Eds.), *Social psychology and teaching* (pp. 1–31). Malden, MA: Wiley-Blackwell.

Gurung, R. A. R., & Daniel, D. (2005). Evidence-based pedagogy: Do pedagogical features enhance student learning? In D. S. Dunn & S. L. Chew (Eds.), *Best practices for teaching introductory psychology* (pp. 41–56). Mahwah, NJ: Erlbaum.

Gurung, R. A. R., Kerns, N., Ansburg, P., Alexander, P., & Johnson, D. (2008). The scholarship of teaching and learning in psychology: A national perspective. *Teaching of Psychology, 35,* 249–261. doi:10.1080/00986280802374203

Gurung, R. A. R., & Martin, R. (2007, July). *Code of conduct: Internationalizing the ethics of SoTL.* Poster session presented at the meeting of the International Society for the Scholarship of Teaching and Learning, Sydney, Australia.

Gurung, R. A. R., & Schwartz, E. (2009). *Optimizing teaching and learning: Pedagogical research in practice.* Malden, MA: Blackwell.

Hatcher, J. W. (2009, October). Can the ethics of therapy inform the ethics of teaching? In R. E. Landrum & M. A. McCarthy (Chairs), *When ethics and teaching collide: Should the ethics of teaching be more controversial?* Presentation at the Society for the Teaching of Psychology Best Practices Conference, Atlanta, GA.

Hutchins, P. (Ed.). (2002). *Ethics of inquiry: Issues in the scholarship of teaching and learning.* Menlo Park, CA: Carnegie Foundation for the Advancement of Teaching and Learning.

Irons, J. G., & Buskist, W. (2008). The scholarship of teaching and pedagogy: Time to abandon the distinction? *Teaching of Psychology, 35,* 353–356. doi:10.1080/00986280802373957

Landrum, R. E. (2007). Introductory psychology student performance: Weekly quizzes followed by a cumulative final exam. *Teaching of Psychology, 34,* 177–180.

Pan, D. (2009, January). What scholarship of teaching? Why bother? *International Journal for the Scholarship of Teaching and Learning, 3,* 1–6.

Richlin, L. (2001). Scholarly teaching and the scholarship of teaching. [Special issue] *New Directions for Teaching and Learning: Scholarship revisited: Perspectives on the scholarship of teaching 2001, 86,* 57–68.

Shulman, L. S. (2002). Foreword. In P. Hutchins (Ed.), *Ethics of inquiry: Issues in the scholarship of teaching and learning* (pp. v–viii). Menlo Park, CA: The Carnegie Foundation for the Advancement of Teaching and Learning.

Smith, R. (2005). The classroom as a social psychology laboratory. *Journal of Social and Clinical Psychology, 24,* 62–71. doi:10.1521/jscp.24.1.62.59175

Smith, R. (2008). Moving toward the scholarship of teaching and learning: The classroom can be a lab, too! *Teaching of Psychology, 35,* 262–266. doi:10.1080/00986280802418711

Stowell, J. R., & Bennett, D. (2010). Effects of online testing on student exam performance and test anxiety. *Journal of Educational Computing Research, 42,* 161–171. doi:10.2190/EC.42.2.b

U.S. Department of Health and Human Services, Protection of Human Subjects, 45 C.F.R. pt. 46. (2009). Retrieved from http://www.hhs.gov/ohrp/policy/ohrpregulations.pdf

U.S. Department of Health, Education, and Welfare, National Commission for the Protection of Human Subjects of Biomedical and Behavioral Research. (1979). *The Belmont report: Ethical principles and guidelines for the protection of human subjects of research.* Retrieved from http://ohsr.od.nih.gov/guidelines/belmont.html

Weimer, M. (2006). *Enhancing scholarly work on teaching and learning: Professional literature that makes a difference.* San Francisco, CA: Jossey-Bass.

II

STUDENT BEHAVIORS

7

STRATEGIES FOR ENCOURAGING ETHICAL STUDENT BEHAVIOR

VINCENT PROHASKA

Academic dishonesty, especially cheating and plagiarism, seems to be on the rise in higher education (McCabe, Treviño, & Butterfield, 2001). Some instructors feel powerless to prevent their students from behaving in unethical ways that disrupt students' opportunities for real learning. In this chapter, I argue that instructors can take actions that will reduce academic dishonesty in their classes, and I offer practical advice in how to do so. I answer two specific questions that instructors face in almost every class:

- How do I prevent cheating on my quizzes and examinations?
- How do I prevent students from plagiarizing their written assignments?

Faculty hope that academic dishonesty will cease to exist. However, cheating and plagiarizing have proven resistant to change and are unlikely to disappear without concerted effort. Keith-Spiegel, Tabachnick, Whitley, and Washburn (1998) conducted a survey of faculty and found, perhaps not surprisingly, that they identified cheating as the most onerous component of teaching. Even more troubling, evidence reviewed by McCabe et al. (2001) suggests that academic dishonesty is increasing. There are many reasons underlying academic dishonesty, and some are clearly outside of an instructor's control. Nonetheless, despair is not the answer; instructors and institutions can and do influence the incidence of academic dishonesty. Deliberate efforts to prevent cheating and plagiarism are necessary and can be effective. The alternative to prevention is the likely continued increase in academic dishonesty. Indeed, Davis and Ludvigson (1995) argued that increases in academic dishonesty might be tied to decreases in instructor standards. That is, if instructors are "watering down" course content, grading mediocre work as excellent, and generally "going through the motions," then students may see no benefit from engaging in the honest and difficult work of learning. A similar argument, that faculty may be responsible for allowing dishonest behavior to flourish, was made more recently in a commentary by Young (2010). In other words, researchers are suggesting that students seem willing to rise (or fall) to the ethical levels set by institutions and instructors.

It has been long established that institutional honor codes can be effective deterrents to academic dishonesty (McCabe et al., 2001; Whitley & Keith-Spiegel, 2001; see also Chapter 8, this volume, for specifics about honor codes). But it is not simply the presence or absence of a code that matters. Establishing an honor code is not sufficient. An institution must implement and maintain its honor code with a systematic set of programs, workshops, and day-to-day activities. For example, Roig and Marks (2006) surveyed students both before and 1 year after a code was established. Although they found no changes in students' attitudes toward cheating, they noted that the college had not implemented programs to support the code. An honor code can only be expected to be effective if that code creates a climate in which academic honesty is expected and enforced (McCabe et al., 2001).

A climate of academic honesty affects students' perceptions of how ethically they are behaving. Research has consistently demonstrated that the most important factor in whether students behave honestly is their perception of their peers' behavior (Caldwell, 2010; McCabe & Bowers, 2009; McCabe, Butterfield, & Treviño, 2006; McCabe & Treviño, 1993; Pulvers & Diekhoff, 1999; Whitley, 1998). If students believe that everyone else is cheating, then they will cheat too. Similarly, Engler, Landau, and Epstein (2008) asked students to estimate their own, their friends', and the average college student's willingness to cheat and plagiarize. Not surprisingly, students overestimated the dishonesty of both their friends and other students compared with their own. Thus, although students reported themselves as relatively honest, they felt most other students were not. Jordan (2001) also found that students who self-identified as having cheated in the past believed that more students cheated, and they reported actually seeing more students cheat.

Engler et al. (2008) advised institutions to continually and consistently express expectations for academic honesty. Similar recommendations, and strong reminders that honor codes must be backed by institutional programs that educate students and encourage academic honesty, have been made by Caldwell (2010), Macdonald and Carroll (2006), McCabe et al. (2001), Roig and Marks (2006), and Whitley and Keith-Spiegel (2001).

My central assumption is that even in institutions lacking honor codes, instructors can create climates in their own classes that either support or undermine academic honesty. Thus, I suggest that instructors create their own classroom atmosphere that leads students to perceive that everyone is honestly and ethically attempting to learn. Moving the expectation of academic honesty from the institution to the classroom level is central to Engler et al.'s (2008) social-norms-based suggestion to keep academic honesty at the forefront of academic activities. Similarly, Macdonald and Carroll (2006) advocated a holistic approach to prevention, that is, an approach that involves all levels of the institution, even students, and focuses on educational activities to reinforce the value of academic honesty in lieu of a focus on detection and punishment.

PREVENTING CHEATING

I have been arguing that faculty play a central role in fighting academic dishonesty. Furthermore, that role should be proactive rather than reactive. So, what can a faculty member do to be proactive in preventing cheating? Consider the following scenario:

> Michael is teaching abnormal psychology. He wants to test his students frequently with a combination of scheduled examinations and pop quizzes, predominantly using multiple-choice questions. But his classrooms tend to be crowded, and he is worried that using multiple-choice questions might make cheating too easy. Michael's first step in preventing cheating and in establishing a climate of ethical behavior is answering this question: Why should students learn the material in my course? Cheating is a lot easier than learning. Why should his students invest the additional time and effort?

Thinking about why students should work to achieve the learning objectives of the course prepares instructors to explicitly explain their objectives, either in the syllabus or on the first day of class or both. A climate of ethical behavior begins when an instructor prepares a course to improve students' knowledge, skills, and abilities and then explains the importance of acquiring knowledge, skills, and abilities. Admittedly, explaining the relevance of psychology courses may be more difficult than explaining the relevance of professional courses. Yet every psychology course must have some relevance to students' futures. Instructors have an ethical responsibility not to waste students' time, effort, and money. Instructors can stress that academic dishonesty eliminates any value added for the student because academic dishonesty eliminates student learning. Thus, academic honesty is then directly and immediately linked to student learning and development.

Including a statement about academic honesty in the course syllabus becomes the gateway for discussing ethics in class, preferably early in the semester. Just as an honor code alone is insufficient, a mere statement on academic dishonesty alone is insufficient. An instructor must convey that the statement in the syllabus has real meaning. Davis and Ludvigson (1995) suggested that instructors should stress how cheating actually interferes with learning. Although it is important to remind students of the seriousness of academic dishonesty (i.e., that students can and have been expelled and that people have lost jobs and careers), it is also important to avoid an exclusive focus on detection and punishment (e.g., "Don't cheat because I'll catch you"). Davis and Ludvigson found that statements about academic honesty and sanctions do serve as a deterrent. Remind students that behaving dishonestly conflicts with their self-image as honest people.

The preceding discussion indicates that the first steps in preventing cheating start before the course begins. I continue here with the earlier scenario:

> After discussions with his colleagues and students enrolled in last semester's classes, Michael places an academic integrity statement in his syllabus and spends considerable time discussing both the policy and the importance of the policy relative to his learning goals. He further explains his rationale for regular testing and links repeated testing to student learning.

In addition to effectively communicating standards for ethical behavior and penalties for unethical behavior, it is also essential for Michael to take concrete steps during the class to actively discourage cheating. For example, when administering examinations Michael can take several small steps (Hollinger & Lanza-Kaduce, 2009; McCabe et al., 2006) to make in-class cheating more difficult:

1. Space desks and students as far apart as possible. Granted, in today's overcrowded classrooms this might be difficult to accomplish. The old procedure of leaving an empty desk between students is probably long gone. However, try to keep students from being so close that seeing one another's papers is unavoidable.
2. Tell students to turn off phones, pagers, and other electronic devices. Do not allow such devices to remain on desks or in view (or in students' ears).
3. Remind students that they cannot leave the room during the exam; trips to the restrooms or to food machines should be completed before the exam begins.

4. If using multiple-choice questions, use several forms of the exam so that questions and/or answer orders are scrambled. Most test bank programs produce multiple versions of a test with relative ease. Hollinger and Lanza-Kaduce (2009) found that both cheaters and noncheaters reported multiple versions of an exam as the most effective technique for preventing cheating.

5. Avoid reusing the same examination questions from semester to semester or allowing students to keep graded exams, especially if those exams are to be reused. Certainly the safest course is never to allow students to keep exams. Students can not only share exams locally but also broadly with students from other institutions. If an instructor is using questions from a test bank, it is even more important to safeguard the exams so that students cannot share them.

These prophylactic measures not only make cheating more difficult but, perhaps more important, they also establish that the instructor is aware of potential opportunities for cheating and is actively combating them. When instructors convey to students a high probability of being caught, it may reduce the perception that others are cheating successfully. Nath and Lovaglia (2009) found that instances of cheating decreased after they began using a computer program to help identify cheaters on their multiple-choice tests. Despite the preliminary and anecdotal evidence suggesting that these actions may reduce cheating, their effects on students' perceptions or behaviors have not been systematically studied.

In-class examinations require careful proctoring. Active proctoring means monitoring the room, periodically moving around, or at least looking around. In a commentary offering a graduate student's view of academic honesty issues, Bates (2009) reported observing students exchanging examination papers when the instructor left the room to make a phone call. An instructor who leaves the room during an examination or who sits in front but is clearly absorbed in another task risks conveying that cheating will be successful. Vigilance is important because if students observe cheating, then they are more likely to engage in unethical behavior (Keith-Spiegel et al., 1998).

Online quizzes or examinations present special difficulties (Young, 2010). For example, instructors cannot control whether student use textbooks or other resources during quizzes and exams. Instructors also cannot prevent early exam takers from noting specific questions and sharing them with classmates. However, as Watson and Sottile (2010) noted, there is little empirical research on whether online students are more likely to cheat than students in traditional classroom settings. The self-report studies that have been conducted have yielded inconsistent results. Nonetheless, instructors should still use proactive measures to prevent online cheating. Brothen and Wambach (2001) suggested that strict time limits should be applied to each question so that even if students are taking the test with a peer or with an open textbook there will be insufficient time to discuss or look up answers. A second strategy includes randomly selecting test questions from a much larger pool of questions so that students cannot simply pass the questions to one another. Because it is easy for online students to collaborate, instructors must be explicit about whether collaboration is allowed and, if so, the precise parameters of that collaboration.

PREVENTING PLAGIARISM

A second major form of academic dishonesty is plagiarism. As with cheating, there is much instructors can do proactively to avoid receiving the papers so many of us dread. Consider a new scenario:

> Angela is teaching cognitive psychology and wants to assign written assignments, mostly reviews and analyses of journal articles. How does she prevent getting plagiarized papers?

Angela's starting point is to establish a climate of ethical behavior and showing her students how ethical writing is important to their learning and development. That is, as I suggested earlier, instructors should explain to their students how plagiarism interferes with their opportunities to learn.

There is considerable debate concerning what students know about plagiarism (Belter & du Pré, 2007; Blum, 2009; Roig, 1997). Roig (1997) suggested that students have some difficulty in identifying plagiarized passages, but faculty also vary considerably in their views of the definition of plagiarism. Roig (2001) found moderate disagreement among professors when they were asked if a specific passage was plagiarized. Perhaps even more disturbing, when presented with a difficult passage to paraphrase, 30% of professors copied some of the original text into their paraphrases.

Perceptions of plagiarism also may be evolving in light of current technologies (Young, 2010). Leask (2006) argued that plagiarism should be seen as culturally constructed and that the definition will therefore vary across cultures. Therefore, instructors should convey their expectations clearly to their students. For example, because the amount of cutting and pasting individual instructors allow might differ, an instructor must establish clear standards. Instructors cannot assume that their individual standards are shared by their students' other instructors.

A second step that instructors can take to reduce plagiarism is to explicitly teach students about plagiarism. That is, they can require students to complete assignments focused on avoiding plagiarism. There is evidence that such time is well spent. For example, Schuetze (2004) compared two classes taught by the same instructor. In both classes, students received a lecture on proper citation and plagiarism, but in one class the lecture was followed by a homework assignment. Schuetze found that students who completed the homework made fewer citation mistakes on their term papers, felt they had a better understanding of plagiarism, and were more confident that they could avoid plagiarizing. Similarly, Belter and du Pré (2007) found that students who completed an online exercise to learn about plagiarism were less likely to plagiarize. Students must understand the material if they are to avoid plagiarism. Roig (1999, 2001) demonstrated that students and faculty were more likely to plagiarize a difficult passage than an easy one. Thus, the ability to paraphrase without plagiarizing is clearly linked to the ability to understand the material read. In practice, instructors need to consider the appropriateness of their assignments and the instruction that students may need to successfully complete those assignments.

A third way to reduce plagiarism is to provide students with specific instruction on proper paraphrasing. As with general knowledge about plagiarism, there is evidence that giving students explicit instruction and practice pays off. Landau, Druen, and Arcuri (2002) found that when students received instruction about appropriate ways of paraphrasing, they were less likely to plagiarize.

Barry (2006) and Walker (2008) also found that students who completed exercises designed to teach them proper paraphrasing techniques were able to demonstrate an increase in their knowledge about plagiarism. Paraphrasing can be taught and reinforced through practice. However, the real value in instructing students about plagiarism and paraphrasing is that students develop an awareness of appropriately citing research. Furthermore, students learn the instructor's criteria and expectations. Students will assume that the likelihood of successfully plagiarizing when an instructor has explicitly provided instruction on plagiarism is low.

SUMMARY

Many instructors lament the current state of academic honesty. Regardless of whether an institution has an effective honor code and programs to support it, the instructor can still affect the ethical climate. Academic honesty is important because it contributes to a student's education and development (Bates, 2009; Blum, 2009; Davis & Ludvigson, 1995). Indeed, the climate must begin with the assertion that student learning is central to all course activities. Students must work to master the course material, and instructors must engage students in learning. Without such engagement and without a bond or commitment between instructors and students to work together, academic honesty is not required.

The recommendations for reducing cheating and plagiarism are relatively straightforward. More important, faculty should attend to implementing strategies that will reduce academic dishonesty. Systematically attending to teaching students how to appropriately learn is central to increasing ethical practice.

REFERENCES

Barry, E. S. (2006). Can paraphrasing practice help students define plagiarism? *College Student Journal, 40*, 377–384.

Bates, C. (2009, February 20). A student's view: Why cheating matters. *The Chronicle of Higher Education, 55*(24), A36.

Belter, R. W., & du Pré, A. (2007, August). *Plagiarism: Ignorance is not bliss.* Poster session presented at the meeting of the American Psychological Association, San Francisco, CA.

Blum, S. D. (2009, February 20). Academic integrity and student plagiarism: A question of education, not ethics. *The Chronicle of Higher Education, 55*(24), A35.

Brothen, T., & Wambach, C. (2001). Effective student use of computerized quizzes. *Teaching of Psychology, 28*, 292–294. doi:10.1207/S15328023TOP2804_10

Caldwell, C. (2010). A ten-step model for academic integrity: A positive approach for business schools. *Journal of Business Ethics, 92*, 1–13. doi:10.1007/s10551-009-0144-7

Davis, S. F., & Ludvigson, H. W. (1995). Additional data on academic dishonesty and a proposal for remediation. *Teaching of Psychology, 22*, 119–121. doi:10.1207/s15328023top2202_6

Engler, J. N., Landau, J. D., & Epstein, M. (2008). Keeping up with the Joneses: Students' perceptions of academically dishonest behavior. *Teaching of Psychology, 35*, 99–102. doi:10.1080/00986280801978418

Hollinger, R. C., & Lanza-Kaduce, L. (2009). Academic dishonesty and the perceived effectiveness of countermeasures: An empirical survey of cheating at a major public university. *Journal of Student Affairs Research and Practice, 46*, 587–602.

Jordan, A. E. (2001). College student cheating: The role of motivation, perceived norms, attitudes, and knowledge of institutional policy. *Ethics & Behavior, 11*, 233–247. doi:10.1207/S15327019EB1103_3

Keith-Spiegel, P., Tabachnick, B. G., Whitley, B. E., Jr., & Washburn, J. (1998). Why professors ignore cheating: Opinions of a national sample of psychology instructors. *Ethics & Behavior, 8*, 215–227. doi:10.1207/s15327019eb0803_3

Landau, J. D., Druen, P. B., & Arcuri, J. A. (2002). Methods for helping students avoid plagiarism. *Teaching of Psychology, 29*, 112–115. doi:10.1207/S15328023 TOP2902_06

Leask, B. (2006). Plagiarism, cultural diversity and metaphor—implications for academic staff development. *Assessment & Evaluation in Higher Education, 31*, 183–199. doi:10.1080/02602930500262486

Macdonald, R., & Carroll, J. (2006). Plagiarism—a complex issue requiring a holistic institutional approach. *Assessment & Evaluation in Higher Education, 31*, 233–245. doi:10.1080/02602930500262536

McCabe, D. L., & Bowers, W. J. (2009). The relationship between student cheating and college fraternity or sorority membership. *Journal of Student Affairs Research and Practice, 46*, 573–586.

McCabe, D. L., Butterfield, K. D., & Treviño, L. K. (2006). Academic dishonesty in graduate business programs: Prevalence, causes, and proposed action. *Academy of Management Learning & Education, 5*, 294–305. doi:10.5465/AMLE.2006.22697018

McCabe, D. L., & Treviño, L. K. (1993). Academic dishonesty: Honor codes and other contextual influences. *The Journal of Higher Education, 64*, 522–538. doi:10.2307/2959991

McCabe, D. L., Treviño, L. K., & Butterfield, K. D. (2001). Cheating in academic institutions: A decade of research. *Ethics & Behavior, 11*, 219–232. doi:10.1207/S15327019EB1103_2

Nath, L., & Lovaglia, M. (2009). Cheating on multiple-choice exams. *College Teaching, 57*, 3–8. doi:10.3200/CTCH.57.1.3-8

Pulvers, K., & Diekhoff, G. M. (1999). The relationship between classroom dishonesty and college classroom environment. *Research in Higher Education, 40*, 487–498. doi:10.1023/A:1018792210076

Roig, M. (1997). Can undergraduate students determine whether text has been plagiarized? *The Psychological Record, 47*, 113–122.

Roig, M. (1999). When college students' attempts at paraphrasing become instances of potential plagiarism. *Psychological Reports, 84*, 973–982. doi:10.2466/PR0.84.3.973-982

Roig, M. (2001). Plagiarism and paraphrasing criteria of college and university professors. *Ethics & Behavior, 11*, 307–323. doi:10.1207/S15327019EB1103_8

Roig, M., & Marks, A. (2006). Attitudes toward cheating before and after the implementation of a modified honor code: A case study. *Ethics & Behavior, 16*, 163–171. doi:10.1207/s15327019eb1602_6

Schuetze, P. (2004). Evaluation of a brief homework assignment designed to reduce citation problems. *Teaching of Psychology, 31*, 257–262. doi:10.1207/s15328023top3104_6

Walker, A. L. (2008). Preventing unintentional plagiarism: A method for strengthening paraphrasing skills. *Journal of Instructional Psychology, 35*, 387–395.

Watson, G., & Sottile, J. (2010). Cheating in the digital age: Do students cheat more in online courses? *Online Journal of Distance Learning Administration*, *13*(1). Retrieved from http://www.westga.edu/~distance/ojdla/spring131/watson131.html

Whitley, B. E., Jr. (1998). Factors associated with cheating among college students: A review. *Research in Higher Education*, *39*, 235–274. doi:10.1023/A:1018724900565

Whitley, B. E., Jr., & Keith-Spiegel, P. (2001). Academic integrity as an institutional issue. *Ethics & Behavior*, *11*, 325–342. doi:10.1207/S15327019EB1103_9

Young, J. R. (2010, April 2). High-tech cheating abounds, and professors bear some blame. *The Chronicle of Higher Education*, *56*(29), A1.

8

THE HONOR SYSTEM: INFLUENCES ON ATTITUDES, BEHAVIORS, AND PEDAGOGY

BETH M. SCHWARTZ, HOLLY E. TATUM, AND JERRY W. WELLS

> I pledge absolute honesty in my academic work and in all personal relation-
> ships at Randolph College. I will maintain the integrity of my word, and I
> will respect the rights of others. Realizing that these standards are an inte-
> gral part of life at Randolph College, I assume my obligation to uphold this
> honor pledge. If at any time I fail to live up to my obligation of this pledge,
> I will report myself to the Chair of the Judiciary Committee. I will also ask
> others to report themselves for any infraction of this pledge.
> —Randolph College Honor Code Pledge

Academic integrity has received a great deal of attention as institutions of higher education look for ways to deal effectively with dishonest behaviors, including cheating and plagiarism, which some believe is the most critical issue facing academia today (Davis, Drinan, & Gallant, 2009). Given the prevalence of the problem, Davis and colleagues (2009) challenged educational institutions to determine ways to prevent cheating and suggested cultivating a culture in which academic dishonesty is clearly unacceptable.

An honor system has been shown to effectively reduce dishonest behaviors such as cheating (e.g., McCabe & Treviño, 1993). There is a growing trend of revitalizing honor systems (e.g., Melgoza & Smith, 2008) or introducing new modified honor systems (e.g., McCabe & Pavela, 2000). Although there is a long history of honor codes at many institutions of higher learning, most researchers have focused on how an honor code affects the attitudes and behaviors of students rather than on pedagogy. In this chapter, we provide a brief history of honor systems in higher education, explain how an honor code influences academic dishonesty, examine how an honor system can impact pedagogy, and offer practical advice for implementing an honor code in a classroom.

HISTORY OF HONOR CODES

Academic integrity was first associated with an honor system in 1736 at the College of William and Mary in Virginia. The code stated that "special care must be taken of their morals, that none of the Scholars presume to tell a Lie . . . or do any Thing else that is contrary to good Manners" (College of William and Mary, 1736). Honor codes developed during this time included rules about the personal lives of students, such as dress and classroom decorum. In the late 18th century, colleges began to develop the traditional honor codes that still exist today. As Woodrow Wilson (1905, p. ES1) aptly stated, "The honor system is the name given to the practice of conducting examinations, not under the surveillance of proctors . . . but under the self-direction of the pupils themselves."

The college-bound population began to increase in the 1940s, resulting in a term paper industry that threatened the integrity of honor codes (Gallant, 2008). College administrators and faculty began to fear that there was a lack of academic integrity in higher education; they responded by adding faculty-run judiciary committees designed to improve the effectiveness of the existing honor codes. However, these committees only widened the gap between the students and the professors and administration, further damaging the state of academic integrity. Honor codes all but disappeared from institutions in the 1950s. In the late 1990s, illicit term paper sales increased exponentially with the emergence of the Internet. As a result, traditional and modified versions of the honor code reemerged because colleges needed to take some type of action to decrease the perceived rise of academic dishonesty (Gallant, 2008).

Both modified and traditional honor systems continue to be a part of the academic culture at many colleges and universities. A traditional honor system is ingrained in a college's culture, deriving from a long history in the college's life. A traditional system is marked by dual responsibility, that is, the obligation for students to report themselves and others when the honor code has been violated. An honor pledge is signed in a formal assembly or acknowledged on written assignments and exams. The traditional system operates through a student-run adjudication process (McCabe & Pavela, 2000). Some of the privileges associated with traditional honor systems include unproctored tests and self-scheduled final exams. At most institutions with these systems, the honor code influences not only academic behavior but also all aspects of college life.

In contrast, a modified honor code may not allow for unproctored exams and does not require a pledge, and a combination of students, faculty, and administrators play a role in both the judicial system and promoting academic integrity (McCabe & Pavela, 2000). Often in the modified honor system there is no obligation to report oneself or a peer if the honor code is violated. The following example helps to clarify the difference between traditional and modified honor systems.

> In an introductory psychology course, a student discovers that a peer turned in the same paper for both a psychology and sociology class assignment. The student who is aware of the violation has a responsibility to confront the peer who committed the infraction and ask her to turn herself in to the chair of the judiciary committee. A meeting between the accused student and the chair of the judiciary committee is required within 2 days. If a violation is believed to have occurred, the case goes to the judicial committee, which holds a hearing, determines whether an honor violation occurred, and if needed, recommends sanctions. Professors decide whether to apply the sanctions recommended by the committee or impose alternative consequences.

Dual responsibility requires that all members of the academic community uphold the honor pledge for themselves and for others. In this example, this same incident would be handled differently at an institution with a modified system; it is unlikely that the student who observes the honor violation would be required to bring it to the attention of the professors and very unlikely that the student would be required to confront her peer and contact a member of the judiciary system. In a modified honor system, faculty have the autonomy to either pursue the incident on their own or turn it over to the committee.

Academic dishonesty is not a new concern for educators. Bowers (1964) published the first large-scale study on academic dishonesty. Then, 30 years later, data were collected again at nine of the same colleges and showed increases in academic dishonesty, especially in the form of cheating on exams (McCabe & Treviño, 1997). This increase in academic dishonesty is most consistently shown in large universities, especially those without an honor code. The greatest increase in dishonesty is students cheating on tests, rather than on other written work such as homework (McCabe, Treviño, & Butterfield, 2001). Some of the cheating on tests occurs in online courses in which students are less likely to cheat overall but more likely to cheat on a test than in live classes (Watson & Sottile, 2010). Furthermore, there is growing concern about an increase in plagiarism, which has been attributed in part to the ease with which students can now simply cut and paste material from a myriad of online sources (Gilmore, 2010). For a comprehensive review of student cheating, see Davis et al. (2009), who discuss what constitutes academic cheating, the prevalence of cheating, and the types of strategies institutions use to confront academic dishonesty.

Findings from numerous studies indicate that the presence of an honor code reduces academic dishonesty (e.g., McCabe & Pavela, 2000; McCabe & Treviño, 1993). For instance, McCabe and Pavela (2000) reported that the percentage of students who admit to cheating on written work was lower on college campuses with an honor code (45%) than on those without an honor code (56%). Findings indicate significant reductions in cheating both on tests and written assignments, ranging from one third to one half (Dodd, 2007). These findings are based on self-report data; therefore, one must consider that perhaps those who attend an institution with an honor code would not admit to cheating because it goes against the institutional culture, deflating that percentage. However, there is enough empirical evidence to conclude that honor codes influence both attitudes and behaviors.

RESPONDING TO ACADEMIC DISHONESTY

How do faculty respond when they become aware of academic dishonesty? Several research studies indicate that professors do not deal with the majority of cases that occur in their own classrooms. In fact, Nadelson (2007) found that faculty reported only 38% of the suspected academic dishonesty cases at one institution. Faculty may not report infractions for several reasons, including the stress created by confronting a student, time constraints, fear of retaliation or legal action, or the belief that students will eventually experience consequences. However, the primary reason faculty do not report incidents of academic dishonesty is a lack of clear evidence (Keith-Spiegel, Tabachnick, Whitley, & Washburn, 1998). Addressing student cheating was rated by faculty as one of the most negative aspects of their role as instructors; however, an institutional honor code creates an obligation for all faculty and students to address each occurrence of academic dishonesty. A well-structured honor system provides clear procedures for dealing with instances of academic dishonesty and reduces the time and effort required by the faculty to address cases of academic dishonesty. Not surprisingly, faculty are more likely to report academic dishonesty when an honor code is present (McCabe, 1993).

In an honor system, there is less ambiguity and a clearer procedure for how to handle instances of academic dishonesty. For example, if a faculty member suspects that a student has cheated on a test, the system requires the faculty member to question the student about the behavior and then determine if the honor code has been violated. At this point the student is given the opportunity to explain the suspected behavior—an opportunity that could potentially eliminate the need to pursue the issue of academic dishonesty any further. Consider the following example:

> In an abnormal psychology class, a professor received a test from a student that raised suspicion. The professor was concerned that the student might have used additional resources in completing a closed-book take-home exam. This student had earned mediocre grades throughout the first half of the semester. However, the student submitted very high-quality work on

the third test. The professor scheduled a meeting with the student during which he expressed his concern about the test. The student replied that she had taken a course on the specific topic covered on the test and then discussed her knowledge in detail. The conversation satisfied the professor, who concluded that the student had not violated the honor code.

If the faculty member determined that the student violated the honor code, the student would be asked to turn him- or herself in to the chair of the judiciary board. The process that follows includes an investigation by student members of the judiciary committee, a hearing in which all parties have an opportunity to provide evidence, and finally, recommended sanctions determined by the committee. At institutions with honor systems, faculty cannot simply determine consequences for suspected academic dishonesty on their own. It is important to record each incident so that an institution can address multiple offenses by the same student. The presence of an honor system is particularly helpful for untenured faculty, who may be concerned about reporting infractions and who worry about the effect that reporting an infraction may have on teaching evaluations as well as relationships with students, colleagues, and the administration. At schools with a well-defined honor system, students know that regardless of who is teaching a class, all issues of academic integrity are handled through the same institutional system. At many institutions with traditional honor systems, students are given 24 hours to turn themselves in to the judiciary chair, at which point the burden is removed from the faculty member.

EMBEDDING THE HONOR CODE WITHIN INSTITUTIONAL CULTURE

The level of academic integrity is determined not merely by the presence of an honor code but also by the extent to which the policy is embedded in the culture and understood and accepted by students, faculty, and administration. How often academic honor is discussed, whether student work is pledged (i.e., student signature on submitted work), and whether the honor pledge is posted in classrooms are all important factors in promoting academic integrity on a college campus. The honor system can be embedded within the ongoing dialogue on campus in many ways. For example, Randolph College holds an honor assembly before each final exam week to review the policies and procedures of the honor system; during the assembly students reaffirm their pledge to uphold the honor code. The repeated "conversations" about the honor system are inversely related to academic dishonesty because the dialogue improves student understanding and acceptance of the policies. Even at schools without an honor code, a commitment to the discussion of academic honor significantly decreases cases of academic dishonesty (McCabe & Treviño, 1993). In fact, even when an honor code is implemented, if it is not part of the culture and climate of the institution, it will not be effective at reducing academic dishonesty (Vandehey, Diekhoff, & LaBeff, 2007).

To ensure the effectiveness of an honor system, discussions on academic integrity should include the requirement that all students act in accordance with the honor code. The presence of an honor code creates greater awareness of students' own sense of morality, focusing on why it is important to do the right thing, and contributes to a sense of community and trust on campus (McCabe & Treviño, 1993). An honor code decreases the perception that others on campus are cheating, which in turn affects whether a student engages in academically dishonest behavior. Students who believe their peers are cheating may feel disadvantaged and therefore engage in dishonest behaviors to maintain their academic standing. One of the variables that distinguish cheaters from noncheaters is the belief that most students approve of cheating (Vandehey et al., 2007). This belief is consistent with the finding we discuss subsequently, that students' perceptions of their peers' behavior with regard to cheating is the strongest predictor of academic dishonesty (McCabe & Treviño).

Here we consider how an honor code can be influential in reducing the incidence of academic dishonesty in one's classroom. Instructors require different types of assignments with varying expectations or rules about how students may complete them. Too often, faculty assume that students are well aware of how the honor code applies within their classes. For example, in the Psychology Department at Randolph College, when students are writing papers for their collaborative senior research project, they are allowed to write the method and results sections together, but they must write the introduction and discussion sections independently. Faculty provide explanations and examples of how students may collaborate in their writing and when they must work independently. Discussing expectations about appropriate collaboration and academic integrity specific to each course is integral to the success of the honor system. One way to achieve this is to include a statement on the syllabus as to how the honor code applies to each assignment in the course. Explaining the importance of the honor system as it applies in the course further illustrates to students that academic integrity is a priority in the classroom and at the institution.

In addition to encouraging clear expectations with regard to academic work, the presence of an honor system allows faculty to extend privileges not typically available without an honor system. For instance, an instructor can make exams available to students during a specified period of time. A time limit is imposed; students are not allowed to use any materials when taking the test; and they are asked to return the test when completed. Tests can be used from one semester to the next with the understanding that old tests are not to be shared. Take-home exams can also be given with a clear understanding of what material can and cannot be used when completing the test. This testing environment is in stark contrast to the testing environment in institutions where a clear lack of trust is present and proctors are encouraged to closely monitor student behavior. Perhaps one of the most valuable components of an honor code is the availability of self-scheduled exams. Students schedule their exams during exam periods throughout the final exam week. Because students are taking the same exams at different times, they are expected to keep both the difficulty level and test material confidential (McCabe, Butterfield, & Treviño, 2003).

Although honor codes are often found at smaller schools, large universities have been successful in both introducing and revitalizing integrity policies. The University of Maryland introduced a modified honor system in 1990 (see McCabe & Pavela, 2000). Texas A&M University was able to revitalize an honor code that has ties to the institution's roots as a Reserve Officers' Training Corps school. During the revitalization process, the university not only established an honor council and honor system office but also organized a campaign to promote them (Melgoza & Smith, 2008). This campaign included the slogan Know the Code as well as programs aimed at educating the campus community on academic integrity. The Texas A&M model is a test case worth reviewing given its reliance on empirical evidence and collaboration among faculty, administrators, and students.

Faculty who advocate for an honor system are likely to face resistance both from other faculty and from students (McCabe et al., 2003). Resistance to adopting an honor code may stem from a belief that faculty will no longer be involved in decisions regarding students' work in their classroom and that student involvement will create more burden than help. The empirical research and case studies reviewed in this chapter can be used to support a proposal for establishing a new honor code. Implementing a modified code that is less rigid may lead to less resistance. Faculty may also involve those who have experience at institutions with honor codes to help colleagues understand the benefits of an honor system and its positive influence on institutional culture (McCabe et al., 2003).

HOW AN HONOR CODE CAN ENHANCE STUDENT–FACULTY RELATIONSHIPS

Student–faculty relationships are also influenced by an honor code. Guidelines for addressing dishonest behavior take the decisions regarding sanctions out of the hands of the faculty and place the responsibility with a jury of peers. An honor system creates uniformity in response to the cases occurring on campus, providing a system of fairness. Therefore, the consequences for different instances of academic dishonesty are not determined by the individual instructor. When an honor system is present, faculty assume less responsibility for handling incidents of academic dishonesty (McCabe et al., 2003). Under an honor system, when sanctions are determined by a jury of peers, the student–teacher relationship focuses solely on teaching and learning. An effective honor system requires a level of maturity, allowing students to regulate their own behavior and creating a sense of mutual respect and trust.

The quality of the student–faculty relationship directly impacts academic honesty. When students perceive that an instructor is caring, fair, and friendly, they are less likely to engage in dishonest behaviors (Stearns, 2001). Overall evaluations of instructor behaviors are directly related to an increase in academic integrity on the part of the students. When a student perceives a favorable student–faculty relationship, the likelihood of cheating, such as writing a paper for another student, copying others' work, studying old tests, or taking a test for someone else, is reduced (Waugh, Godfrey, Evans, & Craig, 1995).

In the absence of a universitywide honor system, individual faculty can implement strategies intended to reduce cheating. For example, students might be required to sign an honor pledge such as the one provided by Konheim-Kalkstein (2006, p. 3), "I promise to abide by an honor code in this class and that I will neither give nor receive aid on any quizzes or exams, and that I will not plagiarize someone's work." When students signed an honor pledge, they reported a greater sense of trust and respect and a higher level of comfort in the classroom, and they committed fewer dishonest behaviors (Konheim-Kalkstein, 2006). To identify the components of an honor code necessary to reduce cheating, Gurung (2010) tested three versions of an honor pledge. Students were less likely to cheat after signing an honor code statement of greater formality that also included consequences for any violations. When adopting a course-specific honor code, faculty should be mindful that the code adhere to any existing campus rules and regulations.

CONCLUSION

Research provides evidence that the presence of an honor code reduces the prevalence of academic dishonesty (McCabe & Treviño, 1993). However, it is clear from this literature that the mere presence of an honor code will not suffice in providing students with the guidance needed to act ethically. Faculty need to be aware of the measures they can take to increase students' academic integrity and in turn decrease behaviors such as cheating and plagiarism. When teaching at an institution with an honor system, instructors may consider using some of the suggestions included in this chapter to clarify how the honor system applies in the classroom and how the specific procedures address instances of questionable academic behavior. When no honor system is in place, instructors may want to consider developing an honor code for their courses. In either case, the literature illustrates the need to discuss the honor code and its implications with students to clearly communicate the importance of academic integrity to impact the likelihood that a student will act honestly when it comes to academic work. The presence of an honor code, whether at the level of the institution or the classroom, can have a significant impact on the student–faculty relationship, leading to a climate of mutual respect and trust and optimizing teaching and learning.

REFERENCES

Bowers, W. J. (1964). *Student dishonesty and its control in college*. New York, NY: Columbia University, Bureau of Applied Social Research.

College of William and Mary. (1736). Statutes of the College of William and Mary in Virginia. *Bulletin of the College of William and Mary, 7*, 13–14.

Davis, S. F., Drinan, P. F., & Gallant, T. B. (2009). *Cheating in school: What we know and what we can do*. Malden, MA: Wiley-Blackwell.

Dodd, T. M. (2007). *Honor Code 101: An introduction to the elements of traditional honor codes, modified honor codes and academic integrity policies*. Retrieved from http://www.academicintegrity.org/educational_resources/honor_code_101.php

Gallant, T. (2008). Revisiting the past: The historical context of academic integrity. *ASHE Higher Education Report, 33*, 13–31.

Gilmore, B. (2010). Write from wrong. *Independent School, 69*, 106–113.

Gurung, R. A. R. (2010). *Establishing honor codes that minimize cheating*. Manuscript in preparation.

Keith-Spiegel, P., Tabachnick, B. G., Whitley, B. E., & Washburn, J. (1998). Why professors ignore cheating: Opinions of a national sample of psychology instructors. *Ethics & Behavior, 8*, 215–227. doi:10.1207/s15327019eb0803_3

Konheim-Kalkstein, Y. L. (2006). Use of a classroom honor code in higher education. *The Journal of Credibility Assessment and Witness Psychology, 7*, 169–179.

McCabe, D. L. (1993). Faculty responses to academic dishonesty: The influence of honor codes. *Research in Higher Education, 34*, 647–658. doi:10.1007/BF00991924

McCabe, D. L., Butterfield, K., & Treviño, L. K. (2003). Faculty and academic integrity: The influence of current honor codes and past honor code experiences. *Research in Higher Education, 44*, 367–385. doi:10.1023/A:1023033916853

McCabe, D. L., & Pavela, G. (2000, September/October). Some good news about academic integrity. *Change, 32*, 32–38. doi:10.1080/00091380009605738

McCabe, D. L., & Treviño, L. K. (1993). Academic dishonesty: Honor codes and other contextual influences. *The Journal of Higher Education, 64,* 522–538. doi:10.2307/2959991

McCabe, D. L., & Treviño, L. K. (1997). Individual and contextual influences on academic dishonesty: A multicampus investigation. *Research in Higher Education, 38,* 379–396. doi:10.1023/A:1024954224675

McCabe, D. L., Treviño, L. K., & Butterfield, K. D. (2001). Cheating in academic Institutions: A decade of research. *Ethics & Behavior, 11,* 219–232. doi:10.1207/S15327019EB1103_2

Melgoza, P., & Smith, J. (2008). Revitalizing an existing honor code program. *Innovative Higher Education, 32,* 209–219. doi:10.1007/s10755-007-9048-6

Nadelson, S. (2007). Academic misconduct by university students: Faculty perceptions and responses. *Plagiary: Cross-Disciplinary Studies in Plagiarism, Fabrication, and Falsification, 1,* 1–10.

Stearns, S. A. (2001). The student–instructor relationship's effect on academic integrity. *Ethics & Behavior, 11,* 275–285. doi:10.1207/S15327019EB1103_6

Vandehey, M. A., Diekhoff, G. M., & LaBeff, E. E. (2007). College cheating: A twenty-year follow-up and the addition of an honor code. *Journal of College Student Development, 48,* 468–480. doi:10.1353/csd.2007.0043

Watson, G., & Sottile, J. (2010). Cheating in the digital age: Do students cheat more in online courses? *Online Journal of Distance Learning Administration, 13*(1). Retrieved from http://www.westga.edu/~distance/ojdla/spring131/watson131.html

Waugh, R., Godfrey, J., Evans, E., & Craig, D. (1995). Measuring student perceptions about cheating in six countries. *Australian Journal of Psychology, 47,* 73–80. doi:10.1080/00049539508257503

Wilson, W. (1905, August 12). The honor system in school and college. *The New York Times,* p. ES1.

III

CONSIDERATIONS IN THE DIVERSE CLASSROOM

9

ASPIRING TO ETHICAL TREATMENT OF DIVERSE STUDENT POPULATIONS

MELANIE M. DOMENECH RODRÍGUEZ AND SCOTT C. BATES

Competent teaching promotes critical thinking and requires the use of strategic persuasion to socialize students into a field of inquiry. In this case, that field is psychology, and it requires competent teachers to attend to diversity broadly (see Principle D and Standards 2.01, Boundaries of Competence; 2.03, Maintaining Competence; 2.04, Bases for Scientific and Professional Judgments; 3.01, Unfair Discrimination; and 7.03, Accuracy in Teaching, of the American Psychological Association's [APA's] *Ethical Principles of Psychologists and Code of Conduct* [hereinafter referred to as the Ethics Code]; APA, 2010). The ethical teacher brings diversity into the classroom through course content. Teachers of psychology also manage diversity within the classroom, for example, adjusting evaluations of learning and including methods of teaching that meet the needs of a diverse student body (see APA, 2003). Attempting to follow the APA Ethics Code as well as the "Guidelines on Multicultural Education, Training, Research, Practice, and Organizational Change for Psychologists" (hereinafter referred to as the Multicultural Guidelines; APA, 2003) and at the same time engaging in the gold-standard methods of teaching (e.g., persuasion, critical thinking) can be difficult challenges for teachers and students alike. In this chapter, we introduce the challenges of attending to diversity in the context of core teaching practices and ethical and diversity guidelines. Case examples serve to elucidate the issues and illustrate potential approaches and solutions to specific dilemmas.

ETHICS AND MULTICULTURAL GUIDELINES

The APA Ethics Code (APA, 2010) includes both aspirational principles and enforceable standards for psychologists who teach. Psychologists who teach are responsible for the proper design (Standard 7.01, Design of Education and Training Programs) and description (Standard 7.02, Descriptions of Education and Training Program) of programs and courses (Standard 7.03, Accuracy in Teaching). They are also responsible for protecting students' rights and well-being (Standards 7.04, Student Disclosure of Personal Information; 7.05, Mandatory Individual or Group Therapy; 7.07, Sexual Relationships With Students and Supervisees), including appropriate and timely evaluation of progress toward course goals (Standard 7.06, Assessing Student and Supervisee Performance). Perhaps the most challenging enforceable standard in the context of diversity, Standard 7.03b states that "when engaged in teaching or training, psychologists present psychological information accurately."

These ethical standards are challenging in the context of competing demands of a teacher (e.g., keeping a course up-to-date while being timely and accurate, monitoring student progress). Teaching in a multiculturally competent way is particularly challenging if one considers that psychologists adhere to the complete Ethics Code, which requires psychologists to (a) attend to the boundaries of their competence (Standard 2.01, Boundaries of Competence), (b) maintain their competence (Standard 2.03, Maintaining Competence), (c) base their work on scientific knowledge (Standard 2.04, Bases for Scientific and Professional Judgments), and (d) avoid engaging in unfair discrimination (Standard 3.01, Unfair Discrimination). These standards are critical to contextualizing the ethical imperative to integrate diversity issues into teaching. Indeed, the Ethics Code presents two principles (i.e., values) that frame these expectations well: Principle C (Integrity) and Principle D (Justice). A teacher with integrity promotes "accuracy, honesty, and truthfulness" in teaching. A just teacher recognizes

> that fairness and justice entitle all persons to access to and benefit from the contributions of psychology and to equal quality in the processes, procedures, and services being conducted by psychologists. Psychologists exercise reasonable judgment and take precautions to ensure that their potential biases, the boundaries of their competence, and the limitations of their expertise do not lead to or condone unjust practices. (APA, 2010, Principle D: Justice)

The Ethics Code is clear and consistent in its commitment to teaching and diversity. However, constructs such as *culture* and *diversity* are complex and multidimensional and have varied meanings. Teachers find themselves having to transport the aspirations and mandates of the profession into specific actions in their classrooms. Following the competence language of the Ethics Code, teachers might turn to the literature to see how one gains cultural competence. To make matters more complex, cultural competence lacks a clear definition and, not surprisingly, lacks a gold-standard measurement (Ridley & Kliner, 2003).

Cultural Competence

Definitions of *multicultural competence* typically include three domains: self-awareness, knowledge, and skills. In this context, *self-awareness* refers to the ability to gauge one's own biases and attitudes and to observe responses to diversity issues and diverse others. *Knowledge* refers to having specific information about the cultural group of interest as well as broader sociopolitical influences that contextualize that knowledge. Finally, the *skills* domain refers to an effective skill set for engaging diversity issues and diverse others. It is important to note that the field has not arrived at a consensus on the ultimate definition of multicultural competence or even agreement about whether there should be a uniform definition (Ridley & Kliner, 2003). What is clear is that cultural competence resides in the person (e.g., teacher) and requires proactive information seeking and gathering as well as a specific skill set that is interpersonal in nature (e.g., for use with students).

When developing cultural competence, it is normal to develop a heightened sensitivity around existing knowledge (e.g., that it is all relative and thus difficult to settle on certainties and the "truth"). Thankfully, Trimble (2003) expressly stated that a psychologist need not discard existing knowledge in psychology to be culturally competent. Teachers can turn to the Multicultural Guidelines (APA, 2003) for helpful guidance on how to build on existing knowledge and use it to strengthen cultural competence. The guidelines explicitly state that teachers should "employ the constructs of multiculturalism and diversity in psychological education" (p. 386). Fouad and Arredondo (2006) specified that culturally competent educators have knowledge regarding five distinct points: (a) statements of philosophy and principles and how to integrate them in syllabi, (b) course design based on content that is also culture centered, (c) learning models to target different learners, (d) students' possible emotional reactions and how to facilitate productive discussion, and (e) research findings as they pertain to diverse ethnocultural groups. These areas of knowledge can facilitate planning (Points a and b) and execution (Points c, d, and e) of a course that successfully integrates diversity into the curriculum and does so transparently.

Specific Teaching Challenges

Teaching challenges in adhering to ethical and professional values of integrating diversity into the curriculum can be broadly divided into challenges around course materials and challenges resulting from student characteristics and ensuing classroom process. Major challenges are listed in Table 9.1, and they follow three broad areas of cultural competence: self-awareness, knowledge, and skills. We consider an example of cultural competence that is related to the necessary knowledge base of multicultural competence:

> A seasoned instructor for an undergraduate developmental psychology course, Dr. Mayo, receives distressing feedback on her course syllabus following a departmentwide review of syllabi. She is told that her syllabus does not reflect an adequate integration of diversity issues in her course objectives, course requirements, or reading list. A review of her otherwise acceptable course evaluations reflects numerous comments from students over the past 5 years on a lack of information regarding the applicability of course material to diverse populations. Dr. Mayo asks for a meeting with the department chair. She states that she is "a developmental psychologist, not a multicultural psychologist," and she was not trained in diversity

TABLE 9.1
Cultural Competence Dimensions

Cultural competence area	Specific challenges
Self-awareness	■ The instructor's ability to observe and evaluate his or her own awareness and attitudes about diversity issues. ■ The teacher's ability to observe and evaluate students' awareness and attitudes about diversity issues.
Knowledge	■ Integrating diversity into a course when the teacher lacks the knowledge about diverse findings in the literature. ■ Integrating diverse methods of teaching and evaluation when the teacher lacks the knowledge about how to do so.
Skills	■ Managing the balance between covering core course content (e.g., developmental psychology theories) and diversity issues. ■ Stimulating an interest in diversity material in an otherwise uninterested group of students. ■ Managing different levels of students' awareness, attitudes, knowledge, and skills (i.e., cultural competence) in class discussions and evaluations.

issues. She is concerned that she is not competent (Standard 2.01, Boundaries of Competence) to address diversity issues in her course and that she could do more harm than good (Standard 3.04, Avoiding Harm) by trying to integrate diversity into the curriculum. The department chair states that these are fine concerns but that psychologists are required to maintain their competence (Standard 2.03, Maintaining Competence) over the course of their professional career and that psychologists present accurate information in courses (Standard 7.03b, Accuracy in Teaching). Given recent changes to the field, materials that integrate diversity into Dr. Mayo's course are absolutely needed to ensure accurate teaching.

Analysis of Case Illustration

The issues presented here are relatively common among more senior faculty who might receive external pressure to modify and update course preparations to include diversity issues. Indeed, all parties involved in this case have important and relevant points: The students' desire for the professor to address diversity issues is warranted by advances in the field and likely is evident as a result of the changing demographics that make ethnic, racial, and cultural context more visible within classrooms. Dr. Mayo's concerns regarding her competence are quite relevant, and her assertion that she could "do more harm than good" is very accurate in the absence of improved competence. The administrator's push for ensuring that programs are current is also important to the long-term sustainability of the department. This push also proactively responds to issues related to design and description of training programs (Standards 7.01, Design of Education and Training Programs, and 7.02, Descriptions of Education and Training Programs). This is a real dilemma that requires a problem-solving process to bring all parties to a common ground.

The problem-solving process was already underway with the gathering of data regarding student evaluations. The first step in any problem-solving process is clarifying the problem itself. Finding data specific to students' wants or needs is an important consideration in strengthening the argument for integrating diversity issues into developmental psychology. Further data from institutional expectations (e.g., APA, 2003) regarding integration of diversity issues in teaching support the necessity of integrating diversity issues into developmental psychology. Thus, the problem is not whether to integrate diversity issues but rather how to do so while setting the professor and the students up for success. Once the problem is specified, potential solutions must be generated to address it. In this phase of problem solving, it would be ideal to include all of the stakeholders (i.e., teacher, student, administrator) in generating a list of possible solutions. Only after all solutions have been presented does an analysis occur to retain, reject, or combine solutions. Brainstorming generated many potential solutions, and the students were informed in writing of the adjustments to be made in the course. Dr. Mayo and the department chair resolved to select three potential solutions for an incremental plan to address the need to integrate diversity issues into the developmental psychology course. In the short term, the solution to bring in guest speakers to address diversity issues serves a dual function of exposing both students and Dr. Mayo to diversity issues in developmental psychology. This intermediate solution provides an immediate observable action toward the desired ultimate goal of supporting the development of Dr. Mayo's competence. A guest speaker will not only address content but also presumably have the expertise to manage the group process, giving Dr. Mayo a model for handling diversity processes in the classroom.

A second short-term solution is to have students do a special diversity project. The students can present the material so everyone benefits. The chair and faculty member resolve to bring in a local consultant to support the development of the project (including an explanation on the syllabus and evaluation criteria) and to be present during the presentations. After the presentations, the local consultant and Dr. Mayo would jointly evaluate the presentations. Dr. Mayo would have the needed support for accurate content and evaluation as well as gain the critical experience for future independent application.

The department chair supports Dr. Mayo in acquiring competence by sending her to continuing education courses and specialty conferences (e.g., recent programs of the Society for Teaching of Psychology would be an excellent venue) and through the identification of resources for Dr. Mayo to read and integrate into her course. For example, Dr. Mayo may be excited by her opportunity to gain a deeper understanding of culture but concerned about her time commitments during the academic year. Dr. Mayo and the department chair decide that she will receive a partial summer salary to compensate her for the time she spends in these activities. Dr. Mayo, in turn, will provide a full report of her activities, including references read and how they were used in making changes to the course. The agreement is written and shared with the student members of the brainstorming committee. In addition, Dr. Mayo and the department chair will meet in mid-July to assess progress toward goals and plan next steps and a long-term solution.

It is important to note that at the institutional level the department chair may want to engage in additional activities that might support a systemic change. For example, the chair might want to conduct a broader assessment of courses and approach comprehensive curricular changes so that no faculty member feels singled out. She could also use faculty meeting time to present relevant department goals (e.g., to integrate diversity into all coursework) and materials that will facilitate meeting these goals (e.g., the Multicultural Guidelines; APA, 2003). The department chair might find that it is an optimal investment of the department's financial resources to bring a consultant in to present a uniform process for integrating diversity into the curriculum and to support all faculty in implementing a plan (i.e., one consultant for all instead of a consultant for each faculty member each time a need is identified). Finally, an evaluation system could be put in place to examine the success of the integration of diversity issues that includes student assessment, behavioral observations of instructors, and instructor self-assessment at a systemwide level. Systemic changes have the benefit of creating more uniform culture shifts that may lead to smoother short-term and more stable long-term transitions in teaching practices.

We consider how teachers might incorporate multiculturally sound ethical pedagogies into a practicum course.

A counseling center practicum course is beginning. During the third seminar meeting of the semester, the instructor, a Latino psychologist, Dr. Marcom, leads the group of 10 students on a privilege walk exercise. This activity is intended to create and/or enhance self-awareness in students. Focusing on privilege, students can examine the areas in which they have had advantages (e.g., if one of your parents was laid off or unemployed involuntarily, take one step back; see Ipas, n.d., for this exercise) that they may not have been previously aware of. Typically, students take steps forward and steps back depending on the scenario, although there are many variations of this exercise (e.g., http://www.whatsrace.org/images/privwalk-short.pdf). The exercise creates self-awareness in students (e.g., How much privilege have I had?) and awareness in relation to others (e.g., Where am I in relation to others in this room?).

The room is prepared to leave open space for the exercise, and the graduate students are nine White Americans (seven women, two men) and one Latina, Ms. Gallardo. As the privilege walk comes to an end, the White American students are all toward the front of the room, with heterosexual men basically touching the front wall, and Ms. Gallardo is in the back of the room, touching the back wall. The configuration leads to a discussion of how privilege influences educational opportunities, either directly or indirectly. The result of the group exercise highlights the difference in where the White students and the one minority student were located. Dr. Marcom, who participated in the exercise, is somewhere in the middle and notes that he was born to college-educated parents and enjoyed great financial and social stability during his upbringing. He also notes that his parents "worked hard to keep us kids away from other Latinos so we wouldn't take a wrong path." A lively discussion on privilege ensues, led by Dr. Marcom. White American students report getting "a lot out of this exercise." The Latina graduate student, who is outraged and marginalized, manages to walk away quietly and at the next meeting with her faculty advisor breaks down in tears and reports that she felt "humiliated . . .

I don't know how I'm supposed to return to that classroom and look my peers in the face."

Analysis of Case Illustration on Skills

In this example, the issues are much more complex. Dr. Marcom's approach to teaching has several strengths; chief among them is the attempt to integrate diversity issues into the practicum curriculum. The incorporation of experiential exercises also provides multiple methods of teaching for diverse learners. Using experiential exercises is a definite strength and consistent with both the Multicultural Guidelines (APA, 2003) and associated recommendations (Fouad & Arrendondo, 2006). It is important to note that there are risks, and in this case, the risk resulted in real harm to an ethnic minority student. Therefore, when implementing exercises like the privilege walk, it is wise to seek advice and counsel from a variety of colleagues, especially ones experienced with experiential exercises and/or multicultural skills development.

Pettigrew and Tropp (2008) suggested that it is not contact alone that creates positive between-groups relationships but rather meaningful, positive intergroup contact. In this instance, the intergroup contact has been positive for nine people and negative for one person. From a broader social perspective, it is critical to note that the person harmed was also the person most vulnerable to the consequences of misuse of power and privilege. Additionally, the facilitator for the group was a Latino psychologist, lending further complexity to the situation.

The challenges in this case are compounded by the potential difficulty in identifying a problem, and to some, it might seem as though the opportunity to intervene has passed. Indeed, as with the previous illustration, the problem-solving process was already underway as the Latina graduate student sought consultation with a faculty advisor with expertise in multicultural issues. Ms. Gallardo and a faculty advisor sought advice from faculty with expertise in multicultural issues.

Simply stated, real harm (Standard 3.04, Avoiding Harm) occurred. From an aspirational perspective (i.e., Principle D: Justice), the lesson that White American students learned was built on the "back" of the Latina graduate student, not unlike railroads in the West were primarily built on the backs of Chinese immigrants. Questions about Dr. Marcom's competence (Standard 2.01, Boundaries of Competence) were also at issue. The team resolved that there must be action to repair the harm done to the Latina student as much as possible through a return to the debrief process for White American students. After much discussion, Ms. Gallardo felt confident that she could undertake the conversation with Dr. Marcom. She will present ideas to Dr. Marcom about returning to the exercise and adding a "resilience walk" component that will

lead to Ms. Gallardo ending toward the center of the room with the rest of her colleagues to address her feelings of alienation from the group and bring back a sense of group cohesion. Ms. Gallardo will also deliver to Dr. Marcom an article regarding the complexities of supervisory relationships within Latino dyads (Field, Chavez-Korell, & Domenech Rodríguez, 2010) that can serve to support Dr. Marcom's awareness regarding his own level of ethnic identity development, cultural competence, and supervisory skills development.

Written agreements are very important to ensure that all the parties can reference the problem and agreed-on solutions. Accordingly, Ms. Gallardo summarized the problem, solutions discussed and selected, and the plan for action to implementation.

CONCLUSION

Teaching is a process of persuasion (Friedrich & Douglass, 1998). Indeed, teaching is a process of socialization for entry into the intellectual elite of a particular society. These elite, in turn, become the resource pool from which knowledge is gathered to shape important outcomes (e.g., public policy). This process of developing an intellectual elite has systematically excluded non-majority knowledge, learning processes, and perhaps most critical, persons. This systematic exclusion of persons and perspectives can lead to a significant loss for a whole society.

Psychology has made enormous contributions to knowledge on teaching and learning. Evidence from cognitive science reveals that specific facts are not easy to retain over time, and deeper processing of material is superior for long-term recall (Craik, 2002). Thus, instructors target processes such as the development of critical thinking skills to best prepare students to reengage with course material over the course of their professional development. Supporting the development of critical thinking skills has long been a goal of instructors (Wade, 2009), and this is reflected in the APA *Guidelines for the Undergraduate Psychology Major* (APA, 2007). The optimal engagement of critical thinking skills may require that teachers take some risks, such as using experiential exercises to bring materials to life and make them personally relevant and meaningful to the learner. The ethical teacher is not reactively avoiding all potential risks but rather proactively considering the full range of possibilities for classroom experiences that will benefit students, proceeding thoughtfully, and responding in a timely manner and with sensitivity when issues arise. The process of proceeding thoughtfully presents a valuable opportunity for students to learn about becoming multiculturally competent; that is, there is no final destination; competence is a journey. Remaining engaged with diversity issues, remaining open to feedback and observant of impact, and being ready to repair

situations and relationships as needed are more powerful models of multicultural skills than the flawless delivery of carefully crafted, "safe" pedagogical materials.

For teachers of psychology, the process represents a higher order skill that can present great challenges and opportunities. Teachers may find that flexibility may make the integration of diversity content into curricula more doable. However, there are many challenges because teachers are not trained in diversity issues and may lack the self-awareness, knowledge, and skills necessary to move forward with confidence in integrating diversity issues into their courses.

Teachers have a tall order, especially in light of limited resources. When it comes to the study of diversity issues, the field is critiqued by those who study it (Arnett, 2008) and by those who write textbooks on diversity (Hogben & Waterman, 1997). The critiques are neither new (Guthrie, 1976) nor resolved (Haeffel, Thiessen, Campbell, Kaschak, & McNeil, 2009). New calls for inclusion of diversity-related topics and a renewed focus on diversity in the undergraduate curriculum were addressed in *Undergraduate Education in Psychology: A Blueprint for the Future of the Discipline* (Halpern, 2010). It is our hope that this chapter has provided readers with challenges that will support increased awareness and ideas as to how to improve knowledge and skills for greater cultural competence. As James (1899) so aptly wrote, teachers advance the field of psychology and provide a critical model for future psychologists. Current knowledge dictates that such a model include cultural competence.

REFERENCES

American Psychological Association. (2003). Guidelines on multicultural education, training, research, practice, and organizational change for psychologists. *American Psychologist, 58*, 377–402. doi:10.1037/0003-066X.58.5.377

American Psychological Association. (2007). *APA guidelines for the undergraduate psychology major*. Retrieved from http://www.apa.org/ed/resources.html

American Psychological Association. (2010). *Ethical principles of psychologists and code of conduct (Amended June 1, 2010)*. Retrieved from http://www.apa.org/ethics/code/index.aspx

Arnett, J. J. (2008). The neglected 95%: Why American psychology needs to become less American. *American Psychologist, 63*, 602–614. doi:10.1037/0003-066X.63.7.602

Craik, F. I. M. (2002). Levels of process: Past, present . . . and future? *Memory, 10*, 305–318. doi:10.1080/09658210244000135

Field, L., Chavez-Korell, S., & Domenech Rodríguez, M. M. (2010). No hay rosa sin espina: Conceptualizing Latina–Latina supervision from a multicultural developmental supervisory model. *Training and Education in Professional Psychology, 4*, 47–54. doi:10.1037/a0018521

Fouad, N. A., & Arredondo, P. (2006). *Becoming culturally oriented: Practical advice for psychologists and educators*. Washington, DC: American Psychological Association. doi:10.1037/11483-000

Friedrich, J., & Douglass, D. (1998). Ethics and the persuasive enterprise of teaching psychology. *American Psychologist, 53*, 549–562. doi:10.1037/0003-066X.53.5.549

Guthrie, R. V. (1976). *Even the rat was white: A historical view of psychology*. New York, NY: Harper & Row.

Haeffel, G. J., Thiessen, E. D., Campbell, M. W., Kaschak, M. P., & McNeil, N. M. (2009). Theory, not cultural context, will advance American psychology. *American Psychologist, 64*, 570–571. doi:10.1037/a0016191

Halpern, D. F. (Ed.). (2010). *Undergraduate education in psychology: A blueprint for the future of the discipline*. Washington, DC: American Psychological Association. doi:10.1037/12063-000

Hogben, M., & Waterman, C. K. (1997). Are all of your students represented in their textbooks? A content analysis of coverage of diversity issues in introductory psychology textbooks. *Teaching of Psychology, 24*, 95–100. doi:10.1207/s15328023top2402_3

Ipas. (n.d.). *Privilege walk*. Retrieved from http://www.ipas.org/Publications/asset_upload_file357_3785.pdf

James, W. (1899). *Talks to teachers on psychology—and to students on some of life's ideals*. New York, NY: Metropolitan Books and Henry Holt. doi:10.1037/10814-000

Pettigrew, T. F., & Tropp, L. R. (2008). How does intergroup contact reduce prejudice? Meta-analytic tests of three mediators. *European Journal of Social Psychology, 38*, 922–934. doi:10.1002/ejsp.504

Ridley, C. R., & Kliner, A. J. (2003). Multicultural counseling competence: History, themes, and issues. In D. B. Pope-Davis, H. L. K. Coleman, W. M. Liu, & R. L. Toporek (Eds.), *Handbook of multicultural competencies in counseling & psychology* (pp. 3–20). Thousand Oaks, CA: Sage.

Trimble, J. E. (2003). Foreword. In D. B. Pope-Davis, H. L. K. Coleman, W. M. Liu, & R. L. Toporek (Eds.), *Handbook of multicultural competencies in counseling & psychology* (pp. x–xiii). Thousand Oaks, CA: Sage.

Wade, C. (2009). Critical thinking: Needed now more than ever. In D. S. Dunn, J. S. Halonen, & R. A. Smith (Eds.), *Teaching critical thinking in psychology: A handbook of best practices* (pp.11–22). Malden, MA: Wiley-Blackwell.

10

CHALLENGING STUDENTS' CORE BELIEFS AND VALUES

STEPHEN L. CHEW

Teaching thus has an ethical dimension, for the teacher has the capacity
to help or harm others.

—Cahn (1986, p. 10)

Students often possess deeply held beliefs and values, some of which
may restrict their ability to incorporate or interact with new knowledge based
on psychological research. Teachers have an ethical responsibility to teach
information accurately and effectively, yet they must also consider the consequences of changing a student's worldview in a way the student neither
sought nor expected. In this chapter, I frame the ethical issues and summarize relevant research related to challenging core student beliefs. I begin by
illustrating how challenging student beliefs can result in an ethical dilemma.

> It isn't unusual for me to have students from devout evangelical Chris-
> tian families. In my general psychology course, I discuss the anatomy of
> the human eye and how the retina is wired "backward" so that light had
> to filter through nonreceptor cells before reaching the rods and cones. I
> contrast the human eye with that of the mantis shrimp, which has a
> much more complex eye and can see in dimensions people cannot. After
> class, a student approached me and asked, "If what you say is true, then
> how can man be God's perfect creation?" I did not have an answer for the
> student, but this incident, among others, helped foment a deep personal
> crisis about her core beliefs and upbringing. She eventually stopped com-
> ing to class and later left the college.

Undergraduate students entering the discipline of psychology usually possess some accurate information about psychology along with simplistic or naïve understandings, misconceptions, and erroneous beliefs about it. Teachers' responsibility is to bring students to a better understanding of how psychological science is supported by empirical evidence. However, an ethical issue arises when teachers' responsibility causes students to question their core beliefs and values and leads to personal distress and upheaval. People hold core beliefs and values as truths across situations, and these truths inform much of their behavior and judgments of right and wrong.

EXAMPLES OF CONFLICTS BETWEEN BELIEFS
AND EMPIRICAL FINDINGS

Because of psychologists' natural emphasis on the human condition, evidence-based conclusions about behavior may present values-based challenges for some students who hold core beliefs about God, behavior, health, and so on. How often do psychological knowledge and core beliefs and values come into conflict? Perhaps more often than teachers like to think. Consider the following issues:

- People refuse to have their children vaccinated out of fear the vaccine might cause autism despite clear evidence that the fear is invalid; they thereby put their children and others at risk for dangerous diseases (Harris, 2010).
- Parents of children with autism are increasingly turning to alternative medical treatments, such as chelation, despite a lack of any evidence that the treatments are effective (Tsouderos & Callahan, 2009).
- In 2006, the Catholic Charities of Boston ended all adoptions rather than comply with a state law requiring that gays and lesbians be allowed to adopt (Wen, 2006). Psychological research indicates no differences in parenting skills between gay and heterosexual parents and no deficits in children of gay parents (American Psychological Association [APA], 2004).
- A Christian-oriented organization holds public seminars on how homosexuality is a sinful choice that can be cured through prayer (Garrison, 2009) despite the findings of an APA task force report that efforts to change sexual orientation are unlikely to be helpful and involve risk of harm (APA, 2009).

All of these issues might come up in an introductory psychology class. The conflict between psychological research and popular beliefs has a long history (Lilienfeld, Lynn, Ruscio, & Beyerstein, 2009; Mercer, 2009). People advocate some antidrug programs despite the lack of evidence for their effectiveness. People promote abstinence-until-marriage sex education programs despite the lack of supporting evidence. An estimated 26% of parents spank their children who are younger than 3 years old despite research linking spanking to a variety of negative outcomes (Regalado, Sareen, Inkelas, Wissow, & Halfon, 2004). Psychological research has also played a key role in challenging popular but incorrect beliefs, such as the accuracy of eyewitness testimony, the validity of memories "recovered" during therapy, the veracity of confessions obtained through interrogation, the impact of subliminal messages, and the existence of paranormal phenomena (Benassi & Goldstein, 2005), among others.

Most teachers take extra care when discussing obviously sensitive or controversial topics such as sexuality, but conflicts between research and core beliefs cannot always be anticipated. Among the students at my university are "young earth" creationists and students who believe that Freudian theory is inherently evil. Some students fear that talking to Jewish or Hindu people could endanger their souls. Many students believe psychotherapy consists of being a good listener and offering commonsense advice. Some of my deeply religious students believe that mental illness shows a weakness in faith and a truly faithful person will not experience mental illness. Students at other universities may have different beliefs and values, but they may still be at odds with psychological research. For example, they may believe in past life regression through hypnosis or that behavior disorders stem from unconscious memories of traumatic birth.

Perhaps the solution is to be on the lookout for the occasional student who has not yet had the opportunity to examine how his or her beliefs have been constructed and to compare that with findings from empirical inquiry. Theories of intellectual development, however, indicate that people can be sophisticated thinkers in some areas yet unsophisticated thinkers in others. Moseley et al. (2006) conducted an exhaustive review of frameworks for the development of student thinking, including Piaget's stages of cognitive development, Bloom's taxonomy, and Perry's developmental scheme. These frameworks assume that students progress from some form of simplistic, primitive thinking to more sophisticated, critical thinking. Such development is a major goal of education. Thus, teachers can expect conflicts between psychological research and the beliefs of students to occur with some regularity.

The extent that teachers are concerned with a clash between what they teach and what students believe depends on what they see as the goal of teaching. If teachers believe the goal is simply to provide information without regard to whether students learn, then their concern will be minimal. If, however, teachers believe the goal of teaching is to develop student understanding, then clashes between what they teach and student values and beliefs pose a serious challenge. In this chapter, I take the latter position.

Teachers may focus on helping students understand the world in more sophisticated ways without giving sufficient consideration to any negative personal consequences that a challenge to fundamental beliefs or values might provoke. Some teachers might dismiss this kind of dissonance and distress as an expected, even desirable, consequence of effective teaching, but the matter is not so simple. The *Ethical Principles of Psychologists and Code of Conduct* (hereinafter referred to as the Ethics Code; APA, 2010) makes clear the ethical obligations of teachers of psychology in these situations. The first principle of the Ethics Code states, "Psychologists strive to benefit those with whom they work and take care to do no harm" (Principle A: Beneficence and Nonmaleficence). The Ethics Code also states,

> Psychologists are aware of and respect cultural, individual, and role differences, including those based on age, gender, gender identity, race, ethnicity, culture, national origin, religion, sexual orientation, disability, language, and socioeconomic status and consider these factors when working with members of such groups. (Principle E: Respect for People's Rights and Dignity)

Teachers of psychology have an ethical obligation to be aware of and try to mitigate the distress that might occur when learning about psychology. Steven Cahn, a philosopher who studies the ethics of teaching, pointed out the damage teachers can do to students:

> An unsuccessful education can ruin you. It can kill your interest in a topic. It can make you a less-good thinker. It can leave you less open to rational argument. So we do good and bad as teachers—it's not just good or nothing. (quoted in Glenn, 2009, para. 3)

To summarize, conflicts between student beliefs and values and psychological research can be expected to occur with some regularity. Faculty, especially teachers of psychology, have an ethical duty to both promote the intellectual development of students while trying to avoid or minimize any tensions between student values and psychological research.

MISCONCEPTIONS AND CULTURAL CLASHES

Many, if not most, conflicts between core beliefs and values and psychological theories and research can be traced to two sources: misconceptions and clashes between the cultural values students possess and the empirical values of psychology. Misconceptions about psychology are common among the public (e.g., Lilienfeld et al., 2009; Mercer, 2009). Many misconceptions are relatively harmless, but some can have dangerous consequences. Students bring these mistaken beliefs into their courses where they come into conflict with course content.

Misconceptions originate from and are maintained by various sources (Benassi & Goldstein, 2005; Chew, 2005). Regardless of the source, misconceptions can be remarkably difficult to correct. Chew (2005) investigated the use of ConcepTests to counter the misconception that negative correlations are weaker than positive ones. ConcepTests force students to confront their misconceptions and compare them with scientifically based evidence. It would seem a misconception about correlations should be easy to correct, but the results showed otherwise. Even though ConcepTests led to a significant improvement in performance, almost half of the students still could not apply the information to a novel situation without falling prey to the misconception.

Although the results have been mixed, research indicates that refutational approaches such as ConcepTests are the most effective way of countering misconceptions (Kowalski & Taylor, 2009; Winer, Cottrell, Gregg, Fournier, & Bica, 2002). Even when misconceptions are corrected, the accurate information is fragile, and students often revert to the misconception. Benassi and Goldstein (2005), for example, found that even after a course on critical thinking about paranormal beliefs, students were still susceptible to uncritical acceptance of a demonstration of psychic phenomena.

As difficult to correct as misconceptions are, they probably do not cause as much distress as when the cultural values and the beliefs that flow from those values come into conflict with the findings of psychology. Students may hold beliefs that are based on spiritual or religious tenets. For example, the belief that the Bible indisputably condemns homosexuality usually entails the belief that homosexuality is a choice that can be changed. People who believe that a person's spirit survives the death of the body may also believe that the spirit can communicate with the living in various ways. People who believe in extrasensory perception may also believe that some people are especially gifted with this ability. These are the kinds of beliefs that, when challenged, also challenge core values that people believe are grounded in transcendent and immutable truths.

A MODEL FOR TEACHING THE CULTURE
OF PSYCHOLOGICAL SCIENCE

The conflicts that can arise between psychological research and values are similar to the differences that arise between cultures. Thus, one can examine research on acculturation for methods of understanding, preventing, and resolving such conflicts. *Acculturation* refers to the changes in cultural patterns that occur when one group of people from a given culture interact with and adapt to the culture of another group (Berry & Sam, 1997). The experience can change the culture of either or both groups. Berry and Sam (1997) described a framework of adaptive strategies for acculturation. Handelsman, Gottlieb, and Knapp (2005) adapted the framework for the purpose of teaching professional ethics to psychology students. Here I adapt the framework more generally to address teaching psychology in an ethical manner.

According to Berry and Sam (1997), there are two dimensions for determining an acculturation strategy. The first is *cultural maintenance*, or students' beliefs in the importance of the cultural values they bring to a course and their commitment to maintaining those values. The second dimension is *contact and participation*, or students' willingness to consider and potentially embrace the culture of psychology. Each dimension is a continuum, but if one considers only the extremes of each dimension, they yield four possible acculturation strategies.

When students are high on both dimensions, they pursue the strategy of *integration* in which they strive to create a new cultural identity that successfully incorporates key elements of both cultures. Integration allows students to retain identity with their original culture while also embracing the new one. If students are low on cultural maintenance but high in contact and participation, then they use an *assimilation* strategy. These students shed their original identity and completely embrace the new culture. Students who are high in cultural maintenance and low in contact and participation practice a *separation* strategy in which they either reject or refuse to consider the new culture. Finally, students who are low in both cultural maintenance and contact and participation practice *marginalization* in which they identify with neither their original nor their new culture.

This framework helps identify different ways in which acculturation strategies can be successful or unsuccessful and the ways in which the process of acculturation can be stressful to students. The most successful strategy is a form of integration that leads to a new and satisfactory sense of personal identity that incorporates psychological values with a student's cultural values. Students who pursue integration recognize the conflicts between their beliefs and psychological research, and they understand that resolving such conflicts will be an effortful but worthwhile process. They may think of their beliefs and values as a "work in progress." Although the process of integration can include acculturative stress, in successful acculturation such stress is eventually resolved.

Assimilation occurs when students abandon their original identities and fully embrace the culture of psychology. The problem here is that student understanding of and commitment to the values of psychology are superficial. Students who practice assimilation are more fans of psychology than scholars. Such students may shed the culture of psychology as easily as they shed their original culture if something more appealing comes along. They may have been persuaded by a charismatic teacher to accept the values of psychology, but they may just as easily be persuaded to believe something else. Although there is little acculturative stress, there is no true internalization of values.

Students who practice separation may be willing to give the teacher the appropriate answers for exams or papers, but the student does not truly accept the values of psychology. Such students distinguish between psychologically correct beliefs that they must report to pass a course and their own true beliefs. These students likely experience the most acculturative stress because they may feel that teachers are being intrusive and threatening when they teach the values of psychology. They may believe that teachers are promoting "political correctness." Such students hold their own values in higher regard when they conflict with the values of other cultures.

Finally, students who practice marginalization lack a defined cultural identity, and their cultural values may change with time and context. They may not experience much acculturative stress, but neither do they have a deep understanding or commitment to the values of psychology. There are no formal assessments to classify students into the categories listed previously or to measure the prevalence of each type of student. The framework, however, is helpful in giving teachers a way to think about the stresses students might experience when their personal values conflict with psychological ones.

Schwartz, Unger, Zamboanga, and Szapocznik (2010) presented a more refined and updated model of acculturation that makes two points relevant to teaching. First, acculturation can be broken down into separate components of practices, values, and identifications. Acculturation may move at different rates among the three components. Thus students may show greater acceptance of psychology in one area over others. Second, a critical factor in acculturation is the *context of reception*, which refers to the attitudes and expectations of the receiving culture. That means that the teacher's attitude toward the culture of the student, which can range from tolerant and empathetic to hostile and dismissive, plays a major role in the process of student acculturation. Thus, teachers must be aware of their own biases, expectations, beliefs, and values.

The likelihood of cultural integration depends on the disparity and compatibility between students' original culture and the culture of psychology. If students see their culture as fundamentally incompatible with the culture of psychology, no integration is possible without a profound and stressful cultural transformation. Clearly there are some highly conservative religious denominations that see science as incompatible with faith, and there are scientists whose views of science are clearly incompatible with any sort of religion (Dean, 2005). Short of the two cultures being completely incompatible, there is a wide range of degrees of compatibility (Schwartz et al., 2010). Some cultural values will be easily compatible with psychology, whereas others represent a major teaching challenge. Obviously it is an oversimplification to say that all psychologists share the exact same scientific values. There are wide variations in beliefs and values within any culture. Likewise, acculturative strategies are also likely to change over time and across situations.

To encourage integration between disparate cultures requires more than conveying information or persuading students. It involves getting students to think through issues critically, realize the differences between their current cultural values and those of psychology, resolve those differences successfully, and at least comprehend, if not embrace, the rationale and utility of psychological values regarding research methods, results, and theories. Benassi and Goldstein (2005) made the point that accomplishing such a feat depends not on content but on pedagogy.

Although there is little direct research on how to promote integration, I propose several possible approaches. The first is to develop a willingness on the part of students to think critically. As Halpern (1998) noted, critical thinking is not just a matter of students having the ability to think critically but requires students to willingly engage in critical thinking. If a student's culture does not value critical thinking, then it is unlikely he or she will be able to achieve integration unless a teacher can convince the student of its value.

Teachers must also recognize that learning has a critical affective dimension (Moseley et al., 2006). Students must come to regard studying psychology as both interesting and useful for understanding important issues. Students may enter the class with a negative perception and faulty preconceptions about psychology. Students with a negative view of psychology will not be open to integration. Teachers must model critical thinking and openness to consider different perspectives as an example for students. This means that the teacher must be critical yet respectful of students' beliefs. The teacher should be neither confrontational nor dismissive when dealing with students with different cultural values. The teacher should not seek to indoctrinate or proselytize because this leads to assimilation rather than integration. Teachers must have a clear understanding of the values of psychology and be able to explain them effectively.

Teachers must recognize the role that cognitive development plays in the ability of students to integrate different cultures. By reason of Perry's (1970) developmental scheme, students who are dualists, who judge right and wrong absolutely according to authority, will perceive a cultural conflict as a disagreement among authority figures. Resolving the conflict becomes a matter of deciding which authority figure to believe. Students displaying multiplicity, the idea that one belief is as good as another, will likewise be unable to integrate different cultures successfully. To the extent possible, the teacher should anticipate acculturative stress and prepare students for it. If a teacher regularly encounters a particular kind of cultural conflict, she or he should try

to understand the culture to see the student's point of view and perhaps suggest variations in the students' own cultural view. Oftentimes students may possess a particularly narrow view of a culture; students are not aware of the full range of cultural variation.

Finally, and perhaps most important, the teacher must develop rapport and trust with students. Benson, Cohen, and Buskist (2005) concluded that a key element of being a master teacher is the ability to develop a strong rapport or sense of trust. Rapport should not to be confused with being popular or easy. It means that students believe that the teacher is committed to helping them learn and develop. Students believe that class assignments are more than busy work and the exams are not arbitrary. Class assignments promote learning goals, and exams are valid assessments. In the scenario that began this chapter, even though I could not answer my student's question, the fact that she asked me was, in my view, a sign of trust. She believed that I wanted to help her learn. The presence of rapport and trust encourages students to take intellectual risks, to pursue unfamiliar and perhaps uncomfortable lines of thought, and to persist in working through difficult new ideas.

CONCLUSION

Ethical teaching facilitates a successful resolution of conflicts of values and beliefs. Students might experience conflicts that teachers are not even aware of, but if teachers teach ethically, they will be motivated to try to resolve conflicts in a way that promotes learning and personal development. Psychologists have an obligation to minimize distress while doing their work effectively, regardless of whether they are conducting research, carrying out therapy or teaching.

REFERENCES

American Psychological Association. (2004). *Sexual orientation, parents, & children*. Retrieved from http://www.apa.org/about/governance/council/policy/parenting. aspx

American Psychological Association. (2009). *Report of the American Psychological Association Task Force on Appropriate Therapeutic Responses to Sexual Orientation*. Retrieved from http://www.apa.org/pi/lgbt/resources/therapeutic-response.pdf

American Psychological Association. (2010). *Ethical principles of psychologists and code of conduct (Amended June 1, 2010)*. Retrieved from http://www.apa.org/ethics/ code/index.aspx

Benassi, V. A., & Goldstein, G. S. (2005). Students' beliefs about paranormal claims: Implications for teaching introductory psychology. In D. S. Dunn & S. L. Chew

(Eds.), *Best practices for teaching introduction to psychology* (pp. 225–243). Mahwah, NJ: Erlbaum.

Benson, T. A., Cohen, A. L., & Buskist, W. (2005). Rapport: Its relation to student attitudes and behaviors toward teachers and classes. *Teaching of Psychology, 32,* 237–270. doi:10.1207/s15328023top3204_8

Berry, J. W., & Sam, D. L. (1997). Acculturation and adaptation. In J. W. Berry, M. H. Segall, & C. Kagitcibasi (Eds.), *Handbook of cross-cultural psychology: Vol. 3. Social behavior and applications* (2nd ed., pp. 291–326). Needham Heights, MA: Allyn & Bacon.

Cahn, S. M. (1986). *Saints and scamps: Ethics in academia.* Totowa, NJ: Rowman & Littlefield.

Chew, S. L. (2005). Seldom in doubt but often wrong: Addressing tenacious student misconceptions. In D. S. Dunn & S. L. Chew (Eds.), *Best practices for teaching introduction to psychology* (pp. 211–223). Mahwah, NJ: Erlbaum.

Dean, C. (2005, August 23). Scientists speak up on mix of God and science. *The New York Times.* Retrieved from http://www.nytimes.com

Garrison, G. (2009, November 2) Focus on Family conference in Birmingham, Alabama will draw gay rights protest. *The Birmingham News.* Retrieved from http://www.al.com

Glenn, D. (2009, October). Course reminds budding Ph.D.'s of the damage they can do. *The Chronicle of Higher Education.* Retrieved from http://www.chronicle. com

Halpern, D. F. (1998). Teaching critical thinking for transfer across domains. *American Psychologist, 53,* 449–455. doi:10.1037/0003-066X.53.4.449

Handelsman, M. M., Gottlieb, M. C., & Knapp, S. (2005). Training ethical psychologists: An acculturation model. *Professional Psychology: Research and Practice, 36,* 59–65. doi:10.1037/0735-7028.36.1.59

Harris, G. (2010, February 3). Journal retracts 1998 paper linking autism to vaccines. *The New York Times.* Retrieved from http://www.nytimes.com

Kowalski, P., & Taylor, A. K. (2009). The effect of refuting misconceptions in the introductory psychology class. *Teaching of Psychology, 36,* 153–159. doi:10.1080/00986280902959986

Lilienfeld, S. O., Lynn, S. J., Ruscio. J., & Beyerstein, B. L. (2009). *50 great myths of popular psychology: Shattering widespread misconceptions about human behavior.* Malden, MA: Wiley-Blackwell.

Mercer, J. (2009). *Child development: Myths and misunderstandings.* Los Angeles, CA: Sage.

Moseley, D., Baumfield, V., Elliott, J., Higgins, S., Miller, J., Newton, D. P., & Gregson, M. (2006). *Frameworks for thinking: A handbook for teaching and learning.* New York, NY: Cambridge University Press.

Perry, W. G. (1970). *Forms of intellectual and ethical development in the college years: A scheme.* San Francisco, CA: Jossey-Bass.

Regalado, M., Sareen, H., Inkelas, M., Wissow, L. S., & Halfon, N. (2004). Parents' discipline of young children: Results from the National Survey of Early Childhood Health. *Pediatrics, 113*, 1952–1958.

Schwartz, S. J., Unger, J. B., Zamboanga, B. L., & Szapocznik, J. (2010). Rethinking the concept of acculturation: Implications for theory and research. *American Psychologist, 65*, 237–251. doi:10.1037/a0019330

Tsouderos, T., & Callahan, P. (2009, December 7). Autism: Kids put at risk. *The Los Angeles Times*. Retrieved from http://www.latimes.com/

Wen, P. (2006, March 11). Catholic Charities stuns state, ends adoptions. *The Boston Globe*. Retrieved from http://www.boston.com

Winer, G. A., Cottrell, J. E., Gregg, V., Fournier, J. S., & Bica, L. A. (2002). Fundamentally misunderstanding visual perception: Adults' belief in visual emissions. *American Psychologist, 57*, 417–424. doi:10.1037/0003-066X.57.6-7.417

11

ETHICAL CONSIDERATIONS IN PROVIDING ACCOMMODATIONS FOR STUDENTS WITH DISABILITIES

DAVID W. CARROLL

Many instructors struggle with issues pertaining to accommodations for students with disabilities. There are confidentiality issues that may preclude instructors from understanding the nature of a student's disability, and some students may request accommodations that seem inappropriate. Moreover, some instructors have concerns that the proposed accommodations do not necessarily serve students' long-term interests. Ethical issues emerge when the interests of stakeholders conflict. Four different constituents include the following: (a) students with disabilities, (b) the disability support services (DSS) office that exists on most campuses, (c) instructors, and (d) students without disabilities enrolled in the course. Students with disabilities want to be successful in their college careers and enlist support of the DSS office as a means of achieving their educational goals. DSS offices are interested in protecting the legal rights of students with disabilities and assisting students with accommodations. Although most instructors genuinely want to help students with disabilities, they must also protect the academic integrity of their courses. Students without disabilities sometimes believe that accommodations offered

I wish to thank Rochelle Kohn for her helpful comments and suggestions on earlier drafts of this chapter.

to other students place them at a disadvantage. For some accommodations, such as providing interpreters for students with hearing impairments, there may be little or no conflict between these groups.

In this chapter, I provide a framework to discuss the ethical issues associated with providing accommodations for students with disabilities. I begin by providing some legal background, including a review of the Americans With Disabilities Act of 1990 (ADA) and its subsequent revision in 2008. Next, I present the processes by which these laws are typically implemented on college campuses and identify ethical issues that often arise when providing accommodations, and I propose solutions for how to appropriately balance student needs with academic integrity. I conclude with a discussion of how the concept of universal design may provide a proactive way of dealing with ethical issues regarding reasonable accommodations.

LEGAL BACKGROUND

The legal provisions regarding disability are complex and evolving, and the issues have been discussed in depth elsewhere (see Goodman-Delahunty, 2000; Gordon & Keiser, 1998; Katsiyannis, Zhang, Landmark, & Reber, 2009; Ranseen & Parks, 2005). Nonetheless, the law provides the boundaries within which campuses must operate; hence a brief overview is appropriate. The ADA was crafted with the intention of promoting inclusiveness, a goal that benefits not only individuals with disabilities but also society as a whole. It was modeled after Section 504 of the Rehabilitation Act of 1973. Whereas Section 504 applied to entities that received federal financial aid, the ADA covers most establishments, whether privately owned or assisted with federal or state funds. In light of the new legislation, colleges previously compliant with Section 504 reviewed accessibility to ensure that they were in compliance with the law. Under ADA and Section 504, all campuses were required to develop protocols to document and serve individuals with disabilities as well as define *reasonable accommodations* for such students.

Accommodations provided to students with disabilities may include provisions such as additional time on examinations, adaptation of instruction, recording of lectures, PowerPoint slides, and lecture notes. They may also include modification of assessment procedures, unless such skills are the factors that the tests are intended to assess. As these laws took effect, DSS offices became responsible for validating the existence of a disability and providing recommendations for reasonable accommodations. There is institutional leeway in providing accommodations, and institutions are not required to provide accommodations that would be an *undue burden* on the institution or would fundamentally alter requirements for a degree. Institutions may not charge students or include disability questions on preadmission inquiries. Institutions must also provide procedural safeguards for ensuring appropriate academic accommodations, such as grievance procedures.

> The ADA defines a person with a disability to be any person who is found to:
> (1) have a physical or mental impairment that substantially limits one or more major life activities of such individual [including walking, seeing, hearing, speaking, breathing, learning, and working], (2) have a record of such an impairment, or (3) be regarded as having such an impairment. (Burgstahler, 2008a, p. 10)

The Equal Employment Opportunity Commission, the government agency charged with implementing the ADA, defines *physical* or *mental impairment* as "any mental or psychological disorder, such as mental retardation, organic brain syndrome, emotional or mental illness, and specific learning disabilities" (Goodman-Delahunty, 2000, p. 198). Students may also be protected under the ADA if the student has a record of impairment. The legislative record indicates that this provision was included to protect individuals whose disabilities were currently under control and whose major life activities were no longer impaired (Goodman-Delahunty, 2000).

In addition, a student may be protected under the ADA if the individual is regarded as having a disabling condition. That is, if a student is perceived to have a disability and is subjected to adverse actions as a result, then the individual is protected under the ADA (Goodman-Delahunty, 2000). For example, although a student may be diagnosed with AIDS, yet have the disease under control, if the student is discriminated against, he or she is entitled to assistance under the provisions of the ADA.

Following the passage of the ADA in 1990, a number of legal cases helped sharpen the effect of the law. In some cases, the phrase *major life activity* has been interpreted broadly. However, in a number of cases, courts have adopted a more restricted definition of disability. For example, a court determined that a job applicant with paranoid schizophrenia was not disabled because the applicant was capable of major life activities such as walking, seeing, breathing, and learning (Frierson, 1997). This ruling is inconsistent with prior rulings that generally classify difficulties in learning as a significant impairment; thus, an individual with schizophrenia would be covered on a typical college campus. There has been considerable discussion about whether test anxiety as a specific disability qualifies under the law. Anxiety is considered a normal human emotion, and the mere presence of anxiety associated with performance is generally not considered sufficient evidence for an ADA-based accommodation (Wilhelm, 2003). As with any disability, the student is responsible for providing documentation to demonstrate that he or she has a diagnosable anxiety disorder that not only manifests itself in a test-taking situation but also is a pervasive feature of the individual's life.

Legal scholars (Frierson, 1997), physicians (Thomas & Gostin, 2009), psychologists (Ranseen & Parks, 2005), and special educators (Kiuhara & Huefner, 2008) have concluded that the recent court decisions have narrowed the scope of protection that Congress had intended. Such a narrow view of disability may not be fully consistent with an inclusive view of disability often advocated by mental health practitioners (Ranseen & Parks, 2005). In response to these court cases, Congress passed a series of amendments to the ADA in 2008. The amendments broadened the scope of the ADA by revising the definition of disability in several ways. First, the concept of major life activities was expanded to protect many activities, including some not previously recognized (e.g., reading, bending, communicating). In addition, the amendments stated that mitigating measures (other than eyeglasses and contact lenses) should have no bearing on determining whether a disability qualifies under the law and thus whether an individual with such a disability is entitled to protection under the ADA. For example, an individual who uses prosthetics, assistive technology, mobility devices, or cochlear implants that ameliorate a disability would still be regarded as disabled under the amended law. Finally, the amendments clarified that those impairments that are episodic or in remission are considered as disabilities if they substantially limit a major life activity.

The primary importance of the 2008 amendments (enacted January 1, 2009) is that they broadened the scope of the definition of disability and thus the likelihood that individuals with disabilities would be entitled to protection under the ADA. The number of student disability requests has increased substantially in recent decades (Paul, 2000). For example, the percentage of students reporting attention-deficit disorder increased from 7% in 2000 to 19% in 2008 (Government Accountability Office, 2009). It seems likely that the recent amendments to the ADA will coincide with an increase in the number of requests for accommodations in the coming years.

CAMPUS IMPLEMENTATION OF THE AMERICANS WITH DISABILITIES ACT

Documentation of a learning disability typically includes a comprehensive psychoeducational evaluation conducted by a licensed psychologist. Most directors insist on an evaluation that is no more than 4 years old (i.e., for traditionally aged recent high school graduates). Nontraditionally aged students are also required to submit current documentation. The DSS office or designated campus officer identifies the reasonable accommodation. Reasonable accommodations might include providing a quiet room for a student to take an exam, providing additional time for an exam, or allowing a student to tape-record lectures. If the instructor has no concerns regarding the accommodations, the process may be relatively smooth.

Providing Reasonable Accommodations

A number of ethical issues may arise when determining reasonable accommodations. Many faculty members have legitimate concerns about providing specific accommodations to students. Vogel, Leyser, Wyland, and Brulle (1999) surveyed faculty about their attitudes toward various accommodations. Almost all faculty were willing to allow students to tape-record lectures, and many were willing to comment on drafts of papers. Fewer were willing to provide copies of lecture outlines, and still fewer were willing to allow students to complete an assignment in an alternative format. Confidentiality issues complicate the question of whether accommodations are reasonable. Often, the DSS office will not disclose the nature of the disability because of limitations imposed by the Family Educational Rights and Privacy Act of 1974. This may place instructors in an uncomfortable situation in that they wish to help students, yet they are not informed about the nature of the disability and therefore are unable to directly access information that may aid in providing students additional assistance. Some DSS offices request permission to share the nature of the disability as a standard course of action, or students may wish to freely share the diagnosis with instructors. In either instance, the DSS office serves a facilitative role in that it documents the disability and assists in providing reasonable accommodations.

Another concern is whether the disability and the accommodation are compatible with the goals of a given course. What happens if a student enrolled in a class that requires oral presentations identifies as having a social anxiety disorder and asks to have the oral presentation requirement waived? In some instances, it might be possible to find an alternative assignment for such a student or even an alternative section of the course that does not include an oral presentation requirement. However, if the requirement for an oral presentation is central to the course, then an accommodation that eliminates the requirement is not appropriate. Some instructors may reasonably question whether such reassignment is in the best interests of the student. The DSS office together with the faculty member should carefully evaluate the request for an accommodation relative to the essential components of the course.

Balancing Reasonable Accommodations With Academic Integrity

A sensitive ethical issue related to providing accommodations is that such provisions may provide an unfair advantage to students with disabilities at the expense of students without disabilities. That is, how do educators balance the needs of students with disabilities against academic integrity? A common accommodation on many campuses is to provide additional time on examinations for students with reading disabilities. The provision of additional time (usually 1.5 times the amount of time given to students without disabilities) is based on research that shows that students with learning disabilities take longer to read exam material (Ofiesh, Hughes, & Scott, 2004). Research also suggests that students do not necessarily perform better when given additional time on exams. Brothen and Wambach (2002, 2004; see also Bangert-Drowns, Kulik, Kulik, & Morgan, 1991) found that students in a computer-based course spent less time and performed better on quizzes when there were time limits on the quizzes. Time limits encourage students to adopt a *prepare-gather feedback-restudy* strategy in which students are better prepared for the initial quiz and then restudy selected materials on the basis of the quiz feedback. The absence of time limits encourages students to adopt a *quiz-to-learn* strategy in which they attempt quizzes without good preparation and simply look up material during the quiz. These data suggest that additional time may not always be in the best interests of students.

Similarly, some well-intentioned administrators waive requirements (e.g., foreign language, mathematics) for students with disabilities. Sparks, Philips, and Javorsky (2003) examined the academic records for students who petitioned for course substitutions for a campus foreign language requirement and a comparable group of nonpetitioning students. The petitioning group had lower American College Testing scores than the nonpetitioning group. Moreover, 60% of the petitioning students either had not taken a foreign language college course or had withdrawn from the course before filing their petitions. Although the practice of waiving or providing substitutions for requirements is probably well intentioned, it may lead to the conclusion that students with disabilities are given unfair advantages in not having to take classes that are challenging for many students without disabilities. It is important to note that courses should not be waived if they are essential to the degree. One of the goals of ensuring equal opportunity for students with disabilities is to enable them to achieve their educational goals as well as success in their careers of choice. The belief that students with disabilities are succeeding in college by taking less rigorous coursework might undermine the widespread acceptance of individuals with disabilities in society.

UNIVERSAL DESIGN

The concept of universal design is that products and environments should be designed for everyone, including people with disabilities (see Burgstahler, 2008a; McGuire, Scott, & Shaw, 2006; Pliner & Johnson, 2004). For example, a ramp provides entry to a building for individuals who use a wheelchair as well as students who can walk. Thus, the purpose of universal design is to design courses to be appropriate for all students. Most courses are designed for students without regard for students with disabilities, thus creating the need to make subsequent accommodations, which, in turn, raises the issue of whether these accommodations provide unfair advantages for such students. In contrast, the concept of universal design suggests that instructors should design courses in ways that are appropriate for all students so that subsequent accommodations are unnecessary.

Burgstahler (2008b) identified principles of universal design that may be applied to instructional settings. These include the principle that the design of a course is useful for individuals with and without disabilities. For example, a course website may be designed so that it is accessible to all students (including a blind student who uses text-to-speech software). In addition, the size and shape of the learning environment should be appropriate for individuals with different physical abilities. For example, a flexible science lab would be arranged to be usable by those who need to work from either a standing or a seated position.

Fichten et al. (2001) conducted a series of empirical studies to evaluate the needs of college students with various disabilities. Although the overwhelming majority of students used computers, almost half needed adaptations to use computers effectively. Fichten and colleagues presented a series of recommendations for faculty wishing to incorporate universal design into their courses. These recommendations included putting course information on the web well in advance of the beginning of the semester, making course materials and websites universally accessible, making course materials available in alternative formats (e.g., electronic textbooks), and holding virtual office hours. Rose, Harbour, Johnston, Daley, and Abarbanell (2008) discussed how universal design could be infused into a lecture course. They suggested that lectures could be made available in alternative sensory modalities. For example, the university might provide sign language interpreters whenever there is a student with a hearing impairment in the class. All lectures could be videotaped and posted on the course website. The instructors might also allow all students to post notes on a course website. Rose et al. suggested that the lecture notes perhaps be more universally designed than the lectures themselves because different students capture different aspects of lectures.

Consider an example of how to make an appropriate academic accommodation for a student with a learning disability.

> On the first day of class a student reveals that he has a learning disability and has received accommodations in other classes. He requests a "cheat sheet" of information to assist him in retrieving information for

examinations. Although there is little doubt that the cheat sheet would help the student's performance, is this request appropriate?

Typically, an examination is designed to test student knowledge. If the examination is testing a student's ability to remember terms and definitions, allowing one student to have this information while excluding it from others would be unethical. On the other hand, if the examination is intended to test students' ability to apply concepts, then providing all students with a common set of information is a universal design solution that does not provide an unfair advantage for any student. This solution allows for equitable treatment of all students. This case suggests that instructors need to think, and perhaps rethink, their course goals in light of their ethical implications. Similarly, it may be possible to modify an assignment in a way that is consistent with course objectives but makes the assignment more accessible to all students.

Large introductory courses may include several features that are problematic for students with disabilities. The lecture hall may include seating for students with disabilities only in designated areas, and the distance from the front of the room may pose an issue for students with visual or auditory disabilities. Moreover, the standard lecture format in which the class meets several times per week may be a challenge for students with health issues that prevent them from attending class as a result of frequent hospitalizations. Brothen, Wambach, and Hansen (2002) implemented universal design in a large introductory psychology class. Brothen et al. suggested that the personalized system of instruction (PSI), originally developed by Keller (1968), is well designed to provide appropriate assistance to all students including students with disabilities. PSI courses are typically self-paced and use written materials. The self-pacing feature enables individuals with chronic health issues (that may lead to intermittent hospitalization) to catch up when their health improves. In addition, by using written materials, students with disabilities may access assignments and course materials online.

The PSI program developed by Brothen and colleagues (2002) illustrates some of the key principles of universal design. The class is designed to be appropriate for all students, and thus permits students with disabilities to succeed academically without providing conditions, such as additional time on examinations, that might be perceived as unfair to students without disabilities. Moreover, faculty members report significant satisfaction with universally designed courses (Izzo, Murray, & Novak, 2008). Izzo et al. (2008) found that 92% of faculty members reported increased comfort in meeting the needs of students with disabilities as a result of using the universally designed curriculum.

CONCLUSION

The primary goal of the ADA is to create an inclusive climate that meets the needs of all students. Although some definitional issues are thorny, and a minority of students may wish to take advantage of these statutes, the overriding goal of the ADA benefits not only individuals with disabilities but all of society.

REFERENCES

Americans With Disabilities Act of 1990, as amended, 42 U.S.C. A. 12101 et seq. Retrieved from http://www.ada.gov/pubs/ada.htm

Bangert-Drowns, R. L., Kulik, C. C., Kulik, J. A., & Morgan, M. T. (1991). The instructional effect of feedback in test-like events. *Review of Educational Research, 61*, 213–238.

Brothen, T., & Wambach, C. (2001). Effective student use of computerized quizzes. *Teaching of Psychology, 28*, 292–294. doi:10.1207/S15328023TOP2804_10

Brothen, T., & Wambach, C. (2004). The value of time limits on internet quizzes. *Teaching of Psychology, 31*, 62–64. doi:10.1207/s15328023top3101_12

Brothen, T., Wambach, C., & Hansen, G. (2002). Accommodating students with disabilities: PSI as an example of universal instructional design. *Teaching of Psychology, 29*, 239–240.

Burgstahler, S. E. (2008a). Universal design in higher education. In S. E. Burgstahler & R. C. Cory (Eds.), *Universal design in higher education: From principles to practice* (pp. 3–20). Cambridge, MA: Harvard Education Press.

Burgstahler, S. E. (2008b). Universal design of instruction: From principles to practice. In S. E. Burgstahler & R. C. Cory (Eds.), *Universal design in higher education: From principles to practice* (pp. 23–43). Cambridge, MA: Harvard Education Press.

Family Educational Rights and Privacy Act of 1974, 20 U.S.C. § 1232.

Fichten, C. S., Asuncion, J., Barile, M., Genereux, C., Fossey, M., Judd, D., . . . Wells, D. (2001). Technology integration for students with disabilities: Empirically based recommendations for faculty [Special issue]. *Educational Research and Evaluation, 7*, 185–221. doi:10.1076/edre.7.2.185.3869

Frierson, J. G. (1997). Heads you lose, tails you lose: A disturbing judicial trend in defining disability. *Labor Law Journal, 48*, 419–430.

Goodman-Delahunty, J. (2000). Psychological impairment under the Americans with Disabilities Act: Legal guidelines. *Professional Psychology: Research and Practice, 31*, 197–205. doi:10.1037/0735-7028.31.2.197

Gordon, M., & Keiser, S. (1998). (Eds.). *Accommodations in higher education under the Americans with Disabilities Act (ADA): A no-nonsense guide for clinicians, educators, administrators, and lawyers*. New York, NY: Guilford Press.

Government Accountability Office. (2009). *Higher education and disability: Education needs a coordinated approach to improve its assistance to schools in supporting students*. Retrieved from http://www.gao.gov/products/GAO-10-33

Izzo, M. V., Murray, A., & Novak, J. (2008). The faculty perspective on universal design for learning. *Journal of Postsecondary Education and Disability, 21*, 60–72.

Katsiyannis, A., Zhang, D., Landmark, L., & Reber, A. (2009). Postsecondary education for individuals with disabilities. *Journal of Disability Policy Studies, 20*, 35–45. doi:10.1177/1044207308324896

Keller, F. S. (1968). Good-bye, teacher . . . . *Journal of Applied Behavior Analysis, 1*, 79–89. doi:10.1901/jaba.1968.1-79

Kiuhara, S. A., & Huefner, D. S. (2008). Students with psychiatric disabilities in higher education settings. *Journal of Disability Policy Studies, 19*, 103–113. doi:10.1177/1044207308315277

McGuire, J. M., Scott, S. S., & Shaw, S. F. (2006). Universal design and its application in educational environments. *Remedial and Special Education, 27*, 166–175. doi:10.1177/07419325060270030501

Ofiesh, N. S., Hughes, C., & Scott, S. S. (2004). Extended test time and postsecondary students with learning disabilities: A model for decision making. *Learning Disabilities Research & Practice, 19*, 57–70. doi:10.1111/j.1540-5826.2004.00090.x

Paul, S. (2000). Students with disabilities in higher education: A review of the literature. *College Student Journal, 34*, 200–210.

Pliner, S. M., & Johnson, J. R. (2004). Historical, theoretical, and foundational principles of universal instructional design in higher education. *Equity & Excellence in Education, 37*, 105–113. doi:10.1080/10665680490453913

Ranseen, J. D., & Parks, G. S. (2005). Test accommodations for postsecondary students. *Psychology, Public Policy, and Law, 11*, 83–108. doi:10.1037/1076-8971.11.1.83

Rehabilitation Act of 1973, as amended, 29 U. S. C. 794 § 504.

Rose, D. H., Harbour, W. S., Johnston, C. S., Daley, S. G., & Abarbanell, L. (2008). Universal design for learning in postsecondary education: Reflections on principles and their application. In S. E. Burgstahler & R. C. Cory (Eds.), *Universal design in higher education: From principles to practice* (pp. 45–59). Cambridge, MA: Harvard Education Press.

Sparks, R. L., Philips, L., & Javorsky, J. (2003). Students classified as LD who petitioned for or fulfilled the college foreign language requirement—Are they different? A replication study. *Journal of Learning Disabilities, 36*, 348–362. doi:10.1177/00222194030360040601

Thomas, V. L., & Gostin, L. O. (2009). The Americans With Disabilities Act: Shattered aspirations and new hope. *JAMA, 301*, 95–97. doi:10.1001/jama.2008.912

Vogel, S. A., Leyser, Y., Wyland, S., & Brulle, A. (1999). Students with learning disabilities in higher education: Faculty attitude and practices. *Learning Disabilities Research & Practice, 14*, 173–186. doi:10.1207/sldrp1403_5

Wilhelm, S. (2003). Accommodating mental disabilities in higher education: A practical guide to ADA requirements. *Journal of Law & Education, 32*, 217–237.

IV

FACULTY BEHAVIOR

12

BUILDING RELATIONSHIPS WITH STUDENTS AND MAINTAINING ETHICAL BOUNDARIES

JANIE H. WILSON, K. BRYANT SMALLEY, AND C. THRESA YANCEY

Positive relationships between students and faculty improve many aspects of the learning process, including student attitudes toward the teacher, the course, and course grades (e.g., Wilson, Ryan, & Pugh, 2010). Navigating the multitude of possible relationships between faculty and students is complicated by the fact that college students are adults. Faculty, by virtue of their role as teachers, are engaged in a relationship that contains a power differential. Faculty do not control students, but they can demonstrate professional behavior that is consistent with the aspirational goals of the American Psychological Association's (APA's) *Ethical Principles of Psychologists and Code of Conduct* (hereinafter referred to as the Ethics Code; APA, 2010). Therefore, faculty are held to a higher standard for setting boundaries and establishing limits for acceptable behaviors. In this chapter, we discuss types of relationships with students, potential benefits of rapport, and how to build good relationships with students while maintaining professional boundaries.

As a general rule, faculty strive to create positive learning environments; thus, faculty seek to create a welcoming and accepting classroom for students. Faculty may serve in many capacities during a student's educational career—teacher, research mentor, and academic advisor. A teacher may even serve as an employer (e.g., for teaching and research assistants) or supervisor. Because the teacher is in a position of power, it is incumbent on faculty to balance the multiple roles and demonstrate professional and ethical boundaries. Multiple roles with students are not inherently harmful; however, diverse roles have the potential to harm the student and must be closely monitored, particularly when roles include personal or social interactions. Using a proactive approach to establish clear criteria and procedures can provide faculty with guidance for establishing boundaries and help guide professors and students in appropriate behaviors.

Professors' Responsibility: Power in the Relationship

Researchers have argued that the complex interactions occurring between students and instructors create a type of *fiduciary relationship* similar to that seen between physicians and patients or lawyers and clients (Plaut, 1993). This type of relationship is defined as one in which the client (student) is seeking guidance and direction from the fiduciary (instructor), with the expectation of being able to fully trust the fiduciary to act in good faith on behalf of the client (Garner, 2004; Henshaw, 2008). When considering who is responsible for protecting the relationship (and thus for establishing boundaries), researchers resoundingly agree that it is the professional's responsibility to maintain appropriate boundaries because of the fiduciary nature of the relationship and the resulting distinct power differential that exists between student and instructor (Hermansson, 1997; Kagle & Giebelhausen, 1994; Webb, 1997).

Boundaries are often created to help diminish the possibility of transitioning into an exploitative relationship between instructor and student. In establishing classroom boundaries, instructors are expected to create an environment in which instruction is the top priority (Henshaw, 2008; Pope, Schover, & Levenson, 1980). Boundaries sometimes vary on the basis of the type of relationships teachers might have with a student. For instance, a clinical supervisor might deem it necessary to ask a clinical student how an issue arising in a therapy session might impact the student personally, whereas questions of a personal nature may not be appropriate in another setting. Similarly, a research supervisor may invite a student to her home to work on a research project, but inviting a student home in the absence of an academic purpose might be deemed inappropriate. Flexibility in relationships leaves professors, and in particular psychology professors, without clear guidance about appropriate boundaries.

Biaggio, Paget, and Chenoweth (1997) highlighted the various (and potentially conflicting) types of power that faculty hold over students. These include reward power (approval and grades), coercive power (disapproving or devaluing), referent power (role modeling), information and expert power (dispensing knowledge), and legitimate power (contractually bound to provide a service). Types of power may be more or less prominent given the particular relationship between the faculty member and student. For instance, if a professor is both an instructor and employer, as an instructor she has reward, coercive, information and expert, and legitimate power, whereas as an employer she would focus mainly on reward and coercive power. Because both roles contain reward and coercive power, boundaries can become blurred. If the professor is reprimanding the student for performance, is she reprimanding him as professor or employer?

Boundaries should be examined within the context of the relationship(s) between students and faculty. Every relationship will be unique, and the boundaries of those relationships will depend on their nature. However, faculty should acknowledge the power and responsibility that come with each role, develop a framework for evaluating their relationships with students, and foster a climate that supports ethical relationships with students (Biaggio et al., 1997).

Mentoring and Boundaries With Graduate Students

By virtue of the nature of graduate training, graduate students generally develop closer relationships with faculty than do undergraduate students. These relationships may be more reciprocal than the traditional professor–student relationships that are common in undergraduate instruction (Shore, Toyokawa, & Anderson, 2008) and therefore pose unique ethical challenges (Barnett, 2008; Johnson, 2008; Shore et al., 2008). As students work toward professional independence in practice and research, the relationship becomes more equal, and graduate students often are considered to be junior colleagues.

The faculty role as a mentor is essential for graduate student development (Barnett, 2008). Both the mentor and student benefit from the close relationship, but the mentor maintains the responsibility for ensuring that the relationship does not become exploitative (Shore et al., 2008). The mentor must remain aware of contextual factors such as developmental differences among students, the gender of the mentor and the student (any possible pairing has unique ethical considerations), and the potential influences of culture (Shore et al., 2008). That is, each relationship is unique, and mentors must keep in mind any contextual limitations as well as any personal biases that might affect mentoring.

Close relationships between a mentor and graduate students can cause difficulty with objective evaluation of students' readiness to enter into professional roles. Mentors often come to care for those they mentor, which can compromise impartial assessment of a student's work (Johnson, 2008). Faculty members have a duty (especially when mentoring future clinicians) to ensure that students possess the requisite qualifications and character to enter into a professional career. Consider the following scenario:

> You are a professor of psychology actively engaged in service, research, and teaching. As with all faculty, you interact with your students in various settings and roles. You currently have Mary, a student, working as your graduate assistant. Mary is exceptional: timely, responsible, and self-sufficient. She has been a valuable member of your research team, greatly facilitating your ability to be a productive scholar. Mary has been working with you for a year and has enrolled for the first time in one of your courses. You look forward to being able to contribute to her education, but as the semester progresses, Mary's grade steadily declines to the point that it is unlikely she will be able to successfully pass your course. Although you do not typically tutor students outside the classroom or office hours, you are left in the position of deciding whether to help her, thus preserving her as your graduate assistant, or fail her, thus forcing the department to take away her assistantship. Multiple roles (e.g., teacher and research mentor) add complexity to the relationship. Do you go above and beyond and help this student, or do you let her fail and lose an integral part of your research team?

In this scenario, Mary is a student, a graduate assistant, and a member of a research team. The more roles a professor has with a student, the more likely the professor is to advocate for him or her, even when it is clear that the faculty member is experiencing difficulties with the student (Johnson, 2008). Johnson (2008) suggested that these difficulties can be mitigated with better preparation of faculty mentors, more education on the maintenance of boundaries, the separation of the roles of mentor and evaluator, and the involvement of students with multiple mentors. Professors' diverse roles and the power inherent in those roles lead to a need for teachers to clarify ethical and unethical interactions with both graduate and undergraduate students. How far should educators go to develop rapport with students? What are the limitations?

ETHICAL GUIDELINES

The APA Ethics Code (APA, 2010) provides guidance for ethics in teaching (Section 7, Education and Training), and teaching-related issues are also contained throughout the document (see also Woody, 2006). The general guiding principles are aspirational, and they indicate that psychologists should strive to benefit others, do no harm, build trust in psychology through responsible behavior, practice personal integrity, honestly evaluate their own biases to avoid injustice, and respect others. The APA Ethics Code's General Principles provide an outline of ethical teacher conduct.

Additional guidance regarding aspirational goals is typically available through most colleges and universities, although these statements are often vague. Our own university merely mentions that faculty should uphold mutual trust and respect between students and all university employees with any power over students; intimate relationships with students damage trust and respect (Georgia Southern University, Office of the Provost and Vice President for Academic Affairs, 2011–2012). Surely, teachers can agree on at least two specific, concrete examples of violating an ethical guideline and crossing a boundary with students: (a) Do not have sex with your student, and (b) do not date your student.

Maintaining a clear boundary is problematic for many academic psychologists. In fact, 7% of a large sample of graduate counseling students reported sexual advances from faculty members (Barnett-Queen & Larrabee, 2000). The majority of such teachers defend their behavior by waiting until the student is no longer in their class. Without clear guidance stipulating some period of elapsed time before entering into a relationship, it is not clear that engaging in a relationship is appropriate at any point. If the possibility for an eventual relationship exists, it is likely that subtle flirtations may occur prior to a student's completion of the course. In other words, when faculty are willing to engage in intimate relationships with students after a faculty–student relationship has ended, all students may be viewed as potential relationship partners.

A related problem occurs when students talk (and text and e-mail) with each other. Gossip, especially interesting information about a student–professor relationship, will quickly spread across campus. How will the actions of one professor affect the professor's reputation and the reputation of the department, the college, or the institution?

If sex and dates with students are out of bounds, perhaps instructors can agree to the following expanded list (including the two previously stated items [do not have sex with your student and do not date your student]): (a) Do not invite your student to your home; (b) do not kiss, hug, or touch a student; (c) do not allow your student to work for you (e.g., babysit); (d) do not invite your student to a social event; (e) do not gossip with your student (or discuss any personal issues not related to class); and (f) do not "friend" your student on Facebook. Futhermore, we recommend that an instructor (a) repeat the entire list with a former student who is still an undergraduate and (b) repeat the list again with a former student who has graduated. (It is always a good idea to have the office door open when meeting one-on-one with a student.)

Each instructor would choose a different point at which to separate the list into acceptable and unacceptable behaviors; that is, each faculty member has to decide where to draw his or her line. Choices might depend on values and expectations of the professor, the student population, the college or university, and the culture of the community. The task of writing hard-and-fast rules quickly becomes impossible. Even though few teachers would agree about where to draw the line between ethical and unethical relationships, the act of building positive professional relationships with students remains a valuable process. It may also be the case that the line is drawn in different locations depending on where the faculty member is developmentally in his or her own career.

BUILDING RAPPORT WITH LIMITS

The safest relationships with students are professional rather than personal. As long as teachers exercise good judgment while seeking to build rapport with students, kind and friendly relationships are beneficial for students (e.g., Wilson, 2006; Wilson et al., 2010). To project an image of approachability, teachers often use verbal behaviors such as calling students by name, speaking with them before class, and using appropriate humor (e.g., Gorham, 1988). Nonverbal behaviors also communicate a positive attitude toward students. For example, behaviors such as smiling, moving around the room during lecture to keep students' attention, and making eye contact (e.g., Richmond, Gorham, & McCroskey, 1987) enhance learning. Additionally, teachers may communicate care for students by making themselves more accessible through appropriate instances of self-disclosure in the classroom and using technology to remain in contact with students.

Rapport and Student Outcomes

Lowman (1994) referred to "interpersonal rapport" as a crucial part of effective teaching, and Murray (1997) argued that professor–student rapport is associated with student learning. Students who believed they experienced rapport with their professor reported greater enjoyment of the material covered in the course and more positive attitudes toward the instructor. Students also reported that they were more likely to attend class, be more engaged while in class, study, contact their professor, and engage in other academically helpful behaviors (Benson, Cohen, & Buskist, 2005; Buskist & Saville, 2004). Wilson et al. (2010) also found that rapport predicted student attitudes, motivation, and grades. In other words, many positive student outcomes have been associated with rapport in the classroom.

One well-documented method of building rapport involves immediacy behaviors enacted by the professor (e.g., Gorham, 1988; Richmond et al., 1987; Wilson et al., 2010). A wealth of research offers specific instructor behaviors, both nonverbal and verbal, that communicate immediacy to students (for one version of the scale, see Gorham & Christophel, 1990). Nonverbal immediacy serves as an excellent predictor of student motivation, perceptions of learning, and attitudes toward the course and the instructor (e.g., Christensen & Menzel, 1998). Verbal immediacy is also associated with student motivation, perceptions of learning, and attitudes toward the course and the instructor (e.g., Wilson, 2006). Wilson and Taylor (2001) reported that student perceptions of teacher immediacy correlated positively with perceptions of teachers' attitudes toward students. Thus, there is a great deal of evidence that specific verbal and nonverbal behaviors build immediacy, and immediacy is a good measure of students' perceived relationship with their professor.

In addition to the specific immediacy behaviors, instructors can build rapport by providing competent and engaging lectures, infusing recent research into courses, and treating students with respect and fairness. The majority of rapport-building methods do not involve ethical issues. One obvious exception is teacher self-disclosure.

Self-Disclosure in the Classroom

Ejsing (2007) suggested that self-disclosure engages students and that engaged students have more potential to learn. To this end, sharing a personal story with students should be followed by postdisclosure discussion of course-related material. In fact, Ejsing argued that heightened engagement following self-disclosure creates fertile ground for learning, but only with careful guidance. Ejsing cautioned that "learners have only entered the space where they are ready to learn, just as teachers have only entered the space where they must be prepared to teach" (p. 242).

The relationship between teacher self-disclosure and student attitudes is not always positive; student responses are moderated by instructor status, instructor gender, and student gender (e.g., see McCarthy & Schmeck, 1982). Beyond moderators that cannot be changed, type of disclosure appears to be important in student outcomes. Although results were limited to female students evaluating female professors, Lannutti and Strauman (2006) found that honest, intentional, and positive self-disclosure leads to better student attitudes toward the teacher. Instructors should also consider using self-disclosure only when a personal story is relevant to course material and avoid excessive use of disclosure. Instructor credibility is enhanced by judicious use of self-disclosure that is relevant to students and course material (Myers, Brann, & Members of Comm 600, 2009).

As an ethical consideration, self-disclosure has the potential to make students vulnerable. For example, during a discussion of attachment theory, I (Janie H. Wilson) make a point of explaining to students that my husband is the primary caregiver in the family. Usually, several students respond with shock; a few even communicate disdain. Other students in the class react defensively in the face of disapproval, whether to be kind to me or to support women's rights I am not sure. Regardless, self-disclosure has the potential to create an uncomfortable divide and a judgmental atmosphere. My students and I discuss gender roles until students are comfortable focusing on changing social expectations and the competence of men to care for children. In fact, the post-disclosure discussion is the goal of the story, and students appear to be completely engaged in the process. Nonetheless, self-disclosure can make students vulnerable to judgment from others in the class, making disclosure a risk.

Boundaries and the Use of Technology

Technology offers ever-increasing opportunities to self-disclose (e.g., e-mail, personal websites, blogs, and social networking sites). Hevern (2006) noted that messages sent through any of these media may be misconstrued because they lack nonverbal or other contextual variables. Electronic messages are easily shared, saved, and printed; even those that are deleted may not be completely destroyed, creating additional complications.

Perhaps the most obvious caution is that students and teachers may learn more about each other than is typical in a professional relationship. Information that was once private is now potentially available to many. For example, a professor may create a post about an evening spent at a bar, and his friended students on Facebook may read the information. Students may bring up the personal information in the classroom, and the ensuing discussion can create a peer atmosphere instead of a teacher–learner environment.

To date, few studies have investigated the impact of social networking on faculty–student relationships. Mazer, Murphy, and Simonds (2007) reported that high professor self-disclosure on Facebook correlated with students' anticipated motivation as well as positive affect toward the course material and the classroom climate. However, student responses to open-ended items caution that teachers' use of Facebook may compromise their credibility. In a follow-up study, high professor self-disclosure on Facebook enhanced student perceptions of instructor credibility (Mazer, Murphy, & Simonds, 2009). Although students responded favorably to computer-generated Facebook pages, they cautioned that professors self-disclosing on Facebook may not be well received. These perceptions suggest that some forms of communication with students may not be entirely acceptable and as a result will not enhance a professional relationship. Furthermore, extensive self-disclosure likely crosses the line into a personal relationship rife with potential ethical problems. Perhaps a personal Facebook page and a professional Facebook page (suitable for friending students and former students) may help preserve appropriate boundaries.

CONCLUSION

In this chapter, we discussed types of relationships with students, potential benefits of rapport, and how to build good relationships with students while maintaining professional boundaries. Professors have a great deal of power over students, and most potential roles between student and professor are characterized by the same power differential. Teachers necessarily take on diverse roles, creating overlapping expectations that can be confusing to the student if not clearly discussed. Relationships with graduate students are particularly complex because graduate students are considered to be junior colleagues. The responsibility of delineating between roles as well as maintaining ethical standards resides with the instructor. Given the positive outcomes associated with rapport, establishing a positive relationship while at the same time maintaining boundaries is particularly important. The immediacy literature (e.g., Gorham, 1988; Richmond et al., 1987; Wilson et al., 2010) and emerging empirical research on student–teacher rapport (Benson et al., 2005; Buskist & Saville, 2004) provide ways to build rapport with students both in the classroom and out of the classroom.

We also provided evidence that rapport in the classroom fosters positive student attitudes, behaviors, and grades. However, intimate relationships with individual students may threaten trust in the professor, department, college, university, and the field of psychology. Teachers must ever be conscious of the potential for unethical relationships with students when building a positive classroom environment. Unfortunately, the inherent risk in building rapport is that boundaries may be compromised. We believe that the relationship between rapport and student outcomes is curvilinear. In other words, positive verbal and nonverbal teacher behaviors enhance student outcomes, but excessive use of immediacy compromises student learning. Similarly, self-disclosure is generally well-received but not when a teacher fails to tie the personal story to course material. Increasing use of technology can help to build rapport, but teachers may not want to submerge themselves in students' worlds and cross into the friend zone.

At this point, we trust that teachers know it is unethical to have sex with a student, at least while evaluating the student's work or having power over the student in any way. In fact, some professors consider students to remain "their" students long after graduation. Much like beloved children, former students continue to evoke pride when they complete an advanced degree or join the workforce. And if a student is always a student, strictly professional relationships remain intact for perpetuity. Regardless of where teachers draw the line when engaging in relationships with students, the effort to establish positive interactions is worthwhile.

REFERENCES

American Psychological Association. (2010). *Ethical principles of psychologists and code of conduct (Amended June 1, 2010)*. Retrieved from http://www.apa.org/ethics/code/index.aspx

Barnett, J. E. (2008). Mentoring, boundaries, and multiple relationships: Opportunities and challenges. *Mentoring & Tutoring: Partnership in Learning, 16*, 3–16. doi:10.1080/13611260701800900

Barnett-Queen, T., & Larrabee, M. J. (2000). Sexually oriented relationships between educators and students in mental-health-education programs. *Journal of Mental Health Counseling, 22*, 68–84.

Benson, A. T., Cohen, L. A., & Buskist, W. (2005). Rapport: Its relation to student attitudes and behaviors toward teachers and classes. *Teaching of Psychology, 32*, 237–270. doi:10.1207/s15328023top3204_8

Biaggio, M., Paget, T. L., & Chenoweth, M. S. (1997). A model for ethical management of faculty–student dual relationships. *Professional Psychology: Research and Practice, 28*, 184–189. doi:10.1037/0735-7028.28.2.184

Buskist, W., & Saville, B. K. (2004). Rapport building: Creating positive emotional contexts for enhancing teaching and learning. In B. Perlman, L. I. McCann, & S. H. McFadden (Eds.), *Lessons learned: Practical advice for the teaching of psychology* (Vol. 2, pp. 149–155). Washington, DC: American Psychological Society.

Christensen, L. J., & Menzel, K. E. (1998). The linear relationship between student reports of teacher immediacy behaviors and perceptions of state motivation, and of cognitive, affective, and behavioral learning. *Communication Education, 47*, 82–90. doi:10.1080/03634529809379112

Ejsing, A. (2007). Power and caution: The ethics of self-disclosure. *Teaching Theology & Religion, 10*, 235–243. doi:10.1111/j.1467-9647.2007.00377.x

Garner, B. A. (Ed.). (2004). *Black's law dictionary* (8th ed.). St. Paul, MN: Thomson.

Georgia Southern University, Office of the Provost and Vice President of Academic Affairs. (2011–2012). *Faculty handbook, 2011–2012*. Retrieved from http://academics.georgiasouthern.edu/provost/handbook/facultyhandbook.pdf

Gorham, J. (1988). The relationship between verbal teacher immediacy behaviors and student learning. *Communication Education, 37*, 40–53. doi:10.1080/036345288 09378702

Gorham, J., & Christophel, D. M. (1990). The relationship of teachers' use of humor in the classroom to immediacy and student learning. *Communication Education, 39*, 46–62. doi:10.1080/03634529009378786

Henshaw, C. M. (2008). Faculty–student boundaries in associate degree nursing programs. *The Journal of Nursing Education, 47*, 409–416. doi:10.3928/01484834-20080901-03

Hermansson, G. (1997). Boundaries and boundary management in counselling: The never-ending story. *British Journal of Guidance & Counselling, 25*, 133–146.

Hevern, V. W. (2006). Using the Internet effectively: Homepages and email. In W. Buskist & S. F. Davis (Eds.), *Handbook of the teaching of psychology* (pp. 99–106). Malden, MA: Blackwell Publishing. doi:10.1002/9780470754924.ch17

Johnson, W. B. (2008). Are advocacy, mutuality, and evaluation incompatible mentoring functions? *Mentoring & Tutoring: Partnership in Learning, 16*, 31–44. doi:10.1080/13611260701800942

Kagle, J. D., & Giebelhausen, P. N. (1994). Dual relationships and professional boundaries. *Social Work, 39*, 213–220.

Lannutti, P. J., & Strauman, E. C. (2006). Classroom communication: The influence of instructor self-disclosure on student evaluations. *Communication Quarterly, 54*, 89–99. doi:10.1080/01463370500270496

Lowman, J. (1994). Professors as performers and motivators. *College Teaching, 42*, 137–141. doi:10.1080/87567555.1994.9926844

Mazer, J. P., Murphy, R. E., & Simonds, C. J. (2007). I'll see you on "Facebook": The effects of computer-mediated teacher self-disclosure on student motivation, affective learning, and classroom climate. *Communication Education, 56*, 1–17. doi:10.1080/03634520601009710

Mazer, J. P., Murphy, R. E., & Simonds, C. J. (2009). The effects of teacher self-disclosure via Facebook on teacher credibility. *Learning, Media and Technology, 34*, 175–183. doi:10.1080/17439880902923655

McCarthy, P. R., & Schmeck, R. R. (1982). Effects of teacher self-disclosure on student learning and perceptions of the teacher. *College Student Journal, 16*, 45–49.

Murray, H. (1997). Effective teaching behaviors in the college classroom. In R. Perry & J. Smart (Eds.), *Effective teaching in higher education: Research and practice* (pp. 171–204). New York, NY: Agathon.

Myers, S. A., Brann, M., & Members of Comm 600. (2009). College students' perceptions of how instructors establish and enhance credibility through self-disclosure. *Qualitative Research Reports in Communication, 10*, 9–16.

Plaut, S. M. (1993). Boundary issues in teacher–student relationships. *Journal of Sex & Marital Therapy, 19*, 210–219.

Pope, K. S., Schover, L. R., & Levenson, H. (1980). Sexual behavior between clinical supervisors and trainees: Implications for professional standards. *Professional Psychology, 11*, 157–162. doi:10.1037/0735-7028.11.1.157

Richmond, V. P., Gorham, J. S., & McCroskey, J. C. (1987). The relationship between selected immediacy behaviors and cognitive learning. In M. McLaughlin (Ed.), *Communication Yearbook 10* (pp. 574–590). Beverly Hills, CA: Sage.

Shore, W. J., Toyokawa, T., & Anderson, D. D. (2008). Context-specific effects on reciprocity in mentoring relationships: Ethical implications. *Mentoring & Tutoring: Partnership in Learning, 16,* 17–29. doi:10.1080/13611260701800926

Webb, S. B. (1997). Training for maintaining appropriate boundaries in counselling. *British Journal of Guidance & Counselling, 25,* 175–188.

Wilson, J. H. (2006). Predicting student attitudes and grades from perceptions of instructors' attitudes. *Teaching of Psychology, 33,* 91–95. doi:10.1207/s15328023 top3302_2

Wilson, J. H., Ryan, R. G., & Pugh, J. L. (2010). Professor–Student Rapport Scale predicts student outcomes. *Teaching of Psychology, 37,* 246–251.

Wilson, J. H., & Taylor, K. W. (2001). Professor immediacy as behaviors associated with liking students. *Teaching of Psychology, 28,* 136–138.

Woody, W. D. (2006). Ethical teaching. In W. Buskist & S. F. Davis (Eds.), *Handbook of the teaching of psychology* (pp. 219–227). Malden, MA: Blackwell Publishing. doi:10.1002/9780470754924.ch38

13

WHAT AND WHEN SHOULD UNDERGRADUATES LEARN ABOUT RESEARCH ETHICS?

BLAINE F. PEDEN AND ALLEN H. KENISTON

Acting ethically is a desirable and important outcome of student learning (American Psychological Association [APA], 2007; APA, Board of Educational Affairs, 2008). Because ethics permeates every topic in psychology, questions often arise regarding how to teach about the responsible conduct of research. In this chapter, we present a developmentally appropriate model that ensures "every psychology student is (or should be) presented with a range of ethical considerations as part of his or her undergraduate education" (Landrum et al., 2010, p. 158). Our "scope and sequence" agenda assumes that teaching ethically requires instructors to learn and teach ethics throughout their careers.

Our suggestions for teaching about research ethics across the undergraduate curriculum derive from several sources. The APA (2007) student learning outcomes include objectives specific to teaching ethics. Additional resources include the developmentally coherent curriculum (APA, Board of Educational Affairs, 2008), discussions of ethical acculturation (e.g., Handelsman, Gottlieb, & Knapp, 2005), and guidelines for conducting ethical research (e.g., Aguinis & Henle, 2002; Kimmel, 2007). Throughout this chapter, we describe how teaching about research ethics can be systematically developed as students progress through the major.

TEACHING RESEARCH ETHICS IN THE FIRST YEAR

Introductory psychology courses should produce a basic understanding of research ethics in all students (Dunn, Beins, McCarthy, & Hill, 2010). In our view, teaching and learning ethics begins in the introductory course and becomes more elaborate in subsequent courses. Student learning outcomes regarding the ethical knowledge, skills, and values for undergraduate psychology majors can be found in the APA *Guidelines for the Undergraduate Psychology Major* (APA, 2007). Teachers may impart information about psychology-specific learning objectives using textbooks, lectures, and demonstrations and by having undergraduates participate in research. Subsequent learning objectives should be addressed later in students' educational careers.

During the first year of students' experience, educators should also introduce the APA *Ethical Principles of Psychologists and Code of Conduct* (hereinafter referred to as the Ethics Code; APA, 2010). Instructors should explain that ethics applies to psychologists working as helping professionals, teachers, and researchers. Teachers should explain that psychologists formally adopted their first professional code of conduct in the 1950s and have revised it regularly since then. Instructors should also emphasize that the Ethics Code applies to students. For example, student affiliates of the APA must agree to adhere to the Ethics Code. Finally, first-year students should understand that the APA Ethics Code dictates the conduct of research and fosters thinking critically about research.

Beyond the usual discussion about the Milgram (1963) study of obedience, several authors (Fisher & Kuther, 1997; Handelsman, 2002; Korn, 1984) have offered ways to introduce ethical topics into beginning courses. For example, teachers can promote understanding of the APA Ethics Code, the requirement to follow the Ethics Code in the treatment of human and nonhuman participants, recognition of the necessity of ethical behavior in the science and practice of psychology, the use of information and technology ethically and responsibly, and the regular display of personal integrity with others, all in the students' first year.

Faculty can also help first-year students gain a basic level of ethical proficiency by making a distinction between classroom demonstrations and psychological research intended to produce new knowledge. Demonstrations of obedience (e.g., Lucas & Lidstone, 2000), discussions of Milgram's (1963) original study and the replication by Burger (2009), and assessment of students' opinions and concerns about these materials can be beneficial in helping students learn the basics of research ethics (Harcum & Friedman, 1991). Engaging students in the classroom demonstration and discussing the accompanying classic article (Milgram, 1963) along with the commentaries on the Burger (2009) article from *American Psychologist* should prompt students to think critically about relevant ethical issues and ethically complex situations. Moreover, discussion about the recent replication of the Milgram procedure allows instructors to raise interesting questions about the use of alternative procedures (Slater et al., 2006).

First-year students can also learn about research ethics by participating in research. That is, student research participants should directly learn about ethical issues. Moreover, students should experience ethical practice in the form of letters of invitation, consent forms, the competent and nonthreatening conduct of research, and debriefing, especially in cases of deception. Instructors can and, perhaps should, use videos to enhance student interest and participation in research (Sacco & Bernstein, 2010). Most important, teachers must ensure students' understanding of their roles, rights, and responsibilities in psychological research (Korn, 1988). Finally, instructors should monitor available research opportunities to ensure integrity on the part of participants and experimenters alike.

Student participants should expect ethical treatment by researchers; however, participants should also act ethically. Kimble (1987) provided syllabus language that instructors could use to promote responsible research participation by first-year students and thereby help to ensure quality scientific research. First, Kimble argued that a syllabus should state that participating in research provides experience with experimental procedures that is otherwise unavailable. Second, psychologists do research to find behavioral solutions to real social problems. Third, future students benefit from today's research in the same way that students now benefit from earlier research. In other words, students should understand that they benefit from and can contribute to historical continuity. Finally, students should have equitable alternatives to participating in research in accord with Standard 8.04, Client/Patient, Student, and Subordinate Research Participants, of the Ethics Code (APA, 2010).

Korn (1988) further described how first-year courses might provide opportunities for teachers to educate their students about how to be high-quality research participants and, at the same time, to educate students on their rights as participants. Korn (1984) emphasized that beginning students should learn about their rights as research participants because they are the largest group of individuals participating in academic research today. Instructors who use syllabus language adapted from Kimble (1987) enhance their students' ability to make informed decisions about starting and finishing a psychological study.

Another way to promote teaching and learning about research ethics is to have students be experimenters. First-year students can learn about psychological research by serving as research assistants. Students might read articles on a topic (selected by the instructor), engage in data collection and analysis (using procedures and instructions provided by the instructor), and write reports about the research as a way to learn about the research enterprise. These experiences allow students to engage in multiple levels of the research process. Consider the following scenario:

> A professor was in her office on Friday afternoon, reflecting on the week. The high point had been a demonstration about eyewitness testimony. It had gone well, and many students had enjoyed the demonstration. Some even stated that research on eyewitness testimony was something they would like to do. Sighing contentedly, the professor picked up her newspaper only to read the following: "City police and patrons of a local café were baffled yesterday when they heard a loud report and a scream at the back of the café, followed by a figure 'wearing a trench coat' or a 'green pullover' running out the front door. Also puzzling was the appearance of a student on the scene who immediately asked patrons to complete a survey about what they had just seen."

Rather than merely asking students to read about research, the teacher can use the newspaper article to further illustrate ethics in research. Using guided questions, the teacher might ask students to identify potential breaches in research ethics and to posit ethical practices. Regardless of whether students serve as participants or experimenters, we recommend that students reflect on the relationship between research and ethics by assessing their own experiences. Bashe, Anderson, Handelsman, and Klevansky (2007) provided several suggestions for reflection papers that can be used to meet this goal. In sum, first-year psychology courses provide many opportunities for students to learn about the ethical codes that govern the behavior of researchers. Students who have learned about and experienced ethical research practice will better appreciate the results of psychological studies, make better participants, and be encouraged to become ethical researchers themselves.

TEACHING RESEARCH ETHICS IN THE SECOND YEAR

Undergraduates typically take statistics prior to research methods in their second college year (Peden & Carroll, 2009; Stoloff et al., 2010). In second-year courses, the student learning outcomes generally should move beyond retention and comprehension to analysis and application of proficiencies. Although statistics instructors usually do not focus on ethical practices, they nevertheless should convey Vardeman and Morris's (2003) advice that doing statistics is an inherently ethical endeavor. Their emphasis on personal integrity and the necessity of ethical behavior in all aspects of practice, research, and teaching echoes more advanced learning objectives. For example, statistics instructors can review ethical concerns regarding plagiarism presented in first-year courses and then discuss fabrication and falsification of data. All three concepts apply to statistics homework and real data. Students in a more advanced statistics course should use their knowledge about the roles, rights, and responsibilities of research participants when they volunteer to serve in research (Korn, 1988) as well as use their new knowledge about measurement, sampling issues, and experimental design. Statistics students should be inclined and able to ask questions during the informed consent or debriefing processes and receive clear and reasonable answers.

The research methods course allows psychology students to apply knowledge about both ethics and statistics during the design, planning, and analysis phases of research. More advanced methods courses provide additional venues to teach about ethical guidelines for the design and implementation of research (Aguinis & Henle, 2002; Kimmel, 2007). Students should receive training about the steps involved in obtaining approval to conduct research. More important, students should learn that ensuring ethical treatment of participants is at the heart of the institutional review board (IRB) process. Students with a developing level of understanding about the ethical treatment of research participants should be able to identify ethical issues that arise at each point in the research process. In the second stage of the research process, researchers are focused on securing a sufficiently large and representative sample, which requires methodological competence and ethical sensitivities. At this point students should learn about controversies associated with recruiting participants through subject pools (for a complete review of issues, see Chastain & Landrum, 1999; Dalziel, 1996; Diamond & Reidpath, 1994).

Discussions of recruitment also prompt researchers to consider whether inducements (e.g., extra credit in a class, money, food) unduly influence (i.e., coerce) students to participate in a given study. Evaluating the level of inducement may prove troublesome for student researchers because students have a unique perspective. For example, Miller and Kreiner (2008) demonstrated that members of IRBs regard inducements as much more coercive than do students. Teaching ethically requires educators to understand students' viewpoints and help them resolve contradictory opinions. It is only later in the sequence of educational training that students are in a position to fully realize the complexity associated with current practices in the recruitment of research participants. Undergraduates typically have some knowledge about conducting research from their own experience as participants. We believe that students can benefit from participating again when they are further along in the major. By serving again as participants, student researchers perceive research and responsible conduct in a different light.

Students who are early in their educational careers may be taught about plagiarism at an introductory level. Although these students may learn that plagiarism is unethical, they may be insensitive to subtle ethical issues regarding authorship (e.g., order of listing), misrepresenting their own or the research of others, and censoring data or ideas. It is likely that students will not fully grasp these subtleties until they are in their third or fourth year and can more directly experience "real life" authorship.

TEACHING RESEARCH ETHICS IN THE THIRD AND FOURTH YEARS

Successful completion of the second-year curriculum prepares students for third- and fourth-year courses. Students are apprentices and may possess skills beyond analysis and application of research, developing their own projects. These student researchers now have the potential to do "real" research that meaningfully contributes to the literature. There are two primary venues for this level of training: advanced content courses and independent work with faculty on research projects. In either case, we recommend that students and faculty discuss a range of ethical issues (Dunn, 2010; Goodyear, Crego, & Johnston, 1992).

One approach to communicating research ethics involves infusing the content into the fabric of the course (Carroll, Keniston, & Peden, 2008). In typical content courses, students may write research proposals and even conduct their own research. Students must delve into the literature to learn about the logic and design of specific paradigms. Reviewing the literature should help to make students aware of the ethical challenges and opportunities inherent in specific research designs. For example, studying incidental recall may require deception because participants must recall material they did not expect to remember (e.g., instructions often suggest that the experiment is about something other than remembering). However, the Ethics Code (APA, 2010) generally proscribes the use of deception (see Standard 8.07, Deception in Research); therefore, students now must learn to make more refined, careful, and sophisticated ethical judgments. Less sophisticated ethical reasoning must give way to more complex solutions.

Instructors of content courses should be conversant with the range of methodological and ethical issues related to student research projects. Faculty may scaffold the learning so that students develop a research project, but faculty must help students prepare IRB protocols. Students must learn about appropriate recruitment, informed consent, and debriefing.

A second approach to communicating research ethics is an apprenticeship in which a student may work as a research assistant for a faculty member. In this context, students learn how to conduct a literature search, master a research paradigm, and become skillful at collecting and analyzing data. Professors can and should model the ethical practices. Students might review prior IRB protocols to learn the rationale and procedures for the study.

Educators should convey that the process of planning a study, recruiting participants, conducting the study, and publishing an article often takes years rather than months. Hence, students who become members of a real research team must understand that they now have ethical obligations to the members of the team, to the profession, and to science that extend to the completion of the project. In other words, abandoning a study because the semester ends is ethically unacceptable.

Students who have become competent researchers in upper level coursework are now literate citizens of the psychological research community. At this point, they may begin to train and supervise other students new to the laboratory group. The final level of learning typically occurs in a capstone course or a faculty–student collaborative research project. In a capstone course, a student may refine and conduct research proposed in an earlier course or propose a new project. The capstone course should require students to demonstrate what they have learned about well-conceived, competently executed, and ethically responsible research. At this level, supervising professors act less as guides and more as evaluators of these three components. Educators also help students find financial resources to support the work and possibly provide proof of oversight. Students doing research for capstone courses must demonstrate that they can design research projects and address the ethical issues on their own. Their success provides a final indication of individual and institutional accomplishment. Success in a capstone course documents a psychology program's ability to develop and acculturate its students as academic psychologists (Handelsman et al., 2005).

Students may also become fully empowered collaborators working with professors on research programs. Experienced student collaborators may be able to propose new studies with the promise of results worth presenting at research conferences or publishing in peer-reviewed journals. In addition to mastering the methodological and ethical necessities of their research, students must become knowledgeable about the ethics of publication and collaboration. Failures of academic integrity threaten their coinvestigators. Thus, students must avoid plagiarism or citation errors and must discover such errors in the work of others on a research team. Students may have major responsibility for research protocols submitted to IRBs and must expertly evaluate the ethical concerns raised by their research. They must participate fully in decisions about authorship that fairly represent the relative contributions of all members of the research team. Serving as a coresearcher implies a leadership role in the research.

Undergraduate psychology students who complete the sequence of development required to become ethical researchers become full members of the academic community. They become models and teachers of ethical research practice who demonstrate conceptual and methodological expertise.

After presenting or publishing their work, these advanced undergraduates may begin to identify with an even larger community defined by the individuals and institutions integral to their research. These students are ready for the transition to the next stages of their training as teachers, researchers, or applied researchers. The ultimate test of their training will be understanding that ethical standards are not static and therefore require commitment to further study and reflection. New or revised ethical standards require willing and cooperative accommodation of research practices to the new standards. We hope that students will adapt to changing ethical climates and cultures and make their own contributions to psychologists' evolving understanding about how best to teach and learn ethically.

CONCLUSION

Teaching and learning in psychology are inherently ethical endeavors. We have described how and when undergraduates should learn about ethical practice in the conduct of research (for more on this topic, see Chapter 15, this volume). Our approach is developmental and emphasizes that learning and teaching research ethics are the responsibility of all members of a department (e.g., Hogan & Kimmel, 1992). Learning about research ethics should extend to all coursework. Training in the ethics of research should begin in the introductory psychology course, unfold in the initial methods course, and be elaborated and specialized in advanced courses. Students have much to learn by participating in research and conducting research as undergraduates. By the time they graduate, psychology students should understand fully the roles, rights, and responsibilities of participants and researchers. Moreover, they should have begun the process of professional and ethical acculturation.

REFERENCES

Aguinis, H., & Henle, C. A. (2002). Ethics in research. In S. G. Rogelberg (Ed.), *Handbook of research methods in industrial and organizational psychology* (pp. 34–56). Malden, MA: Blackwell.

American Psychological Association. (2007). *APA guidelines for the undergraduate psychology major*. Retrieved from http://www.apa.org/ed/precollege/about/psymajor-guidelines.pdf

American Psychological Association. (2010). *Ethical principles of psychologists and code of conduct (Amended June 1, 2010)*. Retrieved from http://www.apa.org/ethics/code/index.aspx

American Psychological Association, Board of Educational Affairs. (2008). *Teaching, learning, and assessing in a developmentally coherent curriculum.* Retrieved from http://www.apa.org/ed/governance/bea/curriculum.pdf

Bashe, A., Anderson, S. K., Handelsman, M. M., & Klevansky, R. (2007). An acculturation model for ethics training: The ethics autobiography and beyond. *Professional Psychology: Research and Practice, 38,* 60–67. doi:10.1037/0735-7028.38.1.60

Burger, J. M. (2009). Replicating Milgram: Would people still obey today? *American Psychologist, 64,* 1–11. doi:10.1037/a0010932

Carroll, D. W., Keniston, A. H., & Peden, B. F. (2008). Integrating critical thinking with course content. In D. S. Dunn, J. S. Halonen, & R. A. Smith (Eds.), *Teaching critical thinking in psychology: A handbook of best practices* (pp. 99–115). Malden, MA: Wiley-Blackwell. doi:10.1002/9781444305173.ch9

Chastain, G., & Landrum, R. E. (Eds.). (1999). *Protecting human subjects: Departmental subject pools and institutional review boards.* Washington, DC: American Psychological Association. doi:10.1037/10322-000

Dalziel, J. R. (1996). Students as research subjects: Ethical and educational issues. *Australian Psychologist, 31,* 119–123. doi:10.1080/00050069608260190

Diamond, M. R., & Reidpath, D. D. (1994). Are students really human? Observations on institutional ethics committees. *Australian Psychologist, 29,* 145–146. doi:10.1080/00050069408257339

Dunn, D. S. (2010). *The practical researcher: A student guide to conducting psychological research* (2nd ed.). Malden, MA: Wiley-Blackwell.

Dunn, D. S., Beins, B. B., McCarthy, M. A., & Hill, G. W., IV. (2010). *Best practices for teaching beginnings and endings in the psychology major: Research, cases, and recommendations.* New York, NY: Oxford University Press.

Fisher, C. B., & Kuther, T. L. (1997). Integrating research ethics into the introductory psychology course curriculum. *Teaching of Psychology, 24,* 172–175. doi:10.1207/s15328023top2403_4

Goodyear, R., Crego, C. A., & Johnston, M. W. (1992). Ethical issues in the supervision of student research: A study of critical incidents. *Professional Psychology: Research and Practice, 23,* 203–210. doi:10.1037/0735-7028.23.3.203

Handelsman, M. M. (2002, Fall). Where are the ethics in introductory psychology? *Psychology Teacher Network, 12*(3), pp. 1, 3.

Handelsman, M. M., Gottlieb, M. C., & Knapp, S. (2005). Training ethical psychologists: An acculturation model. *Professional Psychology: Research and Practice, 36,* 59–65. doi:10.1037/0735-7028.36.1.59

Harcum, E. R., & Friedman, H. (1991). Students' ethics ratings of demonstrations in introductory psychology. *Teaching of Psychology, 18,* 215–218. doi:10.1207/s15328023top1804_3

Hogan, P. M., & Kimmel, A. J. (1992). Ethical teaching of psychology: One department's attempts at self-regulation. *Teaching of Psychology, 19,* 205–210. doi:10.1207/s15328023top1904_1

Kimble, G. A. (1987). The scientific value of undergraduate research participation. *American Psychologist, 42,* 267–268. doi:10.1037/0003-066X.42.3.267.b

Kimmel, A. J. (2007). *Ethical issues in behavioral research: Basic and applied perspectives* (2nd ed.). Malden, MA: Blackwell.

Korn, J. H. (1984). Coverage of research ethics in introductory and social psychology textbooks. *Teaching of Psychology, 11,* 146–149.

Korn, J. H. (1988). Students' roles, rights, and responsibilities as research participants. *Teaching of Psychology, 15,* 74–78. doi:10.1207/s15328023top1502_2

Landrum, R. E., Beins, B. C., Bhall, M., Brakke, K., Briihl, D. S., & Curl-Langager, R. M., . . . Van Kirk, J. J. (2010). Desired outcomes of an undergraduate education in psychology from departmental, student, societal perspectives. In D. F. Halpern (Ed.), *Undergraduate education in psychology: A blueprint for the future of the discipline* (pp. 145–160). Washington, DC: American Psychological Association.

Lucas, K. B., & Lidstone, J. G. (2000). Ethical issues in teaching about research ethics. *Evaluation and Research in Education, 14,* 53–64. doi:10.1080/09500790008666961

Milgram, S. (1963). Behavioral study of obedience. *Journal of Abnormal and Social Psychology, 67,* 371–378. doi:10.1037/h0040525

Miller, W. E., & Kreiner, D. S. (2008). Student perception of coercion to participate in psychological research. *North American Journal of Psychology, 10,* 53–64.

Peden, B. F., & Carroll, D. W. (2009). Historical trends in teaching research methods by psychologists in the United States. In M. Garner, C. Wagner, & B. Kawulich (Eds.), *Teaching research methods in the social sciences* (pp. 23–34). Farnham, Surrey, England: Ashgate.

Sacco, D. F., & Bernstein, M. J. (2010). A video introduction to psychology: Enhancing research interest and participation. *Teaching of Psychology, 37,* 28–31. doi:10.1080/00986280903425995

Slater, M., Antley, A., Davison, A., Swapp, D., Guger, C., Barker, C., . . . Sanchez-Vivez, M. V. (2006) A virtual reprise of the Stanley Milgram obedience experiments. *PLoS ONE, 1,* e39. doi:10.1371/journal.pone.0000039

Stoloff, M., McCarthy, M. A., Keller, L., Varfolomeeva, V., Lynch, J., Makara, K., . . . Smiley, W. (2010). The undergraduate psychology major: An examination of structure and sequence. *Teaching of Psychology, 37,* 4–15. doi:10.1080/00986280903426274

Vardeman, S. B., & Morris, M. D. (2003). Statistics and ethics: Some advice for young statisticians. *The American Statistician, 57,* 21–26. doi:10.1198/0003130031072

14

SUPERVISING UNDERGRADUATES IN COMMUNITY-BASED LEARNING EXPERIENCES: AN ETHICAL APPROACH

KAREN BRAKKE AND PHYLICIA THOMPSON

Undergraduate education in psychology often includes components that occur outside of the classroom or research lab. These community-based learning experiences (CBLEs; following CBL in Mooney & Edwards, 2001), be they service learning, practica, internships, or other learning opportunities, expose students to real-world applications of the psychology concepts and principles that they learn on campus or online. Just as important, CBLEs also introduce students to the complexity of real-world professionalism, with all of its ambiguity and challenges. Thus, such experiences provide a relatively safe, supervised context in which students can learn attitudes and dispositions appropriate for working in psychology and related fields as well as practice their emerging skills and develop their knowledge base (Fernald et al., 1982; Grayson, 2010; Hardy & Shaen, 2000).

The pedagogical literature in this area is primarily focused on the benefits of CBLEs to students and others (see Bringle & Duffy, 1998; Hardy & Shaen, 2000; Lundy, 2007) or descriptions of specific course-based experiences (examples are provided in Bringle & Duffy, 1998; Connor-Greene, 2002; Fernald et al., 1982; Kretchmar, 2001; Lundy 2007). A critical aspect of supervising CBLEs that has earned only sparse attention (e.g., Fernald et al., 1982) is the many ethical considerations involved in these experiences. Given the ever-changing educational, societal, and even legal landscapes that faculty face, it is perhaps time to revisit faculty responsibilities and roles in supervising students as they engage in these experiences. In this chapter, we define CBLEs and their goals. We also address challenges faced by supervisors of these experiences; the educational, legal, and ethical issues that must be acknowledged by institutions and faculty; and recommendations for avoiding ethical dilemmas and meeting these supervisory challenges.

COMMUNITY-BASED LEARNING EXPERIENCES

Psychology is a broad field, and the relevant experiences open to its majors (and minors) are diverse. For the purposes of this chapter, we define CBLEs as those experiences that occur in an applied off-campus setting but that earn course credit or graded evaluation. Such experiences may include relatively brief service-learning assignments as well as semester- or year-long internships or practica that resemble part-time jobs. Here we focus primarily on applied service-oriented experiences that are frequently encountered by psychology majors. These may be characterized as professional education (internships, practica) and civic education (service learning) whose integration "into the curriculum is a dialectical process whereby material appropriate to the content of a specific course [or program] is, through structured reflection, put into dialogue with the experiential input from the [CBLE] setting, activities, and community partners" (Mooney & Edwards, 2001, p. 186).

The APA Guidelines for the Undergraduate Psychology Major (American Psychological Association [APA], 2007) include the application of psychology as one of the goals of undergraduate education in psychology in the 21st century. However, internships, practica, and other fieldwork experiences are not new to education; in fact, formal apprenticeships served as a form of training as early as the 12th century (Snell, 1996) and were brought into modern higher education as "experiential learning" (Dewey, 1938, cited in Johnson & Notah, 1999). Practica and other CBLEs have been offered in psychology departments at least since the 1960s, although they have not always been granted the integral role in the curriculum that they are often awarded in the present day (e.g., Cole & Van Krevelen, 1977; Lunneborg, 1970). The proportion of undergraduate psychology programs that offer CBLEs has increased substantially in the last decade. According to Stoloff et al. (2010), only 30% of programs included a practicum or field experience in 1996 (data from Perlman & McCann, 1999, cited in Stoloff et al., 2010). This percentage increased to 82% of programs in 2005 (Stoloff et al., 2010).

GOALS OF COMMUNITY-BASED LEARNING EXPERIENCES

Bringle and Hatcher (1996) identified the goals of service learning and related experiences as developing effective citizenship among students, addressing complex community needs through application of knowledge, and forming partnerships between the institution and surrounding community. Parilla and Hesser (1998) identified similar goals for related internships within sociology, focusing on the value to the student with regard to acquiring and applying new insights and knowledge in a real-world setting. Thus, the social sciences provide opportunities for students to apply theoretical knowledge in an applied setting.

CBLEs involve several different stakeholders, however, each of whom has a personal perspective and goals. Barton and Duerfelt (1980) described the disparate and sometimes competing goals of different stakeholders in the CBLE. Faculty supervisors aim to establish learning experiences that have well-defined (assessable) outcomes, whereas students are interested in gaining successful experience that can bolster resumes and help them make career decisions. Agencies, meanwhile, may be hoping to reduce employees' workloads while providing students with a rewarding potential career option. Even the clients with whom students interact have their own goals, namely, to have their problems resolved in a congenial manner (Barton & Duerfelt, 1980). Even with all of these disparate perspectives, however, some common goals usually guide successful collaborations.

EDUCATIONAL CHALLENGES ASSOCIATED WITH COMMUNITY-BASED LEARNING EXPERIENCES

As with any learning experience, CBLEs require attention to the educational needs of the student and the desired learning outcomes put forth by the faculty supervisor to support the goals of the program. Because these experiences are often presented as part of the academic curriculum, one challenge is determining what will be assessed and how grades and credit will be assigned (Stone & McLaren, 1999). The current educational climate places strong emphasis on defining and assessing measurable student learning outcomes. It is important, and ethically responsible, that the faculty member not abdicate responsibility for ensuring that learning outcomes are being met. On-site supervisors, however, may not understand the need for specifying such outcomes or may not put priority on following through with regular formative and summative evaluations. For these reasons, the faculty supervisor may need to evaluate documentation of the student's performance or reflection, or if the on-site supervisor is performing the evaluation, the faculty member can provide rubrics and other materials that clearly define what learning gains the student is expected to demonstrate.

A clear difference between CBLEs and more traditional learning contexts is that the setting is not one that is controlled by the supervising faculty member or even the educational institution. The student is, in effect, subjected to a dual chain of command, and the faculty supervisor must provide guidance about how the student can navigate the concerns of both the educational and agency supervisors (Hess et al., 1978). In addition, in many settings, there is also a responsibility to assist the client, who may also press the student to support his or her interests (Minnes, 1987).

In some settings, there is a risk of agency personnel taking advantage of the student's relative inexperience and assigning him or her inappropriate tasks, such as running personal errands or getting coffee. The student may not feel that he or she is in a position to refuse such requests, and thereby challenge the power structure of the agency, without consequence. Such interactions present ethical challenges in that they can distract from the student's learning while exploiting his or her presence as a novice. Students facing these situations may need assistance from the faculty supervisor in recognizing and addressing workplace abuses.

LEGAL AND ETHICAL ISSUES OF COMMUNITY-BASED LEARNING EXPERIENCES

This potential tension between the needs of the client, agency, and educational program can create a climate that interferes with the student's quality of experience and learning (Hess et al., 1978). With most of the student's participation occurring at a distance from campus, communication becomes an especially important consideration in supervising CBLEs. Establishing and monitoring CBLE relationships require time and attention from faculty supervisors (Heckert, 2010) who already devote extensive effort to teaching classes, conducting their own research, participating in institutional and disciplinary service, and perhaps even maintaining a personal life. Because there is often an on-site professional manager to monitor the student's activity, the faculty supervisor may be tempted—deliberately or through default—to rely on the manager's eyes and ears to evaluate student performance. However, this removes any independent oversight of the student–agency relationship and can allow negative situations to develop that in turn interfere with student learning. For example, tensions between student and agency may build gradually over time after minor disagreements, agencies may expect more from the student than he or she is qualified or capable of performing, or managers may not share the same concerns of the faculty supervisor when assigning or monitoring tasks (Fernald et al., 1982).

Given the discrepant goals of CBLE stakeholders as well as the potentially sensitive nature of interactions that accompany many psychology-oriented applied experiences, a number of potential ethical considerations arise in these contexts along with their ensuing legal implications. The most serious of these may occur when students have access to confidential information (Barton & Duerfelt, 1980; Fernald et al., 1982) or are asked to practice psychology beyond the level that their training and qualifications warrant (Fernald et al., 1982). The following two fictional cases, one based on situations related by personal communications from colleagues, illustrate some of the challenges that can arise with ethical implications.

> Ebony attends a regional university in a small town that serves as the county seat for the surrounding rural area. After graduation, she hopes to work to help children who have been emotionally abused by family members. She requests and is placed in a senior-year practicum with the county division of child and family services. This gives her the opportunity to work directly with children in the population that she hopes to serve, and she learns a great deal as she assists with background research and interviews. Ebony performs her duties so well during the first several weeks that the short-handed office gives her additional responsibilities, including occasionally serving as a child advocate in the courtroom.

This case illustrates perhaps one of the most common ethical breaches reported by faculty with supervisory experience (as conveyed in personal communications to the chapter authors). Practicing at psychology should not be confused with practicing psychology. Students, faculty, and agency supervisors must be aware and enforce appropriate limits on the student's duties. Although it may be tempting for agencies, especially in areas otherwise poorly served, to employ students in whatever capacity they can, failure to respect the student's boundaries of competence can result not only in harm to the client but also in legal issues for all involved.

> Sybil is completing her service-learning requirement at a local counseling center. Her primary activity is assisting with group counseling sessions for adult male batterers two evenings per week. Sybil enjoys these sessions and finds that she is very comfortable in this casual interactive setting; she finds that she can establish rapport with many of the group members by sharing some of her personal experiences. However, the group leader with whom she is working becomes increasingly concerned that Sybil does not appreciate the potential risks of her behavior and that her overdisclosure, naïve manner, and inappropriate dress may be sending questionable messages to the group participants.

As illustrated by Sybil's case, along with issues of competence, personal risks to students may also occur in some clinical or criminal justice settings (Hess et. al, 1978). Students may not have the experience or perspective to understand the importance of establishing personal boundaries when acting in a professional capacity, nor may they have the skills to avoid revealing personal information when engaged in conversational settings. Appropriate training and supervision may alleviate these risks; however, any situation that potentially places the student at personal risk should be avoided. In addition, the student's experience must not occur at the cost of the client, whose welfare is paramount (Barton & Duerfelt, 1980; Fernald et al., 1982; Minnes 1987). If students are involved in direct interaction with a client or patient, they must be given guidance on how to avoid overt or adverse reactions to the client's behavior and responses as well as on the importance of avoiding unwarranted judgments or stereotypes about the individuals they are seeing (Hess et al., 1978).

RECOMMENDED SUPERVISION PRACTICES FOR COMMUNITY-BASED LEARNING EXPERIENCES

The existence of ethical and legal considerations accompanying CBLEs need not deter institutions and faculty from pursuing otherwise effective learning experiences for their students (Barton & Duerfelt, 1980; Fernald et al., 1982; Hess et al., 1978). Many of the potential challenges accompanying CBLEs can be averted or mitigated with appropriate planning and communication among all constituents. Planning is especially important because of the many stakeholders and associated ethical issues that we have discussed. To make sure that all concerns are addressed, a checklist such as that provided by Grayson (2010) or a cost–benefit analysis as suggested by Barton and Duerfelt (1980) can be very helpful.

Communication, written and verbal, official and collegial, is key to ensuring a successful experience for all parties involved in a CBLE. As Barton and Duerfelt (1980) and others (Fernald et al. 1982; Grayson, 2010) have noted, it is important that communication between the faculty supervisor and community agency begin before the student steps in the door. Ideally, a long-term relationship will have been established so that each party trusts and knows what to expect from the other. However, new partnerships are critical to maintaining the vitality of the academic program's offerings over time and can readily be worked into a well-managed CBLE portfolio. Regardless of the length or extent of the relationship, a contract specifying the rights and responsibilities of all parties and the criteria on which the student will be evaluated is essential to avoid or address disputes that may arise during the course of the interaction.

To facilitate communication between all parties and ensure that the faculty supervisor stays in touch with the community agency and the student, the number of supervisees for each faculty member should remain small (Blanton, 2001). In addition, Blanton (2001) recommended holding group supervision sessions every 2 weeks to give students a chance to reflect on their experiences while still meeting often enough to monitor activity and head off problems. Asking students to periodically submit journals (either hardcopy or electronically) can assist this monitoring function as well.

Several resources are available to help guide and educate students and community partners who participate in CBLEs. The APA's *Ethical Principles of Psychologists and Code of Conduct* (hereinafter referred to as the Ethics Code; APA, 2010) can be applied to undergraduate experiences as well as professional practice. The Ethics Code charges psychologists with several ethical responsibilities that can be shared with students: Take reasonable steps to avoid harming the client; maintain responsibility to and trust of the client; cooperate with other professionals; respect the rights of clients and other professionals; practice accuracy and honesty in the science, teaching, and practice of psychology; report ethical violations; avoid any work-related duties when personal problems may hinder one from being competent; refrain from taking on a role when there is a conflict of interest; and avoid multiple relationships with the client.

In support of the Ethics Code (APA, 2010), the APA *Guidelines for the Undergraduate Psychology Major* (APA, 2007) suggest that students recognize the possibility of ethical challenges in psychology-relevant settings and behave ethically at all times. Before students are sent to community-based sites, the institution must provide enough training that such behavior can be identified and supported (Barton & Duerfelt, 1980). Part of this training should convey to students the reality that they are limited in their psychological knowledge and skills, so they should not attempt to practice beyond their qualifications. Students can, for example, be introduced to potential ethical scenarios and other issues through readings such as those provided by Bersoff (2003). In addition, interpersonal skills training for interaction with clients and supervisors can help students avoid problematic encounters (LoCicero & Hancock, 2000). If possible, the faculty supervisor in clinical contexts should be licensed so that he or she has the expertise to recognize what constitutes appropriate responsibilities and access for students placed in such settings.

Many community-based placements in psychology occur in clinical settings. The faculty supervisor for CBLE placements in these contexts should be a licensed psychologist. A licensed clinician is most likely to have the expertise to recognize what constitute appropriate responsibilities and access for students placed in such settings as well as the training to know how to address issues and conflicts that arise in such sensitive contexts. If a licensed clinician is not available to serve as faculty supervisor, then alternative placements or supervision guidelines should be considered.

THE FUTURE OF COMMUNITY-BASED LEARNING EXPERIENCES

In this era of reenvisioned education emphasizing authentic learning, CBLEs are likely to remain part of a strong undergraduate education in psychology despite some of the practical and ethical challenges that can accompany them. Currently, 82% of psychology programs offer such an experience, compared with 30% in 1995 (Stoloff et al., 2010). Although the number of students participating remains relatively small (11%; Stoloff et al., 2010), the growing emphasis in undergraduate education on connected and experiential learning (see, e.g., Bok, 2006) suggests that this number will increase in the coming years.

The potential benefits of CBLEs are manifold and distributed among all parties involved. The primary benefits accrue to the students. These experiences provide an opportunity for scholarship and practice to be blended (Dole, 1973), and students learn how theory can be applied in solving real-world problems in a way that would be difficult to achieve in a traditional classroom (Fernald et al., 1982). Through problem solving in these experiences, students can also develop their skills in several areas, including technical, interpersonal, analytic and synthesis, and independent learning (Wayment & Dickson, 2008), aiding in their transition from school to workplace or graduate school (Stone & McLaren, 1999). For these reasons, we anticipate that more students will take CBLE credits in the future.

SUMMARY

In this chapter, we have reviewed some of the potential ethical challenges and possible solutions that can arise when students engage in CBLEs within their undergraduate education in psychology. Faculty supervisors should be aware of the challenges that come along with managing CBLEs. However, with appropriate planning, communication, and follow-through, the experience can be positive for all involved. And, when they "work," CBLEs can ultimately benefit individuals and the community in tangible ways.

REFERENCES

American Psychological Association. (2007). *APA guidelines for the undergraduate psychology major*. Retrieved from http://www.apa.org/ed/precollege/about/psymajor-guidelines.pdf

American Psychological Association. (2010). *Ethical principles of psychologists and code of conduct (Amended June 1, 2010)*. Retrieved from http://www.apa.org/ethics/code/index.aspx

Barton, E. J., & Duerfelt, P. H. (1980). Undergraduate psychology practica pragmatism. *Teaching of Psychology, 7*, 146–149. doi:10.1207/s15328023top0703_4

Bersoff, D. N. (2003). *Ethical conflicts in psychology*. Washington, DC: American Psychological Association.

Blanton, P. G. (2001). A model for supervising undergraduate internships. *Teaching of Psychology, 28*, 217–219.

Bok, D. (2006). *Our underachieving colleges*. Princeton, NJ: Princeton University Press.

Bringle, R. G., & Duffy, D. K. (Eds.). (1998). *With service in mind: Concepts and models for service learning in psychology*. Washington, DC: American Association for Higher Education. doi:10.1037/10505-000

Bringle, R. G., & Hatcher, J. A. (1996). Implementing service learning in higher education. *The Journal of Higher Education, 67*, 221–239. doi:10.2307/2943981

Cole, D., & Van Krevelen, A. (1977). Psychology departments in small liberal arts colleges: Results of a survey. *Teaching of Psychology, 4*, 163–167. doi:10.1207/s15328023top0404_1

Connor-Greene, P. A. (2002). Problem-based service learning: The evolution of a team project. *Teaching of Psychology, 29*, 193–197. doi:10.1207/S15328023 TOP2903_02

Dewey, J. (1938). *Experience and education*. New York, NY: Collier.

Dole, A. A. (1973). A proposed multiple model for supervision. *Professional Psychology, 4*, 7–16. doi:10.1037/h0034684

Fernald, C. D., Tedeschi, R. G., Siegfried, W. D., Gilmore, D. C., Grimsley, D. L., & Chipley, B. (1982). Designing and managing an undergraduate practicum course in psychology. *Teaching of Psychology, 9*, 155–160. doi:10.1207/s15328023 top0903_6

Grayson, J. H. (2010). Capping the undergraduate experience: Making learning come alive through fieldwork. In D. S. Dunn, B. C. Beins, M. A. McCarthy, & G. W. Hill IV (Eds.), *Best practices for teaching beginnings and endings in the psychology major: Research, cases, and recommendations* (pp. 279–297). Oxford, England: Oxford University Press.

Hardy, M. S., & Shaen, E. B. (2000). Integrating the classroom and community service: Everyone benefits. *Teaching of Psychology, 27*, 47–49. doi:10.1207/S15328023 TOP2701_11

Heckert, T. M. (2010). Alternative service learning approaches: Two techniques that accommodate faculty schedules. *Teaching of Psychology, 37*, 32–35. doi:10.1080/00986280903175681

Hess, A. K., Harrison, A. O., Shantz, D. W., Fink, R. S., Zepelin, H., Lilliston, L., . . . Korn, A. H. (1978). Critical issues in undergraduate training in various community settings. *Teaching of Psychology, 5*, 81–86. doi:10.1207/s15328023 top0502_6

Johnson, A. M., & Notah, D. J. (1999). Service learning: History, literature, review, and a pilot study of eighth graders. *The Elementary School Journal, 99*, 453–467. doi:10.1086/461935

Kretchmar, M. D. (2001). Service learning in a general psychology class: Description, preliminary evaluation, and recommendations. *Teaching of Psychology, 28*, 5–10. doi:10.1207/S15328023TOP2801_02

LoCicero, A., & Hancock, J. (2000). Preparing students for success in fieldwork. *Teaching of Psychology, 27*, 117–120. doi:10.1207/S15328023TOP2702_09

Lundy, B. L. (2007). Service learning in life-span developmental psychology: Higher exam scores and increased empathy. *Teaching of Psychology, 34*, 23–27. doi:10.1207/s15328023top3401_5

Lunneborg, P. W. (1970). Undergraduate psychology fieldwork: The unwashed take over. *American Psychologist, 25*, 1062–1064. doi:10.1037/h0030146

Minnes, P. M. (1987). Ethical issues in supervision. *Canadian Psychology/Psychologie Canadienne, 28*, 285–290. doi:10.1037/h0079910

Mooney, L. A., & Edwards, B. (2001). Experiential learning in sociology: Service learning and other community-based learning initiatives. *Teaching Sociology, 29*, 181–194. doi:10.2307/1318716

Parilla, P. F., & Hesser, G. W. (1998). Internships and the sociological perspective: Applying principles of experiential learning. *Teaching Sociology, 26*, 310–329. doi:10.2307/1318771

Perlman, B., & McCann, L. I. (1999). The most frequently listed courses in the undergraduate psychology curriculum. *Teaching of Psychology, 26*, 171–176. doi:10.1207/S15328023TOP260302

Snell, K. D. M. (1996). The apprenticeship system in British history: The fragmentation of a cultural institution. *History of Education, 25*, 303–321. doi:10.1080/0046760960250401

Stoloff, M., McCarthy, M., Keller, L., Varfolomeeva, V., Lynch, J., Makara, K., . . . Smiley, W. (2010). The undergraduate psychology major: An examination of structure and sequence. *Teaching of Psychology, 37*, 4–15. doi:10.1080/00986280903426274

Stone, W. E., & McLaren, J. (1999). Assessing the undergraduate intern experience. *Journal of Criminal Justice Education, 10*, 171–183. doi:10.1080/10511259900084521

Wayment, H. A., & Dickson, K. L. (2008). Increasing student participation in undergraduate research benefits students, faculty, and department. *Teaching of Psychology, 35*, 194–197. doi:10.1080/00986280802189213

15

CULTIVATING A POSITIVE COLLABORATIVE EXPERIENCE WITH UNDERGRADUATES

SCOTT VANDERSTOEP AND SONJA TRENT-BROWN

A generation ago an undergraduate student with significant research experience might have been considered rare; in other words, the research experience might have distinguished him or her from the multitude of graduate school applicants. Recently, however, it has been found that all students generally benefit from the research experience (Nagda, Gregerman, Jonides, von Hippel, & Lerner, 1998). Students are more likely to graduate, and they report greater confidence in their abilities and skills, advances in both written and oral communication skills, improved interpersonal interaction capacities, and greater fortification for their future academic and professional plans (Nagda et al., 1998; Russell, Hancock, & McCullough, 2007; Seymour, Hunter, Laursen, & DeAntoni, 2004). Today faculty more commonly maintain active research programs, seek external funding, and engage undergraduate researchers. Together, faculty and undergraduate students are increasingly presenting their work at regional psychology conferences across the nation. With this increase in research, challenging ethical questions emerge. In this chapter, we describe the process for involving undergraduate students in research, and we explore some of the ethical dilemmas that may arise in faculty–student collaborations.

SELECTING SUITABLE RESEARCH ASSISTANTS: MATCHING STUDENT EXPERIENCE TO TASK COMPLEXITY

The first phase in building successful faculty–student collaborations is to identify students who will both benefit from the experience and assist the faculty member in their work. Although this first step seems ethically innocuous, several ethical issues are present. For example, at most institutions only a limited number of opportunities are available. How should faculty select students for the limited available opportunities? Is it acceptable to select a student because a faculty member had the student in a class? Or should all students be made aware of research opportunities?

A second, related dilemma is deciding how much faculty should weigh the differential value that each student might gain from a research experience. In other words, should faculty privilege students who would be most helped by the research experience? As a concrete example, consider the following scenario:

> A faculty member recruited a highly talented student to assist with a research project. The student had plans to apply to a moderately competitive master's degree program in industrial psychology. The student did great work and later that year secured a spot in his desired program. When recruiting, the faculty member had also considered a second student's request for an opportunity to engage in research. This student was also a senior, but in contrast to the first, she was interested in applying to doctoral programs in social psychology. She was not chosen because, with limited resources, the faculty member worked with the student that he believed would benefit most from access to a research experience.

The dilemma is really whether the student applying to a doctoral program should be provided with more access to research than the student applying to a master's program. It seems plausible that undergraduate research experience would aid the doctoral applicant more than the master's program. Should we weigh the relative benefits for students?

Regardless of whether students are assigned to the faculty member or are individually selected, a consistent selection approach is advisable. A consistent selection process includes an application process requiring documentation and an interview (DeCosmo & Harris, 2008). The application typically includes questions regarding the student's previous course work, including material pertinent to the research topic or methodology, prior research experiences, statistical background, technical skills, computer and technology experience, plans following graduation, and long-term career goals. It may also be beneficial to require a narrative statement as part of the written submission. Essential elements of the written statement include the student's reasons for seeking collaborative research experiences, the student's prior understanding of the research process, what the student hopes to gain from participating in research, and research skills that might be useful in a research collaboration. In programs that do not require students to engage in a collaborative research experience, students who are typically selected demonstrate good grades. Academic success demonstrates potential for future professional and scholarship development.

We see two possible ethical implications in developing a selection process. First, is a screening policy simply a mechanism for the rich to get richer? Students come to us with varying qualifications, motivation, and achievement. Selecting only the best students may not advance the departmental and institutional missions. A second related ethical question is, Are faculty ethically obligated to involve every student who wants a research experience? One could argue that a screening process implies that faculty do not feel ethically obligated to serve all students. Even with this lower number of interested students, it still seems likely that some interested students will not benefit from an individualized research experience. The dilemma in using a selection process is resolving three potentially conflicting goals: providing a meaningful educational experience for students, enhancing the research program of the sponsoring faculty member, and meeting the needs of students in a fashion that meets the institution's mission and culture.

BUILDING A SUCCESSFUL UNDERGRADUATE RESEARCH PROGRAM

In this section, we identify three strategies for building a successful research program. We identify at least one ethical implication that faculty members might encounter when using each strategy.

Strategy 1: Advanced Research Course

A course specifically designed to promote faculty–student research offers an excellent opportunity to engage students in specific research projects. However, these courses tend to have small enrollments. Nevertheless, small enrollments offer several advantages, including ensuring sufficient activity for each student, creating a climate that is intimate enough to foster the building of research community in the group, creating a mechanism for crediting faculty for their research work with students, and allowing for successful management of the team.

The primary ethical dilemma centers on balancing research productivity and quality instruction. An advanced research course provides a clear research framework for both students and faculty. By virtue of providing students with research opportunities in a course format, the requirements are explicitly stated in the syllabus and understood by both parties. If the course is designed well, assignments are clear and ambiguity is low. Faculty can expect students to meet the requirements of the course, and students have the assurance that faculty will be available. However, with this course-based research model, instruction is the priority, with research productivity as a secondary emphasis.

A second ethical issue is determining an appropriate student workload. In a traditional lecture course, expectations are generally well defined. However, in a research practicum course, workload may vary according to the topic of research and unanticipated challenges (e.g., limited subject pool). Balancing the experience with equitable workload is the responsibility of the professor. Faculty should attend to potential conflicts of interest to ensure that the instructor's research agenda does not overshadow student learning.

Strategy 2: Apprenticeship

A second strategy for engaging students in research is through an apprenticeship. This approach can also serve to provide a training mechanism for developing student research skills. In the apprenticeship model, the student works with and learns about research from the faculty member. This approach allows students to develop a one-on-one relationship with the faculty member and a more tailored approach to research. The student is also able to participate in a mentoring relationship with the faculty member. Admittedly, not every collaborative experience will be positive for the student and faculty member, but both will carry forward important lessons learned as they advance to their next collaboration.

The primary ethical issue associated with this approach is the ambiguity of the relationship. Unlike the advanced research course, in which guidelines and expectations are clear, the apprenticeship model can lack clarity and result in an unhealthy power differential. Faculty members must remember that undergraduate apprentices may not have acquired the level of professionalism typically associated with graduate students. Undergraduate students may not have the experience that allows them to negotiate the complexities associated with research collaborations (e.g., authorship). The responsibility for facilitating these skills and ensuring equitable research expectations lies with the faculty member.

Strategy 3: Creating Student Leaders

A third strategy for building a successful undergraduate research program is to promote a student leadership model. Advanced students often have sufficient experience so that they can effectively train novice students. An advanced student may serve as a leader of the group and provide newer students a more familiar point of contact. In other words, a fellow student may be able to provide a student perspective on the research project. For the advanced students, mentoring a novice researcher provides an opportunity to strengthen their own skills, to enhance their comprehension of the research project and protocols, and to develop leadership skills. This approach has the added benefit of showing newer students a potential trajectory of development to which they might aspire. Leadership may be a particularly attractive incentive for students who are seriously considering a career in research.

The primary ethical implication of using this approach is one of pedagogy. With this approach, advanced undergraduate assistants may have more time with other undergraduates. Because faculty may spend less time with junior members of a research team, it is possible that instruction will suffer. A second related concern may be that using student assistants might undermine a teaching-oriented department.

IDENTIFYING APPROPRIATE RESEARCH TASKS FOR UNDERGRADUATES

In this section we identify four different tasks that are appropriate and necessary for the undergraduate research experience. All students should receive ethics training prior to engaging in any form of research. Students should also acquire research skills through structured experiences.

Learning Research Ethics

An essential component of any undergraduate research program is training in research ethics. Although we believe all undergraduate research assistants should receive adequate instruction in ethics, we know that time pressures and other constraints might prompt faculty to place less emphasis on this training. Nevertheless, research training is required of all personnel involved in the research project. Two opportunities for ethics training, in particular, are widely used. Perhaps the most comprehensive is the Collaborative Institutional Training Initiative (http://www.citiprogram.org). The Collaborative Institutional Training Initiative offers online courses for certification in core aspects of ethical treatment of human participants in research, with specific modules for conducting biomedical research, social and behavioral research, and international research (Braunschweiger, 2007). A student researcher module is available for students who may be assisting in a research project.

A second web-based training course is the National Institutes of Health Office of Extramural Research course, Protecting Human Research

Participants (U.S. Department of Health and Human Services, National Institutes of Health, 2008; http://phrp.nihtraining.com/users/login.php). This course replaces a previous National Institutes of Health and National Cancer Institute online training course and offers new content. The course incorporates modules including background and historical coverage, federal codes and regulations, and the basic ethical principles outlined in the Belmont Report (U.S. Department of Health, Education, and Welfare, National Commission for the Protection of Human Subjects of Biomedical and Behavioral Research, 1979)—respect for persons, beneficence, and justice.

Ethical training of student researchers satisfies a general and a specific ethical concern. The general concern is that such training provides broad-based instruction on the relationship between researchers and participants—respect for persons. A more specific ethical implication is that without this training the risk for abuse may be higher. Direct instruction about appropriate conduct is important so that students are well informed about the importance of adhering to ethical guidelines.

Entry-Level Skills

Entry-level skills include recruitment and scheduling of participants for data collection, visiting classrooms to announce studies, managing research appointment websites, posting new appointments, keeping records of participants who have completed the study, and producing participation reports and are appropriate for beginning-level student researchers. One strategy for training students involves asking them to attend research team meetings so that information can be disseminated, progress reports can be reviewed, and elements of the research process (e.g., statistical analysis) can be discussed.

The primary ethical issue for assigning entry-level tasks to new students is the responsibility that the faculty member holds to provide an important educational experience or, at the very least, be clear about what is expected of a student doing entry-level work. Even faculty members in very small departments find themselves doing entry-level tasks themselves because there is no administrative or graduate student support. Thus, asking students to perform these tasks is part of the socialization and practical training that research assistants receive. However, one could say that such tasks, although standard work, do not constitute meaningful educational experiences. Indeed, these tasks further the agenda of the faculty member, so care should be taken to ensure that these experiences add to the student's development.

Intermediate Skills

Intermediate skills include literature review, stimulus generation, and preliminary data analysis. At this level students should have a working knowledge of the ethical considerations of conducting research. Perhaps one of the most exciting aspects for intermediate-level students is the opportunity to work with "real" data. Data analysis and reduction require a mature comprehension of the data entry aspects so that students are capable of discerning errors. Students can then assemble data into a systematic summary format to be submitted for further analysis. Data analysis could include conducting descriptive and inferential statistical analyses, preparing figures and tables, and preparing additional customized analyses.

Providing a healthy faculty–student relationship and affording the students a meaningful educational experience are critical. At this stage of the research process, students are doing more advanced work that better approximates the intellectual challenge of research. So in this regard, educational value becomes less of a concern. Faculty and students at this level may begin to engage more as collaborators than as teacher and student. In either case, the responsibility rests predominately with the faculty member to ensure that the relationship maximizes the educational experience for the student.

High-Level Skills

Students who have advanced to higher levels of research experiences are capable of contributing to the preparation of the research outcomes for dissemination. They have an in-depth comprehension of the project and some exposure to all aspects of the research process. Although some of the subtle nuances and intricacies of the research enterprise will require further academic training, these students are fully capable of preparing poster presentations, oral presentations for conference talks, and written accounts of the research. Advanced students are not only capable of preparing materials for presentation but also of delivering a presentation at a conference or research symposium.

IDENTIFYING APPROPRIATE OUTCOME MEASURES

There is a small but growing literature on assessing research outcomes in psychology education (e.g., Landrum, 2010). Undergraduate research experiences allow students to meet several of the goals initially proposed by McGovern, Furumoto, Halpern, Kimble, and McKeachie (1991). In fact, research has the potential to help students to acquire skills that might otherwise not be possible.

High-level skills are appropriate outcomes for advanced students and include creating a poster for presentation at a research symposium, submitting a conference abstract, or drafting a manuscript for publication. Although these outcomes may not be appropriate for all students, variations of these outcomes may provide viable alternatives. Intermediate students may not be ready for an off-campus conference presentation but would likely benefit from the experience of producing and presenting a poster for a departmental, divisional, or campuswide research event. Intermediate students would also be capable of producing and delivering a research colloquium on campus.

CONCLUSION

Cultivating a positive collaborative research experience with undergraduates is valuable. We have outlined possible components that we believe are involved in cultivating a positive research experience. However, our suggestions are not without ethical cautions. Sometimes the motives of students and faculty diverge. Research productivity may be a priority for faculty, but research experience and skill development may be the priority for a student. Often these two goals are complementary, in which case ethical considerations are minimal. Occasionally, however, competing goals result in ethical dilemmas. Prevention and clarity will be the most helpful in resolving any ethical issues. Professors should be clear about expectations, the role of the student, and the learning outcomes. Students need to articulate their goals for the research experience, assess their role in the research program, and feel empowered to engage in dialogue when ambiguity arises. Such transparency will increase the likelihood that both parties will be satisfied with both the research processes and the outcomes.

REFERENCES

Braunschweiger, P. (2007). The CITI Program: An international online resource for education in human subjects protection and the responsible conduct of research. *Academic Medicine, 82*, 861–864. doi:10.1097/ACM.0b013e31812f7770

DeCosmo, J., & Harris, J. (2008). *Mentoring the undergraduate research experience.* Retrieved from https://catalyst.uw.edu/workspace/file/download/7f7d1f9cac1a41 c8833db1320afc634b2aba12cc385f022ffe4a0ef5439c8052?inline=1

Landrum, R. E. (2010). Skills for undergraduate majors: Because you need it, do we measure it? *Eye on Psi Chi, 14*, 23–25.

McGovern, T. V., Furumoto, L., Halpern, D. F., Kimble, G. A., & McKeachie, W. J. (1991). Liberal education, study in depth, and the arts and science major—psychology. *American Psychologist, 46,* 598–605. doi:10.1037/0003-066X.46.6.598

Nagda, B. A., Gregerman, S. R., Jonides, J., von Hippel, W., & Lerner, J. S. (1998). Undergraduate student–faculty research partnerships affect student retention. *The Review of Higher Education, 22,* 55–72.

Russell, S. H., Hancock, M. P., & McCullough, J. (2007, April 27). Benefits of undergraduate research experiences. *Science, 316,* 548–549. doi:10.1126/science.1140384

Seymour, E., Hunter, A.-B., Laursen, S. L., & DeAntoni, T. (2004). Establishing the benefits of research experiences for undergraduates in the sciences: First findings from a three-year study. *Science Education, 88,* 493–534. doi:10.1002/sce.10131

U.S. Department of Health and Human Services, National Institutes of Health. (2008). *Protecting human research participants.* Retrieved from http://phrp.nihtraining.com/users/login.php

U.S. Department of Health, Education, and Welfare, National Commission for the Protection of Human Subjects of Biomedical and Behavioral Research. (1979). *The Belmont report: Ethical principles and guidelines for the protection of human subjects of research.* Retrieved from http://ohsr.od.nih.gov/guidelines/belmont.html

16

TOWARD A MORE EQUITABLE MODEL OF AUTHORSHIP

MAUREEN A. McCARTHY

The renewed emphasis on advancing science as part of the American Recovery and Reinvestment Act of 2009 (see also National Science Foundation, 2010) only serves to increase the pressure on faculty to mentor undergraduate students conducting research in psychology. There is also an increased expectation that results of scientific investigations with undergraduates will be disseminated through traditional peer-reviewed outlets. Publication of research necessarily requires attention to a multitude of ethical issues. Ethical practices, as they relate to authorship in an undergraduate context, are the central focus of this chapter.

Authorship and order of authorship are important and sometimes contentious issues for researchers. Although authorship is already high stakes in a professional context (Bartle, Fink, & Hayes, 2000; Fine & Kurdek, 1993; Geelhoed, Phillips, Fischer, Shpungin, & Gong, 2007; Oberlander & Spencer, 2006; Sandler & Russell, 2005), authorship at the undergraduate level is becoming increasingly important. In this chapter, I begin with a review of those elements of the *Ethical Principles of Psychologists and Code of Conduct* (American Psychological Association [APA], 2010a; hereinafter referred to as the Ethics Code) that are relevant to evaluating publication credit. I then provide suggestions for a process of ethically determining authorship credit with undergraduate student collaborators.

ETHICS CODE AND AUTHORSHIP CONCERNS

The literature addressing ethical considerations in assessing publication credit focuses primarily on conflicts related to professional colleagues or doctoral students, and few scholars have addressed authorship as it pertains to undergraduate students (Anderson & Shore, 2008). Yet, mentoring undergraduate students in research has become a more frequent practice in most disciplines (Boyd & Wesemann, 2009). With the report of the Boyer Commission on Educating Undergraduates in the Research University (1998), which stated that research-based education should be expanded, and the more recent efforts to increase undergraduate involvement in scientific research (Building Engineering and Science Talent, 2004), efforts to increase undergraduate research opportunities have continued to grow. Not only has undergraduate research become more prevalent but the Association of American Colleges and Universities (2007) has recommended undergraduate research as an effective practice for educating the next generation of students. With the increased growth in undergraduate research across disciplines, and more specifically in psychology, it is important to consider how respective ethics codes address authorship in instances of differential power.

General Principles

The overarching principles of the Ethics Code—Principle A: Beneficence and Nonmaleficence, Principle B: Fidelity and Responsibility, Principle C: Integrity, Principle D: Justice, and Principle E: Respect for People's Rights and Dignity—offer general guidance for determining authorship credit. Psychologists are obligated not to abuse their power (in the case of supervising undergraduate researchers) and to ensure that authorship is awarded when students make a meaningful contribution. Similarly, faculty members are obligated to be responsible when evaluating the relative contributions of all members of the research team. Throughout the research process, faculty have an obligation to be honest, establish a fair process for determining authorship, and follow through with their obligation to award authorship when sufficient contributions are made.

Determining authorship is sometimes a complicated process. Some (Fine & Kurdek, 1993; Winston, 1985) have argued that authorship is determined, in part, by level of professional competence. Following this logic, one might assume that undergraduate students are always less competent than a faculty advisor because they are typically mentored in the research process. Although Fine and Kurdek (1993) acknowledged the possibility that an undergraduate student might perform at a level that warrants authorship, they did not address the possibility that a student might deserve primary authorship. For example, an honors student may independently develop a research project and subsequently ask a faculty member to serve as the supervisor for the project. Much like a master's thesis or a doctoral dissertation, the project is primarily the work of the student, thus warranting first authorship.

Moreover, undergraduate students who write senior theses may meet the criteria for original scholarship (Anderson & Shore, 2008), and undergraduate students may in fact warrant primary authorship when they initiate a project, as illustrated in the following scenario:

> An undergraduate student developed an interest in factors affecting socially acceptable behaviors. She elected to focus her research energies on performing a comprehensive review of the literature in preparation for her senior thesis. On enrolling in the independent study course that would eventually lead to her completed thesis, she conducted an original research study investigating her hypotheses. After completing the study, she received credit for the senior thesis project. The faculty advisor considered the project worthy of publication, so she encouraged the student to submit a manuscript to an undergraduate research journal. The faculty member assisted in writing the manuscript and elected to accept secondary authorship.

Bridgwater, Bornstein, and Walkenbach (1981) found that determining the level of contribution is particularly complicated. They also found that faculty considered design of a study to be the most critical contribution in assigning authorship but believed that other aspects of manuscript preparation should still be considered in the overall assessment of authorship. In this scenario, it seems appropriate for the student to secure primary authorship of the manuscript and for the supervising faculty member to receive credit as well. Because the work was primarily that of the student, the faculty member encouraged the student to submit the manuscript to an appropriate outlet. The order of authorship, student first and faculty second, seems to honor the relative contributions to the manuscript. In this instance, the faculty member attended to the broader ethical principles of beneficence and integrity, thus relying on the general principles to provide general direction for ethical decision making. More specific criteria for determining authorship are also provided in Section 8, Research and Publication, of the Ethics Code.

Standard 8.12, Publication Credit

Although mentoring undergraduate researchers might be considered one aspect of teaching, quite often undergraduate research occurs through individual mentorship. The APA Ethics Code does not specifically address undergraduate research in the context of teaching (Section 7, Education and Training). However, Standard 8.12, Publication Credit, addresses most aspects of the ethical practice of research, with specific attention to making appropriate attributions for publication credit. Standard 8.12 provides general guidance for determining publication credit. In essence, publication credit should be awarded only when an author makes a substantial contribution, and authorship in multiauthor articles should reflect the relative contributions of each author. For decades, interpretations of these guidelines have been a matter of concern, and interpreting the guidelines remains complicated (Bridgwater et al., 1981; Fine & Kurdek, 1993; Spiegel & Keith-Spiegel, 1970; Tryon, Bishop, & Hatfield, 2007). Although the Ethics Code specifies authorship in the case of a dissertation (Standard 8.12c), Fine and Kurdek (1993) suggested that the stipulation of primary authorship for a dissertation is almost redundant because a dissertation is by definition the work of a doctoral student. The most recent edition of the *Publication Manual of the American Psychological Association* (APA, 2010b) goes further and emphasizes the need to carefully assess authorship order whenever a student (master's level or other predoctoral-level student) is involved. This leaves psychologists with the more complicated predicament of assigning authorship when undergraduate students participate in a research experience. Consider the following scenario:

> An undergraduate student developed an interest in factors affecting socially acceptable behaviors. Instead of undertaking an independent project, the student joined a group of undergraduate researchers with similar interests. Under the direction of faculty member, a project evolved, and each of the students assisted in various aspects of the research. On completion of the study, the lead student developed a poster and listed all members of the group as authors. Later, the group explored the possibility of writing a manuscript and submitting the project for publication. The faculty member responsible for the group assumed first authorship and made authorship determinations regarding contributions of the remaining student researchers.

Standard 8.12, Publication Credit, does not specifically address publication credit when undergraduate students are potential authors. It is important to consider the increased power differential that exists between faculty and undergraduate students. When the power differential is great, as is the case when undergraduate students collaborate with a faculty member, determining publication credit may be even more difficult. Although the power differential is inherently larger, the general guidelines do stipulate authorship credit should be determined on the basis of relative contributions. So, if a student provides meaningful contributions during the conceptualization of the study, design of instruments, or writing of the manuscript, it is quite likely that he or she should be awarded authorship credit.

It is often helpful to provide students with an example of a contribution that warrants authorship credit. For example, a student must actually author (i.e., write) part of the manuscript if he or she is to receive credit as an author. If, however, the student's contribution is minimal (e.g., conducting a literature search or running subjects), it is not necessary to award authorship credit. Providing the student with guidance early in the process can help to alleviate future misunderstandings. Exhibit 16.1 lists possible activities associated with producing a manuscript, and only the activities in boldface type are considered in the determination of authorship. It is important to note that even if individual tasks may not warrant authorship, the combination of contributions may warrant authorship. Equitable evaluation of authorship credit is the onus of the faculty member.

When a significant power differential exists, the equitable determination of authorship is even more important (Campbell, Vasquez, Behnke, & Kinscherff, 2009). So, in the second scenario, it is clear that the faculty member invited students to be involved in an existing program of research. If a student merely designs and assembles the poster, a significant intellectual

---

EXHIBIT 16.1
Tasks Associated With Writing a Manuscript

Introduction
- **Developing the research idea or research question***
- Conducting the literature review
- Summarizing articles
- **Writing portions of the introduction for the manuscript (e.g., rationale for the study)**

Method and Analysis
- Selecting surveys
- Creating surveys
- Developing apparatus
- Recruiting participants
- Running participants
- Entering data
- Conducting statistical analyses
- **Writing results of the analysis**

Completing the Manuscript
- **Writing the discussion section of the manuscript**
- Constructing the reference page
- Providing feedback on an initial draft of a manuscript

---

*Items in boldface are intellectual contributions warranting authorship.

contribution is not made and therefore does not necessarily warrant authorship. However, if the student writes a portion of the content for the poster or manuscript, then some level of authorship is warranted.

PROCESS FOR DETERMINING AUTHORSHIP

Because scholarship is a high-stakes endeavor (Geelhoed et al., 2007) and students are potentially vulnerable, the act of supervising student research presents an inherent conflict of interest. Sandler and Russell (2005) surveyed APA members and found that a relatively large percentage (27%) of coauthors perceived some level of impropriety in determining authorship. In fact, in contrast with the number of formally filed ethics complaints, more than one quarter of their respondents reported that they had been involved in some form of unfair authorship assignment. It is important to note that these results reflect cases of perceived unfair authorship of professional colleagues. Fewer than 1% of the respondents were students, thus limiting the generalizations that can be made from the study.

Geelhoed et al. (2007) reported that graduate students perceived less power when discussing order of authorship. Thus, undergraduate students are particularly vulnerable, and therefore the suggestion that students be provided with informed consent (Fine & Kurdek, 1993) is particularly useful. A statement describing authorship criteria and the process for determining authorship might be developed by a department (for an example, see Exhibit 16.2), and the statement can be made widely available to all students. Additionally, the statement may be provided to students enrolling in an independent study course, a capstone experience, or any similar research-based coursework. Providing students with clear authorship criteria is a first step in reducing the imbalance of power that may make undergraduate students particularly vulnerable.

A proactive approach to determining authorship credit will aid in reducing appeals for review of authorship credit. Faculty should engage in the conversation about authorship early in the process (Fine & Kurdek, 1993; Oberlander & Spencer, 2006; Tryon et al., 2007). Regardless of whether the collaborators are faculty colleagues or students, authorship should be discussed early and often. Research tasks should be identified and relative merits of participation established. Fine and Kurdek (1993) also suggested that whenever a student makes a professional contribution, he or she should be included in the discussion of how authorship is determined; they further noted that the process should allow for renegotiation if circumstances change. They also recommended that faculty involve other colleagues in the discussion whenever possible.

EXHIBIT 16.2
Writing Agreement

When is authorship warranted?

Authorship is warranted if a researcher (student or faculty) contributes significantly to the conceptualization, design, or writing of the research study.

How is order determined?

Authorship is based on type and amount of contribution. Each of the contributions is relative in nature. So, if a researcher contributes significantly to writing, the researcher will be given more credit. If a project is primarily that of the student (i.e., an honors thesis or independent study initiated by the student), then the student should be provided with primary authorship.

When should authorship be discussed?

A discussion between the faculty member and all of the members of the research team should occur early in the research process. Ideally, discussion about authorship will occur within the first three meetings.

Whom can I contact if I believe that the authorship process is unfair?

Sometimes misunderstandings or disagreements occur when determining authorship. If a question about authorship emerges before, during, or on completion of a research project, an inquiry can be registered with the chair of the Department of Psychology. To help minimize misunderstandings, it is important that you document each of the contributions that you make to the project. One helpful way to document contributions is to retain not only your written work but also a record of research team meetings, which can help to clarify intellectual contributions that occur during the conceptualization process.

Memorandum of Understanding

I have read the information explaining how authorship credit is awarded, and I understand that I may ask to have the relative merits of my contributions reviewed by the department faculty committee. If I have further questions I will contact the department chair.

Date: _____

Student name:_____

Faculty name:_____

To protect the rights of both the faculty member and the student researcher, both should maintain a written agreement (Fine & Kurdek, 1993; Tryon et al., 2007) clarifying the types of contributions that warrant authorship and how order of authorship is determined. Because the details of an agreement can sometimes fade with time, a written document serves as a record of the original agreement. If all parties are clear on the original apportionment of work, the document can aid in any renegotiation of authorship in the future.

Which factors should be considered when drafting an authorship agreement? Bartle et al. (2000) asked faculty and graduate students to rate the tasks associated with developing a manuscript. They found that writing of the manuscript constituted the most important factor in determining authorship. Similarly, Bridgwater et al. (1981), in a survey of academicians, found that research design and manuscript preparation were rated as highly important when determining authorship. However, merely developing the research idea clearly was the second most important criterion, followed by data analysis, status, and data collection. Although data collection as a single activity typically does not warrant authorship, when collecting data is coupled with other activities, authorship should be considered for all collaborators involved in the project.

Winston (1985) articulated a detailed approach for determining authorship. He suggested that tasks be identified and a weighted system of relative contributions be used. Identifying all of the tasks involved in the project allows the researchers to collectively prioritize each of the activities associated with authorship (i.e., generation of idea, literature search, design, instrument selection or development, selection of data analysis, data collection, data analysis, drafting of manuscripts, editing the manuscript). In other words, the relative importance or difficulty of the task is distinguished from the percentage of time that may be necessary to complete the task. After the tasks are prioritized on the basis of relative importance, each collaborator can evaluate his or her relative contribution to each task. Again, a clear statement of contributions coupled with a record of contributions will facilitate any future discussion of authorship.

Students should be informed about the process for establishing authorship, and they should participate in determining order of authorship. However, using these two processes will not ensure equitable treatment of undergraduate students. The literature clearly indicates (Geelhoed et al., 2007) that when there are differences in power, students are reluctant to register complaints. The inherent power differential can result in direct or subtle repercussions. Therefore, it is incumbent on the department to establish ongoing procedures for monitoring the ethical practices of faculty when determining authorship (Dunn, McCarthy, Baker, Halonen, & Hill, 2007). A committee may be charged with reviewing all research flowing from a department, with particular attention to authorship when undergraduate students are involved in any aspect of a project.

CONCLUSION

As is the case with most ethical dilemmas, authorship decisions are complex. Working with undergraduate students involves an even greater power differential, so determining authorship credit is even more difficult.

In the absence of specific criteria (see Standard 8.12, Publication Credit) for undergraduate research, the general ethical principles provide important overarching guidance for determining authorship. Using clear, documented policies; engaging students in an ongoing dialogue about authorship; and providing students with a nonthreatening process for resolving disagreements are important for ensuring that students are treated with integrity.

REFERENCES

American Association of Colleges and Universities. (2007). *College learning for the new global century*. Washington, DC: Author. Retrieved from http://www.aacu.org/leap/documents/globalcentury_final.pdf

American Psychological Association. (2010a). *Ethical principles of psychologists and code of conduct (Amended June 1, 2010)*. Retrieved from http://www.apa.org/ethics/code/index/.aspx

American Psychological Association. (2010b). *Publication manual of the American Psychological Association* (6th ed.). Washington, DC: Author.

American Recovery and Reinvestment Act of 2009, Pub. L. No. 111-5 (2009).

Anderson, D. D., & Shore, W. J. (2008). Ethical issues and concerns associated with mentoring undergraduate students. *Ethics & Behavior, 18*, 1–25. doi:10.1080/10508420701519577

Bartle, S. A., Fink, A. A., & Hayes, B. (2000). Psychology of the scientist: LXXX. Attitudes regarding authorship issues in psychological publications. *Psychological Reports, 86*, 771–788. doi:10.2466/PR0.86.3.771-788

Boyd, M. K., & Wesemann, J. L. (Eds.). (2009). *Broadening participation in undergraduate research: Fostering excellence and enhancing the impact*. Washington, DC: Council on Undergraduate Research.

Boyer Commission on Educating Undergraduates in the Research University. (1998). *Reinventing undergraduate education: A blueprint for America's research universities*. Retrieved from http://naples.cc.sunysb.edu/Pres/boyer.nsf/

Bridgwater, C. A., Bornstein, P. H., & Walkenbach, J. (1981). Ethical issues and the assignment of publication credit. *American Psychologist, 36*, 524–525. doi:10.1037/0003-066X.36.5.524

Building Engineering and Science Talent. (2004). *A bridge for all: Higher education design principles to broaden participation in science, technology, engineering and mathematics*. Retrieved from http://www.bestworkforce.org/PDFdocs/BEST_BridgeforAll_HighEdDesignPrincipals.pdf

Campbell, L., Vasquez, M., Behnke, S., & Kinscherff, R. (2009). *APA ethics code commentary and case illustrations*. Washington, DC: American Psychological Association.

Dunn, D. S., McCarthy, M. A., Baker, S., Halonen, J. S., & Hill IV, G. W. (2007). Quality benchmarks in undergraduate programs. *American Psychologist, 62,* 650–670. doi:10.1037/0003-066X.62.7.650

Fine, M. A., & Kurdek, L. A. (1993). Reflections on determining authorship credit and authorship order on faculty–student collaborations. *American Psychologist, 48,* 1141–1147. doi:10.1037/0003-066X.48.11.1141

Geelhoed, R. J., Phillips, J. C., Fischer, A. R., Shpungin, E., & Gong, Y. (2007). Authorship decision making: An empirical investigation. *Ethics & Behavior, 17,* 95–115.

National Science Foundation. (2010). *NSF information related to the American Recovery and Reinvestment Act of 2009.* Retrieved from http://www.nsf.gov/recovery

Oberlander, S. E., & Spencer, R. J. (2006). Graduate students and the culture of authorship. *Ethics & Behavior, 16,* 217–232.

Sandler, J. C., & Russell, B. L. (2005). Faculty–student collaborations: Ethics and satisfaction in authorship credit. *Ethics & Behavior, 15,* 65–80.

Spiegel, D., & Keith-Spiegel, P. (1970). Assignment of publication credits: Ethics and practices of psychologists. *American Psychologist, 25,* 738–747. doi:10.1037/h0029769

Tryon, G. S., Bishop, J. L., & Hatfield, T. A. (2007). Doctoral students' beliefs about authorship credit for dissertations. *Training and Education in Professional Psychology, 1,* 184–192. doi:10.1037/1931-3918.1.3.184

Winston, R. B. (1985). A suggested procedure for determining order of authorship in research publications. *Journal of Counseling and Development, 63,* 515–518.

17

PREPARING TO TEACH: BECOMING PART OF AN ETHICAL CULTURE

MEERA KOMARRAJU AND MITCHELL M. HANDELSMAN

Teaching can be an exciting and rewarding experience when instructors feel well prepared and confident about their performance. However, many first-time instructors begin teaching without the advantage of adequate training or mentoring (Buskist, Tears, Davis, & Rodrigue, 2002). In this chapter, we examine departments' responsibilities to graduate teaching assistants (GTAs), adjunct faculty, and new faculty for enhancing teaching skills, clarifying ethical assumptions, and developing professional identities. We also propose a positive approach for building on a department's teaching resources and strengths rather than simply providing a list of rules and disciplinary consequences for noncompliance.

THE NATURE OF THE ACADEMIC CULTURE

One model of ethics training posits that the process of becoming ethical is similar to acculturation—the process of adapting to a new culture (Anderson & Handelsman, 2010; Handelsman, Gottlieb, & Knapp, 2005). Even though graduate students have been students for a long time, the culture

191

that exists in academia—including (a) the general academic culture; (b) the mission, values, and policies of individual colleges; and (c) the specific climate in individual departments—can be quite different once they become responsible for teaching a course. A major task of ethical acculturation for new instructors is to integrate their existing values and virtues with those of the new culture (Handelsman et al., 2005). The corresponding tasks for training programs are to (a) make the culture as effective and ethical as possible and (b) facilitate the acculturation of their newest teachers. One way to conceptualize and capture the complexity of the culture at the departmental level is by looking at the obligations that departments and their faculty members have to a variety of constituencies.

Obligations to Undergraduate Students

When community members send their children to college, they expect instructors to teach with dedication and sincerity, and they expect that their trust in the institution will not be violated or exploited. Departments can respond to these expectations by showing their commitment to undergraduate education in many ways: by being responsive to students' curricular needs, by ensuring that courses listed in brochures and catalogs are indeed offered, by scheduling required courses in a timely manner, or by offering courses at times that are useful for students rather than only working around faculty members' preferences. More importantly for our purposes, departments can fulfill their obligations to students by actualizing the ethical principle of competence. When students sign up for courses, they may have some choice regarding which section of a course they enroll in, but often, they have little or no choice of who teaches the section. Hence, both departments and instructors have obligations to place competent teachers in classrooms and hold them accountable for providing undergraduates with a quality educational experience.

Obligations to Graduate Students

Likewise, departments have obligations to teach GTAs well and not exploit them, for example, by not placing them in teaching assignments for which they have insufficient background and little preparation. Such assignments might include independently teaching a course with no prior teaching experience or teaching a course without adequate background in course content. Preparing graduate students to teach is part of a program's overall obligation to turn bright people into well-rounded new professionals, along with teaching students to perform research and other skills. Departments are more likely to achieve their mission if they explicitly train their GTAs around ethical issues and model ethical behavior by creating a positive ethical climate (Keller, Murray, & Hargrove, in press). In this regard, Kitchener (1992) suggested that anyone involved in teaching or mentoring graduate students has to be concerned with two important issues: dealing with graduate students who act unethically and being ethical in his or her own interactions with graduate students.

At the beginning of their program, graduate students may be more focused on research or clinical training and less likely to realize the complexity of both the pedagogical and ethical decisions that teaching entails. As such, graduate students may also choose an ethical acculturation strategy called *separation* (Handelsman et al., 2005) in which they believe that being nice people and former undergraduates prepares them adequately for the ethical issues and decisions they will face. In reality, as new instructors, graduate students have a very complex acculturation task. They face the same range of ethical issues as more experienced instructors (e.g., confidentiality, boundaries, competence), yet at the same time, they are still learning to teach and to act professionally.

Graduate students are in a potentially awkward position regarding power: They have influence in some contexts but are still students in related contexts; this can make ethical decision making more difficult regarding boundaries, for example. A unique and delicate boundary issue might potentially arise when a graduate student has a GTA who is also a peer (another graduate student) for whom the graduate student needs to provide a performance evaluation at the end of the semester. In such a situation, the graduate student instructor may believe he or she lacks the expertise and experience to provide a valid performance evaluation for a peer who might also be a classmate. To deal with this issue, the graduate student instructor could request that the faculty member supervising the training assignment conduct the performance evaluation for the GTA. Data for this evaluation might include input from the graduate student instructor, course evaluations from students, and self-evaluation by the GTA. This process may require extra effort on everyone's part, but it has the twin benefits of enabling the graduate student instructor to navigate the delicate boundary issues and providing more comprehensive feedback for the GTA.

Graduate students are also learning to balance the competing demands of their GTA responsibilities with studying for their own courses. Although learning to balance the service, teaching, and research aspects of academics is an essential component of a transition into a faculty position (Kuther, 2003), graduate students typically have little experience with these balancing skills and may not receive adequate supervision from the very faculty members who are placing one or more of these demands on them (e.g., "You realize, of course, that you need to make tomorrow's lab meeting even though it will mean missing class!"). Students thus find themselves in positions in which it is easy to be—and even easier to feel—exploited.

Obligations to New Faculty

New faculty often report having adjustment problems when they start their new teaching assignments because they feel unprepared for the academic culture. It is not surprising that new faculty view this lack of training as unfair and exploitative (Mueller, Perlman, McCann, & McFadden, 1997). Training programs in teaching, when they exist, are not uniformly productive or useful and tend to be implemented more efficiently in bigger departments where larger groups of GTAs are targeted (Meyers & Prieto, 2000). New and adjunct faculty may face different kinds and intensities of issues relative to those of a GTA; yet they, too, need to balance their new responsibilities, acclimate to the environment of their new departments, and prepare to fulfill promotion and tenure expectations. In our experience, many departments mentor their new faculty in research to ensure a successful path toward tenure. However, departments are much less likely to mentor faculty in teaching. Departments would be better served by providing new faculty with explicit and adequate training. This training could use video microteaching and offer specific topics such as designing a course or innovative teaching techniques and could be offered through Centers for Teaching and Learning or summer workshops (Persellin & Goodrick, 2010). Departments that invest in mentoring new faculty are likely to experience several benefits, including new faculty who develop their teaching philosophy and use a wider variety of pedagogical techniques (Pierce, 1998); faculty who have an improved understanding of the teaching expectations for tenure and promotion (Schrodt, Cawyer, & Sanders, 2003); an increased likelihood of retaining new faculty (Smith & Ingersoll, 2004); and increased student learning, higher course evaluations, improved teaching effectiveness, and faculty who gain stronger personal rewards (Brightman, 2006).

TRAINING ETHICAL TEACHERS

Ethics is an integral part of teaching effectiveness, so pedagogical and ethics training are complementary. By providing training in ethical skills, departments also facilitate the goal of preparing instructors who are capable of teaching competently. Teaching involves several tasks, including communicating information effectively, helping students acquire thinking and other skills, and the less obvious task of relating to students and responding to their unique and varied demands in an ethical manner. A new instructor might receive training in how to prepare and deliver a lecture with well-crafted slides, movie clips, and clickers but is less likely to be instructed in dealing with students who come late, talk, and disrupt other students' learning; ask to submit an assignment long after the deadline has passed; complain about another teacher in the department; ask for extra help; or ask the instructor out for a romantic date. Hence, departments can improve their training and supervision of GTAs as well as prepare new faculty to deal more explicitly with ethical issues (McKeachie & Svinicki, 2011). Branstetter and Handelsman (2000) found that only 50% of GTAs believed that their ethics training was adequate. GTAs reported that they did not receive enough training in dealing with a variety of issues, including knowing how to prepare for teaching, teaching a course outside their specialty areas, allowing students to drop courses without officially approved reasons, and dating an undergraduate student. Further, GTAs who received no training in ethics were more likely to believe that having dual relationships with students was ethical than were GTAs who had received some training. These findings are alarming and draw attention to the needs of GTAs who realize they need more training and know they are not receiving it. Graduate students also report that they do not feel properly trained for an academic career, for classroom management, or for handling ethical concerns (Meyers, Reid, & Quina, 1998). If departments provide relevant training, GTAs are likely to be better prepared to enter the workplace, feel socially connected to other GTAs, and perform more competently as faculty (Davis & Kring, 2001). By investing in programs that provide GTAs thorough training and supervision in teaching—and the ethics related to teaching—departments will benefit and teachers will experience increased enjoyment of teaching and higher levels of instructor self-efficacy (Komarraju, 2008).

Initial training for new GTAs is a good first step, but ongoing monitoring and supervision are also necessary. Evidence suggests that although GTAs often know what is ethical or unethical, they may still engage in unethical behavior (Branstetter & Handelsman, 2000). For instance, GTAs know that teaching while unprepared is unethical, yet many report doing so—the data for full members of the American Psychological Association are comparable (Tabachnick, Keith-Spiegel, & Pope, 1991). GTAs need to develop ethical choice-making skills (Anderson, Wagoner, & Moore, 2006) even about such seemingly small behaviors as asking a favor of a student or accepting a student's invitation to a party. GTA training sometimes includes a practicum in the teaching of psychology, observing new teachers during the semester, reviewing student evaluations, and peer supervision, along with other forums for suggesting ways of improving. Folse (1991) suggested distributing a teaching manual with guidelines about a range of issues, including where to take exams for processing, when to assign an incomplete grade, why and how to conduct office hours, the importance of responding promptly to student queries, and procedures for handling emergency situations in a classroom. This information could be combined with more experiential training, such as making GTAs aware of the sexual harassment policy and augmenting that awareness with a mock hearing to allow them to reason through the issues (Shannon, Twale, & Moore, 1998). We believe that with some effort and creativity, all of these methods could be expanded and adapted to prepare GTAs and new instructors to recognize ethical dilemmas, prevent or handle ethically problematic situations, and create their own ethical identities as professionals.

One way to facilitate ethics discussions is through *ethics rounds* (Bashe, Anderson, Handelsman, & Klevansky, 2007) that are regularly dedicated discussions or a part of ongoing supervision sessions. Some examples of ethical dilemmas and issues that could be handled in ethics rounds might include plagiarizing by both students and faculty, cheating, failing to apply rules fairly and consistently across student situations, giving priority to personal convenience over obligation to students, not being prepared for class, applying unfair and inconsistent grading policies, changing grading policies during the semester, displaying favoritism toward specific groups of students, having sexual or romantic feelings toward students, and behaving in ways that reflect derogatory beliefs or attitudes toward students.

One advantage of regularly scheduled ethics rounds is that ethics can be discussed in a routine, positive, and supportive environment rather than, for example, an environment in which the faculty or GTA is called into a special session when a violation is alleged. Supervisors can emphasize specific behaviors and ethical acculturation strategies rather than give a disembodied recitation of policy statements. GTAs and their supervisors can discuss their own professional values, virtues, and beliefs from their cultures (ethical or others) of origin and become familiar with professional values within the culture of teaching. The department could thus provide training that sensitizes teachers to their own values and offer guidance for what is meant by positive or exemplary ethics (Handelsman, Knapp, & Gottlieb, 2009), not just avoiding violations and sanctions.

Ongoing discussions of ethical issues in teaching are necessary; ethics cannot be taught in a 1-hour presentation the week before classes start or in a handbook distributed to new teachers during their orientation. Learning to make ethical choices, like any professional activity, is a developmental process (Handelsman, 2001; Skovholt, & Rønnestad, 1992; Stoltenberg & Delworth, 1987) and, like any skill set, takes practice. Discussions evolve as instructors gain experience, practice the skills involved in analyzing ethical dilemmas, and try out a variety of ethical acculturation strategies. As new instructors encounter ethical dilemmas that defy easy answers, the opportunity to discuss these situations with supervisors, try out a suggested option, and then return for another round of reflection on the consequences of choosing that option would be an invaluable tool. In this regard, Francis (2009) discussed a process of "ethical gradualism" (p. 49) in which supervisors reinforce supervisees for behaviors that are approximations of perfect ethical behavior.

As graduate students progress in their development, they are likely to learn how to find answers to a variety of teaching-related issues ranging from minor questions such as figuring how much time to grant a student who requests extra time for completing an assignment to more complex tasks such as deciding on a teaching philosophy; understanding what it means to be an ethical teacher; learning what it means to display exemplary ethics; and identifying teachers' obligations to themselves, their students, their institution, and their discipline. Discovering answers to such questions allows GTAs to recognize that ethical questions permeate the pedagogical decisions they make every day and that consideration of ethics can improve their teaching performance. The following case study provides an example of a real-life situation that new graduate students might face.

> Ang Shuss has just joined a graduate program to complete her master's and doctoral degrees in clinical psychology. For her first training assignment she will be a GTA for an abnormal psychology course. She is excited about this assignment as "abnormal" was her favorite undergraduate class. She is wondering what she will be expected to do as a GTA assisting the course instructor Dr. Cella Phane. During her first meeting with Dr. Phane 4 days before the start of the semester, she learns about the structure of the course: two weekly lectures and three small breakout sections that meet once a week. Ang will be responsible for meeting these breakout sections, and Dr. Phane asks her to develop some in-class experiential activities that will actively engage students in the course material. Ang realizes she lacks the background or training for creating experiential activities and begins to feel overwhelmed and worried that she will not have sufficient time to get ready for the first day of classes. Dr. Phane ends that meeting with a definitive, "See you on Monday!" Thus, Ang is not sure whether she can ask Dr. Phane for help in developing some of the initial materials. In addition, Ang still needs to figure out several details pertaining to her own schedule, such as determining the classes for which she needs to register, setting up a meeting time with her research mentor, obtaining a parking sticker, getting keys for her office, and meeting with the program director. Where does she begin? How are ethical principles like autonomy, justice, beneficence, nonmaleficence, involved? What choices and options does Dr. Phane have?

In analyzing this scenario, graduate students and faculty can explore both the obvious and more subtle ethical dilemmas and the choices involved. This case could be used with new GTAs, but it also contains elements that would be relevant for more advanced graduate students and for seasoned faculty.

Creating an Ethical Climate

Supportive and positive ethics supervision will clearly be more effective if it occurs in the context of a department with a positive ethical climate (Keller et al., in press). One element of a positive ethical climate may be a holistic and supportive approach to professional development that goes beyond an apprentice model and that trains GTAs to balance their multiple responsibilities, including coursework, thesis or dissertation, and teaching. Most GTAs enter graduate programs with a host of anxieties and problems, including academic and social concerns, that may be difficult for faculty and supervisors to imagine or anticipate (Goodlad, 1997). Anticipating and addressing these issues in a proactive way, not just when obvious problems develop, is a good first step.

Ongoing training, mentoring, and coaching could include everyone in the department, not only junior faculty. Senior faculty members are not immune to ethical lapses (Tabachnick et al., 1991) and could benefit from ongoing discussions. At the same time, senior faculty can be invaluable sources of practical wisdom and inspiration for their junior colleagues. Senior faculty can help monitor the ethical behavior of their GTAs by providing ongoing supervision to help them handle dilemmas for which existing rules do not apply neatly or easily. Senior faculty can also model ethical behavior by being open to discussion and transparent about the ethical elements of their decisions. For instance, cases like that in the previous example could be adapted and presented from the point of view of a faculty member. For example, consider the following scenario:

> Dr. Phane has a student who appears unmotivated, lazy, and always complaining about the amount of work required as a GTA. Dr. Phane wants to be supportive of her GTA and transparent about her own values and methods. She also needs to submit three research papers in the next 3 weeks so they will appear in her tenure dossier. How might Dr. Phane handle this situation? Why? How might she mentor a junior faculty member to become aware of and address the ethical dilemmas inherent in such a situation?

Modeling Ethical Behavior

Departments could formulate and adhere to teaching-related policies that model ethical behavior and are not exploitative of graduate students. For example, in determining teaching assignments, departments could take responsibility for assigning GTAs or faculty only to courses for which they have adequate background or training. Policies can be devised and implemented that are explicitly sensitive to a broad range of concerns, including college targets for enrollments; training of GTAs; the educational mission of the college; and the academic, intellectual, and cultural backgrounds of GTAs.

As we conclude, we are fully aware that we may have moved beyond the realm of positive ethics (Handelsman et al., 2009) into the realm of *impossible ethics*. We understand the imperfections in our adopted academic culture. At the same time, we choose not to let these challenges discourage us. We hope that aspiring to higher goals will result in better outcomes. Such outcomes may involve improved academic performance of students, better pedagogy, and better ethical decision making by both students and faculty.

SUMMARY

Preparing teachers to be ethical is not only a matter of compliance—it requires a more comprehensive and positive approach. GTAs and new faculty can use personal values, virtues, and principles and integrate them with the best values and principles of the academic culture. Departments can support this acculturation process with ongoing and regular attention to the ethical dimensions of teaching and by developing and implementing policies that actualize their highest values. By preparing GTAs and new faculty members to teach effectively, departments can potentially fulfill their obligations to their undergraduate students, graduate students, and new faculty members. Sensitizing new instructors to the ethical dilemmas they are likely to face in their teaching assignments could make long-term contributions toward developing an ethical climate for student learning. Learning to make ethical choices is a developmental process requiring ongoing mentoring and coaching using case studies, ethics rounds, and individualized supervision to increase professionalism in GTAs and faculty members.

REFERENCES

Anderson, S. K., & Handelsman, M. M. (2010). *Ethics for psychotherapists and counselors: A proactive approach.* Malden, MA: Wiley-Blackwell.

Anderson, S. K., Wagoner, H., & Moore, G. K. (2006). Ethical choice: An outcome of being, blending, and doing. In P. Williams & S. K. Anderson (Eds.), *Law and ethics in coaching: How to solve and avoid difficult problems in your practice* (pp. 39–61). Hoboken, NJ: Wiley.

Bashe, A., Anderson, S. K., Handelsman, M. M., & Klevansky, R. (2007). An acculturation model for ethics training: The ethics autobiography and beyond. *Professional Psychology: Research and Practice, 38,* 60–67. doi:10.1037/0735-7028.38.1.60

Branstetter, S. A., & Handelsman, M. M. (2000). Graduate teaching assistants: Ethical training, beliefs, and practices. *Ethics & Behavior, 10,* 27–50. doi:10.1207/S15327019EB1001_3

Brightman, H. J. (2006). Mentoring faculty to improve teaching and student learning. *Issues in Accounting Education, 21,* 127–146. doi:10.2308/iace.2006.21.2.127

Buskist, W., Tears, R. S., Davis, S. F., & Rodrigue, K. M. (2002). The teaching of psychology course: Prevalence and content. *Teaching of Psychology, 29,* 140–142.

Davis, S. F., & Kring, J. P. (2001). A model for training and evaluating graduate teaching assistants. *College Student Journal, 35,* 45–51.

Folse, K. A. (1991). Ethics and the profession: Graduate student training. *Teaching Sociology, 19,* 344–350. doi:10.2307/1318200

Francis, R. D. (2009). *Ethics for psychologists* (2nd ed.). Chichester, England: BPS Blackwell. doi:10.1002/9781444306514

Goodlad, S. (1997). Responding to the perceived training needs of graduate teaching assistants. *Studies in Higher Education, 22,* 83–92. doi:10.1080/03075079712331381151

Handelsman, M. M. (2001). Learning to become ethical. In S. Walfish & A. K. Hess (Eds.), *Succeeding in graduate school: The career guide for psychology students* (pp. 189–202). Mahwah, NJ: Erlbaum.

Handelsman, M. M., Gottlieb, M. C., & Knapp, S. (2005). Training ethical psychologists: An acculturation model. *Professional Psychology: Research and Practice, 36,* 59–65. doi:10.1037/0735-7028.36.1.59

Handelsman, M. M., Knapp, S., & Gottlieb, M. C. (2009). Positive ethics: Themes and variations. In C. R. Snyder & S. J. Lopez (Eds.), *Oxford handbook of positive psychology* (2nd ed., pp. 105–113). New York, NY: Oxford University Press.

Keller, P. A., Murray, J. D., & Hargrove, D. S. (in press). Creating ethical academic cultures within psychology programs. In S. Knapp (Ed.), *Handbook on ethics in psychology.* Washington, DC: American Psychological Association.

Kitchener, K. S. (1992). Psychologist as teacher and mentor: Affirming ethical values throughout the curriculum. *Professional Psychology: Research and Practice, 23,* 190–195. doi:10.1037/0735-7028.23.3.190

Komarraju, M. (2008). A social-cognitive approach to training teaching assistants. *Teaching of Psychology, 35,* 327–334. doi:10.1080/00986280802374344

Kuther, T. L. (2003). Teaching the teacher: Ethical issues in graduate student teaching. *College Student Journal, 37,* 219–223.

McKeachie, W. J., & Svinicki, M. (2011). *Teaching tips: Strategies, research, and theory for college and university teachers* (13th ed., pp. 315–329). Belmont, CA: Wadsworth Cengage Learning.

Meyers, S. A., Reid, P. T., & Quina, K. (1998). Ready or not, here we come: Preparing psychology graduate students for academic careers. *Teaching of Psychology, 25,* 124–126. doi:10.1207/s15328023top2502_11

Meyers, S., & Prieto, L. R. (2000). Training in the teaching of psychology: What is done and examining the differences. *Teaching of Psychology, 27,* 258–261. doi:10.1207/S15328023TOP2704_03

Mueller, A., Perlman, B., McCann, L. I., & McFadden, S. H. (1997). A faculty perspective on teaching assistant training. *Teaching of Psychology, 24,* 167–171. doi:10.1207/s15328023top2403_3

Persellin, D., & Goodrick, T. (2010). Faculty development in higher education: Long-term impact of a summer teaching and learning workshop. *Journal of the Scholarship of Teaching and Learning, 10,* 1–13.

Pierce, G. (1998). Developing new university faculty through mentoring. *The Journal of Humanistic Education and Development, 37,* 27–38.

Shannon, D. M., Twale, D. J., & Moore, M. S. (1998). TA teaching effectiveness: The impact of training and teaching experience. *The Journal of Higher Education, 69,* 440–466. doi:10.2307/2649274

Schrodt, P., Cawyer, C. S., & Sanders, R. (2003). An examination of academic mentoring behaviors and new faculty members' satisfaction with socialization and tenure and promotion process. *Communication Education, 52,* 17–29. doi:10.1080/03634520302461

Smith, T., & Ingersoll, R. (2004). What are the effects of induction and mentoring on beginning teaching turnover? *American Educational Research Journal, 41,* 681–714. doi:10.3102/00028312041003681

Skovholt, T. M., & Rønnestad, M. H. (1992). *The evolving professional self.* New York, NY: Wiley.

Stoltenberg, C. D., & Delworth, U. (1987). *Supervising counselors and therapists: A developmental approach.* San Francisco, CA: Jossey-Bass.

Tabachnick, B. G., Keith-Spiegel, P., & Pope, K. S. (1991). Ethics of teaching: Beliefs and behaviors of psychologists as educators. *American Psychologist, 46,* 506–515. doi:10.1037/0003-066X.46.5.506

INDEX

Berk, R. A., 15
Bernstein, D. J., 15, 17
Berry, J. W., 118
Bersoff, D. N., 167
Best fit, 51
Biaggio, M., 141
Bidding wars, 48–49
Blanton, P. G., 167
Blignaut, S., 57–58
Bloom, B., 115
Bornstein, P. H., 183
Boundaries
    in community-based learning
        experiences, 165–166
    in student–faculty relationships,
        140–142
    with technology use, 146–147
Boundaries of Competence (APA
    Ethics Code), 10–11
Bowden, R. G., 21
Bowers, W. J., 91
Boyer, E. L., 21
Boyer Commission on Educating
    Undergraduates in the Research
    University, 182
Bransford, J. D., 17
Branstetter, S. A., 195
Bribery, 47–48
Bridgwater, C. A., 183, 188
Bringle, R. G., 163
Brothen, T., 84, 130, 132
Brown, A. L., 17
Brulle, A., 129
Bundling, 49–50
Burbules, N. C., 56
Burger, J. M., 152
Burgoyne, S., 27
Burgstahler, S. E., 131
Burman, M. E., 24
Burton, G., 15
Buskist, W., 121

Cahn, S. M., 113, 116
Callahan, P., 114
Capstone course, 157
Carroll, J., 81
CBLEs. *See* Community-based learning
    experiences
Center for Social Media, 58–59

Cheating
    faculty role in prevention of, 81–84
    honor systems for prevention of, 89
    institutional role in prevention of,
        80–81
    investigative procedures for, 92–93
    student perceptions of, 80, 94
Chenoweth, M. S., 141
Chew, S. L., 117
Classroom strategy(-ies)
    for academic honesty, 81
    for cheating prevention, 94–95
    for establishing boundaries, 140–141
    experimental, 27–28
    faculty evaluation and discussion
        of, 24
    honor pledge as, 96
    for multicultural competence,
        105–109
    for rapport building, 121, 144–145
    self-disclosure as, 145
    for universal design, 130–132
    for virtual classrooms, 55–56
Climate, ethical, 81–82, 198
Clinical licensing guidelines, 70
Clinical settings, 167
Cocking, R. R., 17
Coercion, 25, 71–72
Cohen, A. L., 121
Collaboration, 14. *See also*
    Faculty–undergraduate student
    collaboration
Collaborative Institutional Training
    Initiative, 175
Common Rule, 23
Communication, 166–167
Communication technologies, 55, 56,
    146–147
Community-based learning experiences
    (CBLEs), 161–168
    educational challenges with, 163–164
    goals of, 163
    legal and ethical issues with,
        164–166
    supervision practices for, 166–167
Competence
    cultural, 103–104
    multicultural, 102–109
    professional, 182–183
ConcepTests, 117

Monitoring
   of community-based learning
      experiences, 164–166
   of graduate teaching assistants,
      195–196
   of in-class exams, 83
   of teaching innovations, 69–70
Morris, M. D., 154
Moseley, D., 115
Multicultural competence, 105–109
Multiple-choice exams, 37
Multiple Relationships (APA Ethics
   Code), 26
Multiple roles, 140–142, 193–194
Murphy, R. E., 146
Murray, H., 144

Nadelson, S., 92
Nagel, L., 57–58
Nath, L., 83
National Academies, 46
National Commission for the Protection
   of Human Subjects of Biomedical
   and Behavioral Research, 22
National Institutes of Health Office of
   Extramural Research, 175–176
National Research Act, 22
Nelson, C., 11
Netiquette, 61
New faculty, 61–62, 194
Nonverbal behaviors, 144, 145
Nuremberg Code, 23

Obama, Barack, 51
Offenders, first-time, 36
Office for Human Research Protections
   (OHRP), 23
Online discussions, 57
Online teaching, 55–62
   cheating prevention in, 83–84
   digital privacy in, 56–58
   intellectual property in, 58–60
   professional practices for, 60–62
Order of authorship, 181
Outcome measures, 177–178
Outcomes, 144–145, 163–164
Ownership, 59

Paget, T. L., 141
Pallett, W. H., 15

Paraphrasing, 85
Parilla, P. F., 163
Pavela, G., 91–92
Pedagogical imperative, 69
Pedagogical research, 68, 69
Perkins, D. V., 44
Permanence, textual, 57
Perry, W. G., 115, 120
Personalized system of instruction (PSI),
   132
Pettigrew, T. F., 108
Philosophy of teaching, 15, 17
Physical impairment, 127
Piaget, J., 115
Plagiarism
   case example of, 35–36
   increase in, 91
   prevention of, 79–80, 84–85
   and second year undergraduates,
      155–156
Political correctness, 119
Positive ethical climate, 198
Power
   of graduate students, 193
   and publication credit, 184–185, 188
   in student–faculty relationships,
      139–141
Practica, 162
Prepare-gather feedback-restudy strategy,
   130
Primary authorship, 182–183
*Principles for Quality Undergraduate
   Psychology Programs* (APA), 17
Privacy, digital, 56–58
Problem solving, 105–106
Proctoring, 83
Productivity, 173–174
Professional competence, 182–183
Professional development, 17
Promotion, 17
Protecting Human Research Participants,
   175–176
Protection of Human Subjects, 25–26
PSI (personalized system of instruction),
   132
Publication Credit (APA Ethics Code),
   183–186
*Publication Manual of the American
   Psychological Association,* 184
Publishers, 46–49

Quality instruction, balancing research productivity and, 173–174
Quiz-to-learn strategy, 130
Quizzes, 83–84, 130

Randolph College, 89, 93, 94
Rapport, 121, 144–147
Reasonable accommodations, 126, 129–130. *See also* Accommodations (students with disabilities)
Recruitment, 155
Relationships with students. *See* Student–faculty relationships
Religious beliefs, 113, 115, 117
Repeat offenders, 36
Requirements, educational, 130
Research assistants, 172–173
Research ethics, 151–158
    for first year undergraduates, 152–154
    for second year undergraduates, 154–156
    for third and fourth year undergraduates, 156–158
    undergraduate training in, 175–176
Research methods, 155
Research programs, 173–175
Research studies, 153, 155. *See also* Undergraduate research ethics
Respect, 71–72
Respect for People's Rights and Dignity (APA Ethics Code), 116
Rogers, K., 61
Roig, M., 80, 84, 85
Rose, D. H., 131
Royalties, 46, 50
Russell, B. L., 186

Sam, D. L., 118
Sandler, J. C., 186
Scheutze, P., 85
Scholarly teaching, 68–69
Scholarship of teaching and learning (SoTL), 21–28. *See also* Evidence-based pedagogy
    experimenting with methodology in, 27–28
    with human participants, 22
    inducements to participate in, 24–26
    informed consent to use student work in, 27

institutional review board in, 23–24
    journals on, 14
    multiple relationships in, 26
Schwartz, S. J., 119
Scientific disciplines, 12–15
Screening policies, 173
Seaman, J., 55
Second year undergraduates, 154–156
Selection processes, 172–173
Self-awareness, 103
Self-disclosure, 145–147
Self-scheduled exams, 95
Senior faculty, 198
Senior theses, 183
Sensitive topics, 115
Separation strategy, 118, 119, 193
Service learning, 162. *See also* Community-based learning experiences
Sexual relationships, 143, 147–148
Shulman, L. S., 69
Simonds, C. J., 146
Simpson, M., 57
Skills
    for multicultural competence, 103
    research, 176–177
Sloan Survey of Online Learning (Sloan-C), 55
Soltis, J. F., 55
SoTL. *See* Scholarship of teaching and learning
Sottile, J., 83
Spiritual beliefs, 117
Spitzer, T. M., 28
Statistical analyses, 154–155, 177
Stoloff, M., 162
Strauman, E. C., 145
Streaming video, 59
Strike, K., 55
Strike, K. A., 36
Student behavior, 79–86
    cheating, 81–84
    plagiarism, 84–85
Student–faculty relationships, 139–148. *See also* Faculty–undergraduate student collaboration
    ethical guidelines for, 142–144
    and honor systems, 95–96
    multiple roles in, 140–142
    rapport with limits in, 144–147

ABOUT THE EDITORS

R. Eric Landrum, PhD, is a professor of psychology at Boise State University; he received his doctorate in cognitive psychology (with an emphasis in quantitative methodology) from Southern Illinois University at Carbondale in 1989. His research interests center on the study of educational issues, identifying those conditions that best facilitate student success (broadly defined). He has given over 280 professional presentations at conferences and has authored 17 books or book chapters and over 70 professional articles in peer-reviewed journals, such as *Teaching of Psychology, College Teaching,* and the *Journal of College Student Development.* He has worked with over 275 undergraduate research assistants and taught more than 12,000 students in 19 years at Boise State. During summer 2008, he led a working group at the National Conference for Undergraduate Education in Psychology concerned with the desired results of an undergraduate psychology education.

Maureen A. McCarthy, PhD, is a professor of psychology at Kennesaw State University; she earned her doctorate from Missouri State University in research and evaluation. She previously served as president of Division 2 (Society for the Teaching of Psychology) of the American Psychological

Association (APA) and is currently a member of APA Divisions 35 (Society for the Psychology of Women), 5 (Evaluation, Measurement, and Statistics), and 26 (Society for the History of Psychology). She has authored or coauthored numerous publications, including the article in the *American Psychologist* titled "Quality Benchmarks in Undergraduate Psychology Programs." An extension of this work was published in 2010 as a book titled *Using Quality Benchmarks for Assessing and Developing Undergraduate Programs*. This volume offers a comprehensive approach to program assessment and evaluation to help programs and departments in the humanities, social sciences, and natural sciences use assessment data to improve undergraduate education. Dr. McCarthy has authored numerous articles and edited several volumes addressing pedagogical issues, and she continues to pursue scholarship in pedagogical techniques, assessment of student learning, and program evaluation.